ACKNOWLEDGEMENTS

IN HIS CONSTANT WILLINGNESS TO DEEPEN HIS
KNOWLEDGE, THE "CUISINIER" CONTINUES TO
EXERCISE HIS PASSION.

IT IS WITH GREAT PLEASURE THAT, IN THE
REALIZATION OF THIS BOOK, I HAVE BEEN ABLE TO
SHARE MY ENTHUSIASM WITH ALL THOSE WHO
HELPED ME.

I WISH ESPECIALLY TO THANK MY FRIEND LEN
HALPERT OF NEW YORK AND ANDY STEWART,
WHO WILLINGLY GAVE ME HIS CONFIDENCE AND
GUIDED ME IN THIS WORK IN CLOSE COLLABORA-
TION WITH THE TEAM OF EDITOR ROY FINAMORE,
DESIGNER RITA MARSHALL, AND TRANSLATORS
TINA UJLAKI AND CHARLES PIERCE.

MY THANKS ALSO GO TO CHRISTOPHER BAKER,
PHOTOGRAPHER OF GREAT TALENT TO WHOM WE
OWE THE MAGNIFICENT IMAGES, AND TO ROGER
POURTEAU, WHO WITH ALL HIS GOODNESS HAS
SO ENLIGHTENED ME ABOUT THE BOUNTIES OF
NATURE.

I THANK MICHEL GUERARD, JACQUES
MAXIMIN, MARC MENEAU, JOEL ROBUCHON,
AND ALAIN SENDERENS, CREATIVE COOKS WHO
HAVE EACH WILLINGLY DONATED A RECIPE FOR
THIS BOOK.

I AM ALSO MOST GRATEFUL TO MY KITCHEN
TEAM FOR THEIR INVALUABLE HELP IN THE
REALIZATION OF THE PRESENTATION OF DISHES
FOR THE BOOK, AND TO PRISCA VITTE, WHO
HELPED WITH THE STYLING AND GUIDED US TO
THE MOST PICTURESQUE AREAS TO BE FOUND IN
THIS BEAUTIFUL REGION OF FRANCE.

The Natural Cuisine of
GEORGES BLANC

PHOTOGRAPHY BY CHRISTOPHER BAKER

RECIPES TRANSLATED AND TESTED BY
TINA UJLAKI AND CHARLES PIERCE

STEWART, TABORI & CHANG
NEW YORK

Text copyright © 1987 Georges Blanc

Photographs copyright © 1987 Christopher Baker

Captions translated by Paul Stuart Rankin
and adapted by Catherine Bush

Published by Stewart, Tabori & Chang, Inc.
740 Broadway, New York, New York 10003

Library of Congress Cataloging-in-Publication Data

Blanc, Georges, 1943–

    The natural cuisine of Georges Blanc.

    Includes index.

    1. Cookery, French.   2. Vegetarian cookery.

I. Title.

TX719.B5877   1987   641.5′636   87-10768

ISBN 1-55670-008-3

Distributed by Workman Publishing
1 West 39 Street, New York, New York 10018

Printed in Japan

87 88 89 10 9 8 7 6 5 4 3 2 1

First Edition

To gardeners,
superb artisans
whose fruits and
vegetables are
the essence of
quality cooking

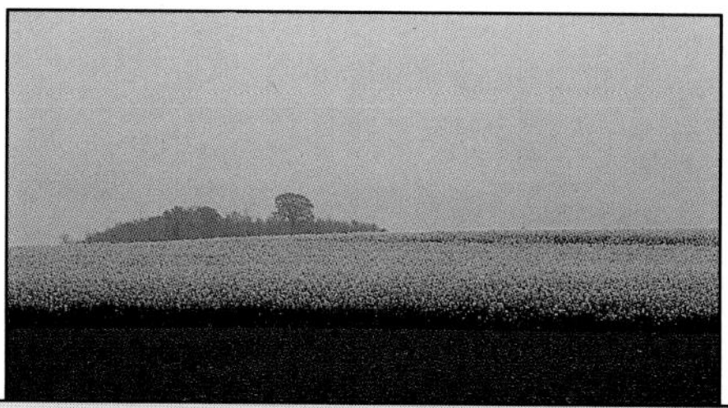

S P R I N G

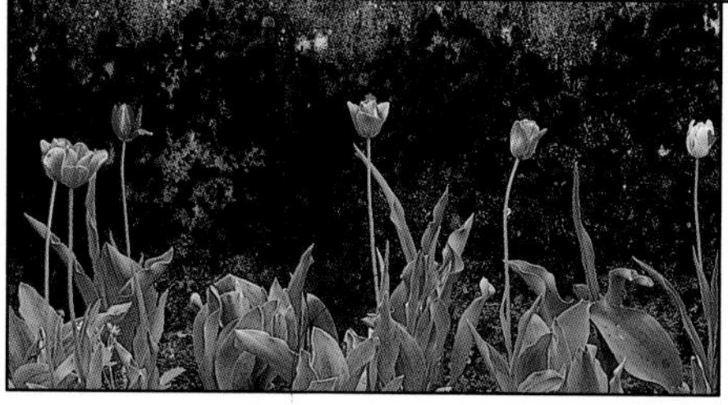

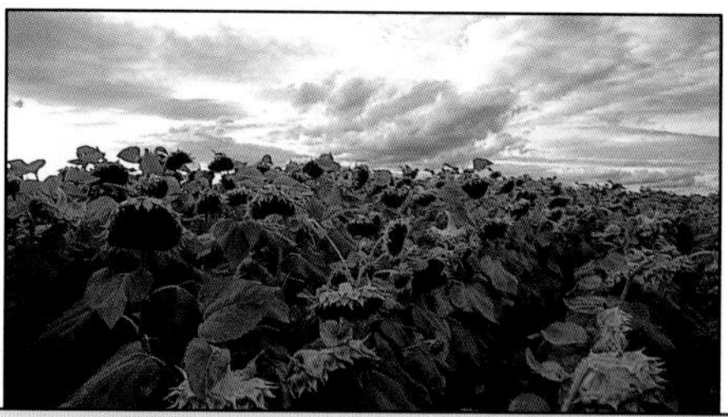

S U M M E R

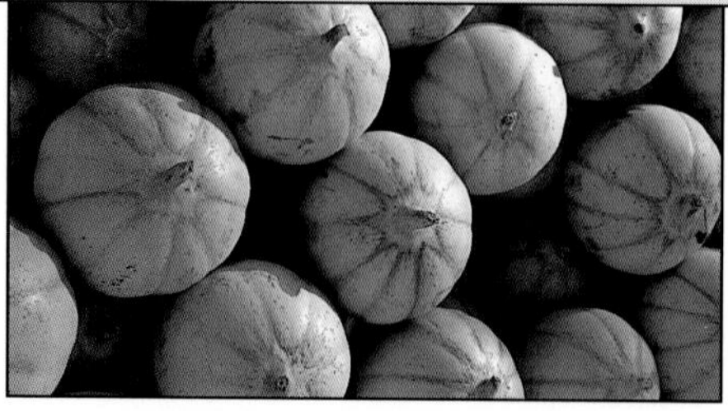

A U T U M N

AUTUMN VEGETABLES 196

AUTUMN FRUITS 236

PREFACE

THE STORY OF LA MÈRE BLANC

IT BEGAN WELL BEFORE THE FRENCH REVOLUTION, in that part of Burgundy called Bresse. Here, the Blanc family cultivated the earth at Marboz, at Cuet (near Montreval), then at Saint-Didier-d'Aussiat.

In 1872, Jean-Louis Blanc and his wife established themselves as innkeepers near the fairgrounds in Vonnas. The main clientele of that time were egg merchants who would arrive by horse-drawn carriage and warm themselves with the Blancs' soup. When the Thursday market was over, they sat down to a large snack. The soup was good, and word spread.

Their son, Adolphe, married Elisa Gervais, and this pair succeeded at the inn in 1902. Elisa was installed in the kitchen and soon became celebrated under the name "la mère Blanc."

Curnonsky, elected prince of gastronomes, called Elisa "the best cook in the world," but she was not what one would call a great chef. Elisa had inherited from her mother, Virginie, the secrets of a culinary art based on butter and she perfected her craft during her apprenticeship at the home of Madame Lambert-Peney, a highly respected hotelier in Vonnas. She did not receive any theoretical culinary training; rather, she learned it all by instinct and by taste. Her cooking was a cuisine of the earth—simple, honest, prepared with love and to perfection with the freshest and finest country produce.

Affairs prospered. People came from farther and farther away to savor the Frog Legs with Herbs, the Bresse Chicken in Cream, and the famed Crêpes Vonnassiennes at La Mère Blanc. On Sundays, the train would bring families from Macon, and the automobile brought even more people to Vonnas. In 1930, the Touring Club of France awarded first prize in its culinary competition to La Mère Blanc. The best gastronomic chroniclers of the period awarded press honors; the Club des Cent and the Academie des Gastronomes equally honored her.

In 1934, Jean Blanc (the eldest son) took over the inn, and his wife, Paulette, took the kitchen in hand. Guided by Elisa, Paulette conserved the same traditional specialties that had made the inn so well known.

Their son, Georges, studied hotel and restaurant management, then worked at a two-star restaurant in the Cote d'Azur. Later, he apprenticed at several other restaurants before returning to La Mère Blanc in 1965 to learn his mother's cooking. In 1968, Georges and his wife, Jacqueline, became the proprietors.

A perfectionist in the kitchen and in the dining room, Georges has transformed the style of cooking at La Mère Blanc. As did other chefs in the 1970s, Blanc felt a need for lighter food. "But," he says, "it must be personalized." Blanc turned to the extraordinary produce of Burgundy and fashioned a light, natural cuisine that is rich in tradition, still reminiscent of his mother's and grandmother's cooking. In 1981, he became the youngest chef to win the coveted three stars from Michelin.

Georges' two sons, Frederic (already a cook) and Alexandre, are preparing themselves to continue the line.

INTRODUCTION

THE GIFTS OF NATURE—GENEROUS, RICH IN FLAVOR—constitute the largest and most precious part of the pantry. In the countryside in the heart of Burgundy, where my family has lived for generations, there has always been great respect for the good products of the earth. In my family it is something of a tradition; my mother and grandmother and great-grandmother offered simple cooking, food that was basically honest, prepared with the best, freshest seasonal ingredients. Today, we find pleasure in rediscovering the simple joys of country savors, of fresh vegetables and fruits as the focus of a meal.

In the exercise of their craft, today's cooks know how much they depend on the quality of goods from the market. They have discovered and rejoiced in the growing interest in a very light cuisine. This, the most natural of nourishments, reflects too the tendency toward a moderate, rather than immoderate consumption of meat. It is a question of being in harmony with nature's cycles, of looking to the seasons to find a healthy cuisine, a cuisine of well-being.

In developing these recipes I have wished to share with you my passion for vegetables and fruits. I have tried to look beyond fad and sophistication to simple and proper combinations of foods, combinations that are equally attractive to the palate and the eye. I recommend that in order to make the best use of this book and the recipes in it, you be very particular concerning your choice of products. The fruits and vegetables you use should be of the best possible quality and of the utmost freshness. The best vegetables or fruits, of course, are those that one cultivates oneself and gathers at the peak of maturity. These are then brought into the kitchen and consumed the same day. For those who have no vegetable garden or orchard there are still excellent resources. In the small markets of our towns and villages and in farmers' markets in larger cities, one meets true artisans who cultivate intensively and economically and grow exquisite produce. Market gardeners in England and truck farmers in the United States know quality and are able to offer it. Search out these gardeners and ask for the best.

In trying to put into this book at least one recipe for each of the principal fruits and vegetables I hope to show that it is possible to conceive of an original, natural, and tasty cuisine without meat. This is not, however, a book just for vegetarians. There are several recipes each season for cuisine that comes from the sea.

Christopher Baker, in his photography of the recipes in the book, has tried to show the relationship of nature to the plate. The food has been photographed as often as possible in a natural setting, and always with the available light of the season.

In the course of putting this book together I have been able to measure my knowledge and enrich it thanks to those I have met and who have taught me a great deal. Gardeners especially have talked with me and allowed me to use their best products. I met daily with these lovers of nature, all of us pursuing the same ideal: the rediscovery of quality. It is for this that I thank them and dedicate this book to them.

S   P   R

SPRING VEGETABLES

IN THE SPRING OUR GARDENS AWAKEN AGAIN AFTER THEIR LONG WINTER SLUMBER AND, AS VICTOR HUGO SAID, THERE ARE "PEARLS EVERYWHERE, IN THE THYME, IN THE ROSES." THE SEASON'S FRESH YOUNG PRODUCE ALSO FILLS THE MARKETPLACE, OFFERING A HOST OF NEW POSSIBILITIES FOR THE INVENTIVE COOK.

MIXED VEGETABLES A LA GRECQUE
GRECQUE DE CHOU-FLEUR ET CONCOMBRE

1	CUP OLIVE OIL	1	SMALL EUROPEAN SEEDLESS CUCUMBER
1	SMALL CAULIFLOWER, DIVIDED INTO FLORETS	12	SMALL SPRING ONIONS, TRIMMED
4	CLOVES GARLIC, PEELED	16	SMALL MUSHROOMS, TRIMMED
1⅔	CUPS DRY WHITE WINE	2	RIBS CELERY, FROM THE HEART, PEELED AND CUT INTO 2-INCH PIECES
2	LEMONS	1	SMALL BOUQUET GARNI
2	SPRIGS OF THYME	1½	TEASPOONS TOMATO PASTE
1	BAY LEAF	10	BLACK PEPPERCORNS
1	LARGE PINCH OF POWDERED SAFFRON	1	BASIL LEAF, FINELY CHOPPED
20	CORIANDER SEEDS	1	SMALL TOMATO, PEELED, SEEDED, AND FINELY DICED
	SALT		
4	SMALL ARTICHOKES	1	TABLESPOON FRESH CHERVIL LEAVES

Heat ⅓ cup olive oil in a medium casserole. Add cauliflower florets and toss to coat with oil. Cover and cook over medium heat for 4 minutes. Add 2 cloves garlic, ½ cup wine, ½ cup water, the juice of ½ lemon, the thyme, bay leaf, saffron, 10 coriander seeds, and a pinch of salt. Bring to a boil over high heat and boil until the liquid emulsifies, about 10 minutes. Reduce heat to medium and simmer until cauliflower is just tender, about 4 minutes longer. Remove from heat and set aside.

Cut off the artichoke stems. Remove all of the tough green leaves around the base and cut the crown to within 1½ inches of the base. Rub the artichokes with a lemon half. Trim off any tough green portions to give the bottoms a nice shape. Remove hairy chokes with a teaspoon. Rub again with the lemon; set aside in a bowl of water with the lemon half.

Peel cucumber with a swivel vegetable peeler, leaving lengthwise strips of green. Cut cucumber crosswise into 2-inch-thick rounds, then quarter the pieces lengthwise. With the knife, shave off any sharp edges to form neat cylinders.

Heat remaining ⅔ cup olive oil in a large nonreactive casserole or saucepan. Add the artichoke bottoms, spring onions, mushrooms, cucumber, and celery and cook over medium high heat, stirring occasionally, for 5 minutes. Add bouquet garni, tomato paste, remaining 2 garlic cloves, juice of 1 lemon, remaining wine, ½ cup water, and a pinch of salt. Tie remaining 10 coriander seeds and peppercorns in a square of cheesecloth and add them to the casserole. Stir well and bring to a boil over high heat; boil for 2 minutes. Reduce the heat to medium high and cook until artichoke bottoms are just tender, 12 to 15 minutes. Remove from heat and discard bouquet garni and cheesecloth sack. Stir in basil.

TO SERVE: Drain cauliflower and discard garlic cloves, coriander seeds, thyme sprigs, and bay leaf. Place an artichoke bottom in the center of each of 4 plates. Remove the cucumber from the vegetable mixture. Heap the vegetables onto the artichoke bottoms. Arrange alternating mounds of the bright yellow cauliflower florets and the cucumber cylinders around the artichokes. Sprinkle each serving with diced tomato and chervil and serve warm, tepid, or cold. *Makes 4 servings.*

THIS NICELY SPICED DISH FEATURES THE CAULIFLOWER, A SPRING VEGETABLE WHICH IS ONE OF THE STARS OF BRETON GARDENS; HERE IT IS BLENDED WITH A VARIETY OF VEGETABLES AND FLAVORINGS IN A FEAST OF COMPLEX TASTES. THE FIRST CAULIFLOWERS TO ARRIVE IN SPRING MARKETS ARE A BIT SMALLER THAN THOSE FOUND IN THE AUTUMN, BUT THEIR QUALITY IS RECOGNIZABLE BY THEIR WEIGHT, THE DENSITY OF THEIR HEADS, AND THEIR WHITE OR SLIGHTLY YELLOWISH COLOR. GOURMETS SAY THAT THE BRETON CAULIFLOWER HAS A PRONOUNCED HAZELNUT

TASTE AND HAS AN ERRONEOUS REPUTATION FOR BEING LESS DIGESTIBLE. ABOVE, THE SUN DISAPPEARS BEHIND POPLAR TREES IN THE BRESSE COUNTRYSIDE.

GREENGROCER'S NAPOLEON
MILLEFEUILLE MARAICHERE

VEGETABLES

⅔ CUP DRIED FLAGEOLET BEANS, SOAKED OVERNIGHT AND DRAINED, OR 1¼ CUPS FRESH

2 CARROTS, PEELED AND CUT INTO ⅓-INCH DICE

1 CUP SHELLED PETITE GREEN PEAS

¼ POUND STRING BEANS, TRIMMED AND CUT INTO ⅓-INCH PIECES

2 MEDIUM TURNIPS, PEELED AND CUT INTO ⅓-INCH DICE

4 TABLESPOONS UNSALTED BUTTER
SALT AND FRESHLY GROUND PEPPER

¼ CUP HEAVY CREAM

PASTRY

¾ POUND PUFF PASTRY, DEFROSTED IF FROZEN

1 WHOLE EGG, BEATEN

1 CUP FINELY GRATED GRUYERE CHEESE
PAPRIKA

⅔ CUP FRESH BREAD CRUMBS, SIEVED

SAUCE

1 CUP MILK

3 TABLESPOONS UNSALTED BUTTER

2½ TABLESPOONS ALL-PURPOSE FLOUR

1 EGG YOLK

¼ CUP HEAVY CREAM

⅓ CUP FINELY DICED GRUYERE CHEESE
PINCH OF FRESHLY GRATED NUTMEG
SALT AND FRESHLY GROUND PEPPER

SERVING

1 CUP *BEURRE FONDUE* OR *BEURRE BATTU* (SEE APPENDIX)
COARSELY CHOPPED FRESH HERBS

PREPARE THE VEGETABLES: In medium saucepan, combine soaked and drained flageolet beans with water to cover. Bring to a boil and cook over medium high heat until tender, adding water as necessary, about 40 minutes; drain well. Alternatively, cook fresh flageolets in a saucepan of boiling water until tender, about 6 minutes; drain well.

Bring another saucepan of water to a boil. Add the diced carrots and cook until just tender, about 8 minutes. Remove carrots with large perforated skimmer and refresh under cold water; drain well. Repeat this process with the peas, string beans, and turnips, cooking them separately until just tender, refreshing under cold water and draining well, about 10 minutes for the peas and 6 minutes each for the beans and turnips.

In large skillet, melt butter. Add all of the cooked vegetables and cook over medium heat, stirring gently, until any liquid has evaporated. Season with salt and pepper to taste and stir in cream; set aside.

PREPARE THE PASTRY: Preheat oven to 375 degrees. Roll out puff pastry on lightly floured surface to a 15-by-10-inch rectangle, about ⅛-inch thick. Trim dough, if necessary, by cutting straight down with a sharp knife. Transfer the rolled out dough to a moistened large heavy baking sheet. Prick dough all over with a fork. Brush beaten egg evenly over the surface of dough and sprinkle with grated Gruyère and paprika. Scatter bread crumbs over the dough and bake on bottom shelf of oven until golden, about 20 minutes. Rotate baking sheet as necessary during baking to ensure even browning. Transfer pastry to a large rack.

PREPARE THE SAUCE: Bring milk to a boil in a medium saucepan. Add butter and whisk until melted. Sprinkle in flour and cook over medium heat, whisking constantly, until sauce is very smooth, about 4 minutes. Remove from the heat and stir in egg yolk, cream, diced Gruyère, and nutmeg. Season to taste with salt and pepper. (The recipe can be prepared ahead to this point.)

TO ASSEMBLE: Reheat vegetables in the cream. Stir in cheese sauce, a little at a time, until the vegetables are thoroughly coated with sauce. Using a serrated knife, cut pastry sheet crosswise into 3 even strips to form 10-by-5-inch rectangles.

Place one band of pastry, cheese-side-up, on a work surface. Spread half of vegetable mixture evenly over pastry and top with a second strip of pastry, cheese-side-up. Spread with remaining vegetables and top with third strip of pastry, cheese-side-up. With a metal spatula, smooth the sides. Using a serrated knife and a gentle sawing motion, slice the napoleon into four 2½-by-5-inch rectangles.

TO SERVE: Pour ¼ cup of *beurre fondue* or *beurre battu* onto each of 4 serving plates and place a napoleon on each one. Sprinkle with fresh herbs and serve hot. *Makes 4 servings*.

NOTE: Don't wait too long to serve this dish as the pastry becomes soggy rather quickly. If necessary, you can keep it hot in a warm oven for a few minutes. This dish could also be presented in rounds, squares, or diamonds. If you like, you can add a little lemon juice to the *beurre fondue* or *battu*.

FRESH SPRING GRASS, CONSUMED BY COWS IN THE MARSHLAND, ENHANCES THE FLAVORS OF THE DAIRY PRODUCTS USED IN THIS ORIGINAL PUFF PASTRY DISH. A COMBINATION OF VEGETABLES, INCLUDING FRESH FLAGOLET BEANS, THAT DELICATE HARICOT BEAN WITH A PALE-GREEN COLOR, ARE ASSEMBLED IN THIS DISH AND TOPPED WITH FRESH HERBS, ALL BOUGHT AT MARKET THAT MORNING.

WARM ASPARAGUS SALAD
FONDUE DE POINTES D'ASPERGES A L'ASPERGE

Like the season's first blossoms, fresh asparagus is one of the annual delights of spring gardens. In antiquity, asparagus was even given as an offering to the gods. Today, as prepared in this warm asparagus salad, all the flavor and freshness of this delicate vegetable comes through.

1¾ POUNDS FRESH ASPARAGUS
8 TABLESPOONS UNSALTED BUTTER
   SALT AND FRESHLY GROUND PEPPER
2 TABLESPOONS OLIVE OIL
2 TEASPOONS RED WINE VINEGAR
   FRESH TRUFFLES (OPTIONAL)

Snap off tough stems of asparagus and discard. Peel the stalks to within 3 inches of tips. With a sharp knife, slice peeled portion of stalks crosswise on the diagonal, about 1/16-inch-thick. Cut green tips lengthwise into fine julienne.

Melt 3 tablespoons butter in each of 2 medium skillets. Add sliced stalks to one skillet and julienned tips to other. Season both with salt and pepper. Cook tips over medium heat, tossing occasionally, for 5 minutes. Add 1 tablespoon butter and cook for 5 minutes more, or until just tender. Meanwhile, cook asparagus stalks over medium heat until just tender, about 10 minutes. (Do not let asparagus brown.)

Add ½ tablespoon butter to each skillet and toss until melted. Add 1 tablespoon olive oil and 1 teaspoon vinegar to each skillet and cook for 1 minute more. Season with salt and pepper to taste and let asparagus cool slightly.

TO SERVE: Mound sliced stalks in the center of each of 4 serving plates. Carefully spoon julienned tips attractively around stalks and serve immediately. If you like, garnish with shavings or strips of fresh truffles. *Makes 4 servings.*

THREE-LAYER OMELET
RUBANEE D'OMELETTE

½ CUP PLUS 1½ TEASPOONS OLIVE OIL
½ RED BELL PEPPER, FINELY DICED
½ GREEN BELL PEPPER, FINELY DICED
2 CLOVES GARLIC
2 BAY LEAVES
2 SPRIGS OF THYME
  SALT AND FRESHLY GROUND PEPPER
12 EGGS
½ CUP HEAVY CREAM
5 TABLESPOONS UNSALTED BUTTER
⅔ POUND FRESH SPINACH, WELL-WASHED, STEMMED, AND CUT INTO THIN STRIPS

⅓ POUND FRESH YOUNG SORREL, WELL-WASHED, STEMMED, AND CUT INTO THIN STRIPS
1 CUP WATERCRESS LEAVES, WELL-WASHED AND THINLY SLICED
1 SMALL ONION, FINELY CHOPPED
1¼ POUNDS TOMATOES, PEELED, SEEDED, AND CHOPPED
2 FRESH BASIL LEAVES, FINELY CHOPPED
SERVING
  FRESH TOMATO *COULIS* (SEE APPENDIX)
  SNIPPED FRESH CHIVES (OPTIONAL)

Heat ½ cup olive oil in a small saucepan. Add the diced red and green bell peppers, 1 garlic clove, 1 bay leaf, 1 sprig of thyme, and ⅛ teaspoon salt. Bring to a simmer and cook over medium heat until peppers soften slightly, about 5 minutes. Drain peppers in a strainer and discard garlic, thyme sprig, and bay leaf.

Preheat oven to 325 degrees. Butter an enameled or porcelain 5-cup terrine very well and line the bottom with parchment paper; butter the paper.

In a medium bowl, beat 4 eggs with ¼ cup cream. Stir in drained peppers and season with ⅛ teaspoon each salt and pepper, or to taste. Pour mixture into terrine and set in a larger pan filled with warm water to reach halfway up sides of terrine. Bake until the top is set, about 30 minutes.

Meanwhile, melt 4 tablespoons butter in a large casserole over medium heat. When butter foams, add spinach, sorrel, and watercress and cook, stirring, until greens are wilted and tender, about 5 minutes. Drain greens and press or squeeze out as much liquid as possible, either in a strainer or in a towel.

In a medium bowl, beat 4 eggs with remaining ¼ cup cream. Stir in greens and mix well. Season with ⅛ teaspoon each of salt and pepper, or to taste. When the first layer of terrine is set, pour in this mixture and continue baking until set, about 30 minutes more.

Meanwhile, in a medium skillet, heat remaining 1 tablespoon butter with remaining ½ tablespoon olive oil. Add onion and cook over medium heat, stirring occasionally, until translucent, about 3 minutes. Finely chop the remaining garlic clove and add to skillet. Cook, stirring, for 30 seconds, then add chopped tomatoes, the remaining sprig of thyme, bay leaf, and ⅛ teaspoon each of salt and pepper. Let tomatoes cook, stirring occasionally, until all liquid has evaporated, about 15 minutes. Remove from heat and stir in basil.

In a medium bowl, beat remaining 4 eggs. Stir in tomato mixture and season with salt and pepper to taste. When the top of the terrine feels set, pour in this mixture. Continue cooking the terrine just until tomato layer is completely set, about 35 minutes. If top begins to brown, cover loosely with foil.

Remove terrine from water bath and let cool on a rack for 10 minutes. Run a thin-bladed knife or a metal spatula around the edge to loosen terrine; unmold onto a large plate.

TO SERVE: Using a sharp knife, cut terrine into slices. Serve hot, warm, or cold, accompanied with Fresh Tomato *Coulis*. If you like, sprinkle each serving with snipped chives. *Makes 8 servings.*

NOTE: If you would like to prepare this dish in stages, all of the vegetable mixtures can be cooked one day ahead and then combined with the eggs and cream just before baking.

THE LAYERS OF THIS MULTI-FLAVORED OMELET ECHO THE COLORS OF THE LANDSCAPE AND SPEAK TO THE MARVELOUS MARRIAGE OF TASTES THAT FRESH PRODUCE CAN PROVIDE. GREEN AND RED PEPPERS ARE UNITED IN THE BOTTOM LAYER OF THE TERRINE; SPINACH, SORREL, AND WATERCRESS LEAVES ARE COMBINED IN THE MIDDLE; AND TOMATO FLAVORS THE TOP LAYER.

HERBED VEGETABLE CAKES
GATEAU PRINTANIER D'HERBES AUX FEVES ET POIS GOURMANDS

VEGETABLE CAKES

⅔ POUND SPINACH, WELL-WASHED AND LARGE STEMS REMOVED

ONE 6-OUNCE POTATO, PEELED AND SLICED ½-INCH THICK

1 LEEK, WELL-WASHED, TRIMMED, AND QUARTERED

1 CLOVE GARLIC, PEELED

1 BUNCH OF PARSLEY, RINSED AND LARGE STEMS REMOVED

1 BUNCH OF WATERCRESS, RINSED AND LARGE STEMS REMOVED

2 SMALL HEADS OF BOSTON LETTUCE, WELL-WASHED AND CORED

1 BUNCH OF CHERVIL, RINSED AND LARGE STEMS REMOVED

4 EGGS

¼ CUP CREME FRAICHE

FRESHLY GRATED NUTMEG

SALT AND FRESHLY GROUND PEPPER

GARNISH

¾ CUP SHELLED PEAS

¼ POUND SNOW PEAS, TRIMMED AND STRINGS REMOVED

¾ CUP FAVA BEANS

2 TABLESPOONS UNSALTED BUTTER

LEMON BUTTER

JUICE AND GRATED ZEST OF 1 LEMON

1 SHALLOT, THINLY SLICED

3 TABLESPOONS CREME FRAICHE

10 TABLESPOONS UNSALTED BUTTER

SALT AND FRESHLY GROUND PEPPER

SERVING

FRESH CHERVIL SPRIGS

PREPARE THE VEGETABLE CAKES: Bring a very large pot of salted water to a boil. Add 10 of the prettiest large spinach leaves to water and blanch for 15 seconds. Remove with a slotted spoon and refresh under cold water. Spread spinach leaves out on paper towels to drain.

Add potato, leek, and garlic to pot and cook for 8 minutes. Add parsley, remaining spinach, and watercress; cook for 3 minutes. Add lettuce and chervil and cook for 3 minutes longer. Drain all vegetables in large colander and refresh under cold water. Gather vegetables into a ball with your hands and squeeze to extract as much liquid as possible.

Place vegetables in a food processor and puree, scraping down the sides every 20 seconds, until very, very smooth. Add eggs, crème fraîche, and a good pinch of nutmeg. Puree until thoroughly blended. Season mixture with salt and pepper to taste.

Preheat oven to 325 degrees. Generously butter five 6-ounce ramekins or darioles and line them with reserved blanched spinach leaves. Fill lined molds with vegetable puree. Bake in a warm water bath until a cake tester inserted in the center comes out clean, about 35 minutes. Remove molds from water bath. (These vegetable cakes can be prepared ahead and then rewarmed in a hot water bath in the oven until heated through.)

PREPARE THE GARNISH: In medium saucepan, cook the peas in boiling salted water until tender, about 15 minutes. Remove with a slotted spoon, refresh under cold water, and drain well. Add snow peas to saucepan and cook until just tender, about 4 minutes. Remove with a slotted spoon, refresh under cold water and drain well. Add fava beans to water and cook for 4 minutes. Drain the fava beans and refresh under cold water. Remove their tough skins by gently squeezing beans between thumb and index finger. Cut snow peas into diamonds and place in a medium skillet along with fava beans and peas. Add butter to skillet and set aside until serving time.

PREPARE THE SAUCE: In small heavy saucepan, combine lemon juice and zest, shallot, and ¼ cup water. Bring to a boil over high heat and cook until reduced by two-thirds. Add crème fraîche and reduce the heat to medium. When cream simmers, whisk in butter, 1 tablespoon at a time. When all butter has been thoroughly incorporated and mixture is creamy, remove from heat. Season with salt and pepper to taste and strain sauce through a fine-mesh sieve. (Keep sauce warm in a water bath, if you like.)

TO SERVE: Reheat vegetable cakes, if necessary. Warm peas and beans in butter in skillet over medium heat. Run a flexible knife around inner rim of the vegetable cakes to loosen them, then unmold onto 5 rimmed serving plates. Garnish each serving with peas and beans. Spoon some of the lemon butter over all and sprinkle with small chervil sprigs. *Makes 5 servings.*

A HERBED VEGETABLE CAKE NESTLED AMID COUNTRY FLOWERS IS GARNISHED WITH FAVA BEANS, GREEN PEAS, AND SNOW PEAS—ALSO CALLED THE *MANGETOUT* OR EAT-THEM-ALL PEA, BECAUSE THE PEA AND POD ALIKE ARE EATEN. SNOW PEAS, WHICH MUST BE EATEN YOUNG, HAVE COME BACK INTO FASHION, ESPECIALLY WITH THOSE FAVORING A LIGHT CUISINE, AFTER HAVING HAD THEIR HOUR OF GLORY DURING THE RENAISSANCE. THE DELICACY OF THIS DISH PERFECTLY EVOKES AN AURA OF SPRING.

FRESH PASTA WITH LEMON
PATES FRAICHES AU CITRON

PASTA
1⅔ CUPS ALL-PURPOSE FLOUR
1 WHOLE EGG
1 EGG WHITE
1 TABLESPOON OLIVE OIL
⅛ TEASPOON SALT

SAUCE
GRATED ZEST OF 4 WELL-WASHED
   ORGANIC LEMONS
½ CUP DRY WHITE WINE
1 CUP CREME FRAICHE
¾ CUP GRATED GRUYERE CHEESE
LEMON JUICE
SALT AND FRESHLY GROUND PEPPER

THIS RECIPE COMES FROM A ROMAN CHEF WHOM I MET DURING A TRIP TO ITALY, WHERE I FIRST ENJOYED THIS DISH. THE ZESTY FLAVOR OF FRESH LEMON OR ORANGE MAKES THIS A SIMPLE AND UNUSUAL WAY TO REDISCOVER THE PLEASURES OF FRESH PASTA.

PREPARE THE PASTA: In a food processor fitted with metal blade, combine flour, whole egg, egg white, oil, salt, and 4 teaspoons water. Process until dough is smooth and forms a ball, about 1 minute. If the dough seems dry, add a little more water through feed tube until dough coheres. Wrap the dough with plastic wrap and refrigerate for 1 hour.

Alternatively, place flour in a medium bowl and make a well in center. Add remaining ingredients and 4 teaspoons water to well and stir to combine. Gradually work flour into liquids. When dough coheres, transfer to a lightly floured work surface and knead until smooth and elastic, about 3 minutes.

Using a pasta machine, roll out dough into thin sheets. Cut into fettuccine strips. Set aside to dry slightly. Cook pasta in a large pot of boiling salted water until *al dente*, about 4 minutes.

PREPARE THE SAUCE: Meanwhile, in a large sauté pan, combine lemon zest with wine. Bring to a boil over medium heat. Increase heat to high and boil until the wine reduces by half, about 5 minutes.

Drain pasta and add to sauté pan. Stir in crème fraîche and Gruyère and cook over medium heat, tossing constantly, until the cream thickens slightly and pasta is thoroughly coated and piping hot. Add lemon juice to taste and season with salt and pepper. Serve immediately. *Makes 4 servings.*

NOTE: If you are short on time, ⅔ pound of fresh fettuccine can be substituted for the pasta called for here.

CREAM OF FRESH FAVA BEAN AND PEA SOUP
CREME DE FEVES ET POIS AUX CROUTONS

EARLY SPRING IS THE TIME OF THE LAST FROSTS, AS SEEN IN THIS CLEARING IN THE BEOST FOREST. IT CAN ALSO BE A TIME FOR A FORTIFYING BUT SOOTHING SOUP OF FRESH FAVA BEANS AND GREEN PEAS. THE EATING OF PEAS BECAME VIRTUALLY A MANIA IN SIXTEENTH-CENTURY FRANCE; PEAS REMAIN POPULAR.

IT IS STRONGLY RECOMMENDED THAT FRESH PEAS BE SHELLED WITHOUT DELAY, EVEN IF IT MEANS KEEPING THEM IN THE REFRIGERATOR MIXED WITH A BIT OF BUTTER. THREE POUNDS OF PEAS IN PODS ARE NEEDED TO OBTAIN ABOUT 21

OUNCES OF PEAS, EACH POD CONTAINING ABOUT SIX TO EIGHT GREEN PEARLS.

VEGETABLE STOCK
1 CARROT, PEELED AND SLICED INTO THIN ROUNDS
1 LEEK, WHITE AND LIGHT GREEN, WELL-WASHED AND SLICED
1 ONION, PEELED AND THINLY SLICED
1 WHOLE CLOVE
BOUQUET GARNI
SOUP
1½ CUPS SHELLED FAVA BEANS (ABOUT 1¼ POUNDS UNSHELLED)
1½ CUPS FRESH PEAS
10 TABLESPOONS UNSALTED BUTTER

1 SHALLOT, FINELY CHOPPED
1 CUP HEAVY CREAM
SALT AND FRESHLY GROUND PEPPER
FRESHLY GRATED NUTMEG
4 SLICES WHITE BREAD, CRUSTS REMOVED AND BREAD CUT INTO SMALL CUBES
SERVING
4 TEASPOONS TOMATO, CHOPPED, PEELED, AND SEEDED
1 TABLESPOON CHERVIL LEAVES
FRESHLY GRATED PARMESAN CHEESE AND CREME FRAICHE (OPTIONAL)

PREPARE THE VEGETABLE STOCK: In medium saucepan, combine all of stock ingredients with 2¼ cups of water. Bring to a boil over high heat. Reduce heat to medium and simmer for 30 minutes. Strain stock and reserve 1 cup for the soup. Save remainder for another use.

PREPARE THE SOUP: Blanch fava beans in boiling salted water for 2 minutes. Remove with a wire skimmer and refresh under cold water. Add peas to saucepan and boil over high heat until tender, about 15 minutes. Drain and refresh under cold water. Peel off thick outer shell of fava beans.

Melt 2 tablespoons butter in medium casserole. Add shallot and cook, stirring, until translucent, about 2 minutes. Add fava beans, peas, and reserved 1 cup vegetable stock and cook over medium high heat until fava beans and peas are very tender, about 5 minutes. Add cream and bring to a boil over high heat. Transfer mixture to a blender and puree until very smooth. Strain the soup through a fine-mesh strainer set over a saucepan. Season the soup with salt, pepper, and nutmeg to taste.

Melt 4 tablespoons butter in a medium skillet. Add bread cubes and sauté over medium high heat, tossing frequently, until browned on all sides, about 4 minutes. Drain croutons on paper towels.

TO SERVE: In a small skillet, warm chopped tomato over medium heat. Reheat soup. Cut remaining 4 tablespoons butter into small cubes and add to soup, whisking thoroughly until incorporated. Taste for seasoning. Ladle soup into 4 shallow rimmed soup plates and sprinkle with croutons. Place 1 teaspoon of chopped tomato in the center of each serving and sprinkle with chervil leaves and freshly ground pepper. Pass Parmesan and crème fraîche separately, if using. *Makes 4 servings.*

ARTICHOKE BOTTOMS STUFFED WITH MUSHROOMS
FONDS D'ARTICHAUTS FARCIS AUX CHAMPIGNONS

A RELATIVE OF THE THISTLE, THE ARTICHOKE IS OFTEN COOKED IN WATER THAT HAS BEEN ACIDULATED WITH SOME LEMON OR VINEGAR, THEN DRAINED HEAD DOWN IN A COLANDER AND SERVED WITH ANY OF A VARIETY OF SAUCES (HOLLANDAISE OR MOUSSELINE, FOR EXAMPLE). IN THIS DISH (PICTURED ON PAGE 32) THE BOTTOMS ARE STUFFED FOR AN ELEGANT LIGHT MEAL.

ARTICHOKES
4 LARGE ARTICHOKES
  FOUR ⅓-INCH-THICK LEMON SLICES
FILLING
1 POUND FRESH MUSHROOMS, WIPED CLEAN
1½ TABLESPOONS OLIVE OIL
4 TABLESPOONS UNSALTED BUTTER
2 SHALLOTS, FINELY CHOPPED
1 TEASPOON ALL-PURPOSE FLOUR
½ CUP HEAVY CREAM

1 EGG YOLK
¼ CUP FRESH BREAD CRUMBS, DRIED AND SIFTED
1½ TABLESPOONS FINELY CHOPPED PARSLEY
  SALT AND FRESHLY GROUND PEPPER
2 TABLESPOONS GRATED PARMESAN CHEESE
1 CUP *BEURRE BATTU* (SEE APPENDIX)
  SNIPPED CHIVES AND TARRAGON LEAVES FOR GARNISH

PREPARE THE ARTICHOKES: Cut stems from artichokes and trim tips with scissors. Place 1 lemon slice over stem end of each artichoke and secure with string. (The lemon will keep the base moist, tender, and bright.)

In a large pot of boiling salted water, cook artichokes over medium heat until just tender when pierced with a skewer, about 30 minutes. Drain well. When artichokes are cool enough to handle, remove all leaves and place in a large bowl. Scoop out hairy chokes and discard. Using a teaspoon, scrape the edible portions from all of the leaves and set aside in a bowl. (The artichokes can be cooked in advance, if you like. Refrigerate the cooked and prepared bottoms in a little bit of cooking liquid to keep them from drying out.)

PREPARE THE FILLING: Remove stems from mushrooms and finely chop caps. Heat olive oil and 2 tablespoons butter in a large skillet. Add chopped mushroom caps and cook over medium heat, stirring occasionally, until most of their liquid evaporates, about 8 minutes. Add shallots and flour and cook, stirring to incorporate flour, for 1 minute more. Add the cream and artichoke meat that was scraped from the leaves. Stir in egg yolk, 2 tablespoons bread crumbs, and the parsley. Mix well to combine thoroughly and season to taste with salt and pepper. (This filling, too, can be prepared in advance.)

Preheat oven to 325 degrees. Butter a baking dish large enough to accommodate the artichoke bottoms. Encircle each artichoke with a band of parchment paper, forming a collar that extends at least 1½ inches above artichoke. Secure collars with string.

Fill artichokes with mushroom mixture and smooth surfaces. Evenly sprinkle each with 1½ teaspoons bread crumbs and 1½ teaspoons Parmesan cheese. Dot top of each one with ¾ teaspoon of butter. Carefully place artichokes in baking dish and add ⅛ inch water to the dish, along with the remaining 1 tablespoon butter. Bake artichokes on middle shelf of oven until heated through and crumbs are golden brown, about 30 minutes.

TO SERVE: Remove artichokes from baking dish. Discard strings and paper collars. Divide *beurre battu* among 4 plates and place an artichoke in the center of each one. Garnish with snipped chives and tarragon and serve hot. *Makes 4 servings.*

ASPARAGUS FLANS
FLAN AUX ASPERGES, AUX FEVES, ET POIVRONS ROUGES

2 POUNDS ASPARAGUS	2¾ CUPS SHELLED FAVA BEANS (ABOUT 2½
2½ CUPS CREME FRAICHE	POUNDS IN THE SHELL)
2 WHOLE EGGS, BEATEN	3 TABLESPOONS UNSALTED BUTTER
2 EGG YOLKS	1 SHALLOT, PEELED AND THINLY SLICED
SALT AND FRESHLY GROUND PEPPER	1 RED BELL PEPPER

PREPARE THE ASPARAGUS FLANS: Snap woody ends off asparagus and peel stalks. Cut tips into 2-inch lengths. Cook tips in boiling salted water until just tender, about 5 minutes. Remove with a wire skimmer or slotted spoon, refresh under cold water, and drain very well; set aside.

Add asparagus stalks to boiling water and cook until very tender, about 20 minutes. Drain stalks and squeeze in a kitchen towel to extract all moisture. Puree stalks in a food processor and strain through a fine-mesh sieve into a bowl. Whisk in 1¼ cups crème fraîche, the whole eggs, and egg yolks. Season with ½ teaspoon salt and ¼ teaspoon pepper, or to taste, and mix well.

Preheat oven to 325 degrees. Generously butter twelve ⅓-cup dariole molds or eight ½-cup ramekins. Pour flan mixture into prepared molds and set molds in a hot water bath. Bake flans until a cake tester or toothpick inserted in the center comes out clean, about 20 minutes for darioles and 35 for ramekins. Remove molds from water bath and let cool slightly on a rack.

PREPARE THE SAUCE AND GARNISH: While flans are baking, blanch fava beans in boiling water for 3 minutes. Drain and refresh under cold water. Press beans gently between thumb and index finger to remove their tough outer skins.

In medium saucepan, melt 1½ tablespoons butter over medium heat. Add shallot and cook until translucent, about 3 minutes. Add two-thirds of the peeled beans and remaining 1½ cups of crème fraîche; bring to a boil over high heat. Reduce heat to medium and simmer for 5 minutes. Transfer beans and cream to a blender and puree until completely smooth. Strain bean sauce into a small saucepan and season to taste with salt and pepper. (The sauce should be quite thin—if it's too thick, thin it out with a little cream or water.)

Roast red bell pepper directly in a gas flame or under broiler, turning until charred on all sides. Let cool slightly. Peel pepper and discard core and seeds. Cut out any veins with a small knife and cut pepper into diamond-shaped pieces.

TO SERVE: Melt remaining 1½ tablespoons butter in a medium skillet. Add reserved asparagus tips and fava beans and toss over medium heat until warmed through. Reheat fava bean sauce.

Run a sharp, flexible knife around edges of flans and unmold them onto 4 heated shallow-rimmed plates. Spoon fava bean sauce around flans and garnish each serving with red pepper diamonds and beans. Arrange asparagus tips in a crown pattern around flans and serve immediately. *Makes 4 servings.*

WHILE THE ASPARAGUS SEASON IS SHORT, THERE ARE MANY WAYS TO SAVOR THIS HIGHLY PRIZED VEGETABLE. THIS DISH WILL SERVE ON THOSE SPECIAL OCCASIONS WHEN YOU WISH TO SURPRISE AND DELIGHT THE EYES AND PALATES OF THE MOST DEMANDING GUESTS. SERVED HOT OR AT ROOM TEMPERATURE, ASPARAGUS IS TRADITIONALLY ACCOMPANIED BY MELTED BUTTER OR A

VINAIGRETTE, ALTHOUGH THERE IS A NEVER-ENDING ARGUMENT AS TO WHICH IS PREFERABLE. ANOTHER EXCELLENT METHOD OF SERVING ASPARAGUS IS WITH MELTED BUTTER AND SOFT-BOILED EGGS, THE STALK TAKING THE PLACE OF TOASTED BREAD TO SOAK UP THE EGG.

ARTICHOKE-STUFFED SOUFFLES
SOUFFLES FARCIS AUX ARTICHAUTS

THE PERFECT ARTICHOKE IS HEAVY FOR ITS SIZE, FIRM, AND WITH STIFF LEAVES. FOR THIS RECIPE, THE CLASSIC COMBINATION OF ARTICHOKE AND EGG IS GIVEN AN ORIGINAL TWIST.

4	ARTICHOKES, WELL-RINSED	
4	TABLESPOONS UNSALTED BUTTER	
4	SHALLOTS, FINELY CHOPPED	
½	POUND MUSHROOMS, TRIMMED AND VERY FINELY CHOPPED	
	SALT AND FRESHLY GROUND PEPPER	
4	HARD-COOKED EGG YOLKS	
1	TEASPOON CHOPPED PARSLEY	

SOUFFLE MIXTURE

1	CUP MILK
1½	TABLESPOONS UNSALTED BUTTER
1½	TABLESPOONS ALL-PURPOSE FLOUR
6	TABLESPOONS CREME FRAICHE
1	EGG YOLK
½	CUP GRATED PARMESAN CHEESE
1	TEASPOON SNIPPED CHIVES
	FRESHLY GRATED NUTMEG
4	EGG WHITES

Cook artichokes in a large pot of boiling salted water until tender, about 30 minutes. Drain well. Remove leaves from artichokes and set aside. With a small spoon, scoop out hairy chokes. Trim artichoke bottoms to give them a neat shape.

While artichokes are cooking, melt 3 tablespoons butter in a large skillet. Add shallots and cook over medium heat, stirring, until translucent, about 3 minutes. Add mushrooms and cook over medium high heat, stirring, until their liquid evaporates and mixture is dry, about 5 minutes. Season with salt and pepper and remove from the heat; let cool slightly.

On a small plate, mash hard-cooked egg yolks with a fork. Add to mushroom mixture along with parsley and blend well. With a small spoon, scrape meaty portion from reserved artichoke leaves and add to mushroom mixture. Mix well with a fork. (If you like, you can reserve a few of the prettiest artichoke leaves to garnish soufflés.)

Generously butter four 1- to 1¼-cup ramekins. Thinly slice each artichoke bottom and place on bottom of prepared ramekins. Divide mushroom mixture evenly among ramekins and smooth tops. (The recipe can be prepared ahead to this point.)

FOR THE SOUFFLE: Preheat oven to 400 degrees. Bring milk to a boil in a small saucepan. Meanwhile, melt butter in another small saucepan. Add flour and whisk over medium heat until foaming. Whisk in scalded milk and crème fraîche. Bring to a boil over medium high heat, whisking constantly, and boil for 30 seconds. Remove from heat and whisk in egg yolk. Stir in Parmesan and chives. Season to taste with salt, pepper, and nutmeg.

In a bowl, beat egg whites until stiff. Gently fold into Parmesan mixture until fully incorporated. Fill ramekins with soufflé mixture. Place soufflés in a hot water bath and bake in oven until well-risen and browned on top, about 15 minutes. Serve immediately, as is, or garnish soufflés with a few reserved artichoke leaves. *Makes 4 servings.*

QUARTET OF VEGETABLE PUREES
PRINTANIERE AUX SUCS DE LEGUMES

Tomatoes, red peppers, celery root, and string beans are the quartet of colorful vegetables used in this dramatic assemblage of purees. Not only does this dish represent one of the felicitous marriages of taste that a natural cuisine can provide but the dish can also become a visual splendour of marbleized patterns. In its presentation, you may be as artistic as you wish.

1¼ pounds ripe tomatoes, cored and coarsely chopped
1 clove garlic, peeled
  salt and freshly ground pepper
1¼ pounds red bell peppers, cored, seeded, and cut into pieces
1 pound celery root (celeriac), peeled and cut into large chunks
1 pound string beans, trimmed
1 to 1½ cups heavy cream

In a medium skillet, combine tomatoes with garlic. Season with salt and pepper and cook over medium heat, stirring occasionally, until liquid from tomatoes evaporates, about 15 minutes. Strain tomatoes through a sieve or in a food mill set over a small saucepan. Set puree aside.

In a medium casserole, combine red bell peppers with 2 table-spoons water and a pinch of salt. Cover and cook over medium heat, stirring occasionally, until very tender, about 13 minutes. Puree peppers in a food mill or food processor and strain puree through a fine-mesh sieve into a small saucepan.

Cook celery root in boiling salted water until very tender, about 20 minutes. Drain very well and puree in a food mill or food processor; strain through a fine-mesh sieve into a small saucepan.

Soak beans in ice water. Meanwhile, bring a medium saucepan of salted water to a boil over high heat. Plunge beans into boiling water and cook until very tender, about 12 minutes. Drain very well. Puree beans in a food mill or food processor and strain through a fine-mesh sieve into a small saucepan. (The vegetable purees can be prepared ahead and finished just before serving time.)

To serve: Reheat all of the vegetable purees over medium heat. Add enough cream to give each one the consistency of a very thick soup. Season purees with salt and pepper to taste. Spoon equal amounts of each puree into 4 large rimmed soup plates. Tap plates lightly on a flat surface to even them out, then swirl decoratively with a spoon or a knife. Serve immediately. *Makes 4 servings.*

MUSHROOM-STUFFED MUSHROOMS WITH CURRY
CHAMPIGNONS FARCIS

MUSHROOMS

12 VERY LARGE MUSHROOMS, STEMS
   REMOVED
½ POUND SMALLER MUSHROOMS, STEMS
   REMOVED
¼ CUP LEMON JUICE
6 TABLESPOONS UNSALTED BUTTER, PLUS
   ¼ CUP MELTED BUTTER
   SALT
1 SHALLOT, FINELY CHOPPED
1 CLOVE GARLIC, FINELY CHOPPED
3 TABLESPOONS CREME FRAICHE
2 EGG YOLKS
⅔ CUP FRESH BREAD CRUMBS, DRIED AND
   SIEVED
1½ TABLESPOONS CHOPPED PARSLEY

FRESHLY GRATED NUTMEG
PINCH OF CURRY POWDER
FRESHLY GROUND PEPPER
½ APPLE, PEELED AND CUT INTO SMALL
   DICE

SAUCE

⅔ CUP CREME FRAICHE
1 TABLESPOON UNSALTED BUTTER
2 TABLESPOONS MINCED WHITE ONION
1 TEASPOON CURRY POWDER
1 TABLESPOON CHOPPED BLANCHED
   ALMONDS
   SALT AND FRESHLY GROUND PEPPER
½ TOMATO, SEEDED AND CUT INTO SMALL
   DICE FOR GARNISH

THIS MUSHROOM DISH, IN WHICH THE STUFFED MUSHROOMS ARE ENHANCED WITH A CURRIED FILLING AND SAUCE, IS ONE OF MY FAVORITES—A HEARTY AND FLAVORFUL TREAT, GARNISHED WITH SAUTEED APPLE AND TOMATO.

PREPARE THE MUSHROOMS: In a medium saucepan, combine all mushroom caps with 2 tablespoons lemon juice and toss well. Add 1 cup water, 1½ tablespoons butter, and a pinch of salt. Bring to a boil over high heat, cover, and cook for 3 minutes. Drain the mushrooms over a saucepan, reserving cooking liquid.

Preheat oven to 325 degrees. Finely chop smaller mushroom caps, reserving larger ones for stuffing. In a large skillet, melt 3 tablespoons butter. Add chopped mushrooms and cook over medium heat, stirring, until most of their liquid evaporates, about 5 minutes. Add shallot and garlic and cook for 1 minute more. Stir in crème fraîche and egg yolks; add bread crumbs, parsley, a small pinch of nutmeg, and a pinch of curry powder. Mix well and season to taste with salt and pepper.

Fill large mushroom caps with stuffing mixture and place in a buttered baking dish. Sprinkle with remaining 2 tablespoons lemon juice and drizzle with the melted butter. Bake mushrooms until heated through, about 25 minutes.

Meanwhile, melt remaining 1½ tablespoons of butter in a small skillet. Add the diced apple and sauté over medium high heat, tossing, until golden, about 4 minutes; reserve.

PREPARE THE SAUCE: Bring reserved mushroom liquid to a boil over high heat and cook until reduced to ½ cup, about 12 minutes. Stir in crème fraîche, return to a boil, and simmer sauce for 5 minutes; set aside. Melt butter in a small skillet. Add onion and cook over medium heat until softened, about 3 minutes. Stir in curry powder and cook, stirring, until quite fragrant, about 2 minutes longer. Scrape curried onion into sauce, add almonds, and bring to a boil. Simmer sauce over medium high heat until it has a nice consistency and the flavors are blended, about 5 minutes. Season with salt and pepper to taste. Strain sauce through a fine-mesh strainer.

TO SERVE: Reheat sautéed diced apple. Spoon sauce onto 4 serving plates and arrange 3 stuffed mushroom caps on each. Garnish with sautéed apple and diced tomato. Sprinkle each mushroom with a little additional curry powder before serving. *Makes 4 servings.*

FRIED GNOCCHI
WITH ZUCCHINI AND RED BELL PEPPERS
GNOCCHI AUX COURGETTES ET AUX POIVRONS ROUGES

THE TREES OF BUGEY (PAGE 42) ARE IN FLOWER, TRANSFORMING THE HILLS WITH SPRING-TIME HUES. MEANWHILE THIS GNOCCHI DISH (PICTURED ON PAGE 43) PROVIDES ITS OWN TANTALIZING BALANCE OF COLORS AND TASTES. THE GNOCCHI ARE SERVED IN A RED PEPPER SAUCE, SURROUNDED BY A CROWN OF UPRIGHT,

GNOCCHI

2	CUPS MILK
½	TEASPOON SALT
¼	TEASPOON FRESHLY GROUND PEPPER
	PINCH OF FRESHLY GRATED NUTMEG
¾	CUP ALL-PURPOSE FLOUR
1	WHOLE EGG
1	EGG YOLK

VEGETABLES

2	RED BELL PEPPERS
2	MEDIUM ZUCCHINI, TRIMMED AND THINLY SLICED
1	TABLESPOON OLIVE OIL

SAUCE

⅔	CUP CREME FRAICHE
3	TABLESPOONS UNSALTED BUTTER

PREPARE THE GNOCCHI: In a saucepan, bring milk, salt, pepper, and nutmeg to a boil. As soon as it boils, reduce heat to medium high and sift in flour. Stir constantly with a wooden spoon for 5 minutes, until mixture is very smooth and thick. Remove from heat and beat in whole egg and egg yolk, stirring until thoroughly incorporated. Using a spatula, scrape gnocchi dough onto a buttered baking sheet. Dip spatula in water and spread out dough to form an even square about ½-inch-thick. Let cool. Cover and refrigerate until cold and firm. (This can be prepared 1 day ahead.)

PREPARE THE VEGETABLES: Roast peppers directly in a gas flame or under broiler, turning until charred all over. Let cool slightly, then peel peppers and remove the cores and seeds. Using a small sharp knife, cut peppers into 12 neat diamond shapes; reserve all trimmings for sauce.

Blanch zucchini slices in a large pot of boiling salted water for 1 minute. Drain, refresh under cold water, and transfer to paper towels to drain thoroughly.

PREPARE THE SAUCE: In a medium skillet, cook pepper trimmings in olive oil over medium heat until very soft, about 3 minutes. Add crème fraîche and simmer for 5 minutes. Transfer mixture to a blender and puree until completely smooth. Strain pepper sauce into a saucepan and season to taste with salt and pepper.

COOK THE GNOCCHI: Using a lightly floured 4½-inch round or fluted cookie cutter, stamp out four rounds from gnocchi dough. In a medium large skillet, heat 2 tablespoons butter until foamy. Add gnocchi (carefully, because they are quite tender) and fry over medium heat until nicely browned, 3 to 5 minutes per side.

In another skillet, gently reheat zucchini slices in remaining 1 tablespoon butter. Reheat red pepper sauce.

TO SERVE: Place 1 gnocchi in the center of each of 4 serving plates and surround with a crown of upstanding, overlapping zucchini slices. Carefully spoon red pepper sauce around inside of zucchini crown and garnish each serving with red pepper diamonds. Pass remaining sauce separately in a sauceboat. *Makes 4 servings.*

OVERLAPPING ZUCCHINI SLICES AND GARNISHED WITH RED PEPPER DIAMONDS.

ALAIN SENDERENS' ZUCCHINI AND CARROT "SPAGHETTI"

SPAGHETTI DE COURGETTE ET CAROTTE AU THYM D'ALAIN SENDERENS

SAUCE

2   TABLESPOONS UNSALTED BUTTER
2   CARROTS, THINLY SLICED
4   LARGE SHALLOTS, THINLY SLICED
1   LARGE LEEK, WHITE AND LIGHT GREEN, THINLY SLICED
1   SMALL RIB CELERY, THINLY SLICED
1   SPRIG OF THYME
½   BAY LEAF
¼   CUP DRY WHITE WINE
2   CUPS HEAVY CREAM
6   SMALL SPRIGS OF BASIL
2   BUNCHES OF CHIVES PLUS 1 TABLESPOON SNIPPED CHIVES

"SPAGHETTI"

5   LARGE CARROTS, CUT INTO LONG THIN STRIPS (SEE NOTE)
6   TABLESPOONS UNSALTED BUTTER
4   ZUCCHINI, CUT INTO LONG THIN STRIPS
1   TABLESPOON FRESH THYME
    SALT AND FRESHLY GROUND PEPPER
8   GREEN OLIVES, PITTED
8   BLACK OLIVES, PITTED
1   TOMATO, PEELED, SEEDED, AND CHOPPED
2   TEASPOONS CHOPPED FRESH BASIL

ALAIN SENDERENS, A TRUE CREATOR, OFFERS THIS INNOVATIVE RECIPE IN KEEPING WITH MY THEME: THE UNITING OF FRESH PRODUCE AND GREAT COOKING. LONG, THINLY SLICED CARROT AND ZUCCHINI STRIPS ARE ROLLED ON A FORK TO FORM LITTLE NESTS OF VEGETABLE "SPAGHETTI" AND SERVED WITH A SAUCE PERFUMED WITH FRESH BASIL AND THYME. THE RESULT IS LIGHT

PREPARE THE SAUCE: Melt butter in a wide medium saucepan. Add carrots, shallots, leek, celery, thyme, and bay leaf and stir to coat vegetables with butter. Cover and cook over medium heat, stirring from time to time, until vegetables are tender and fragrant, about 10 minutes. Add wine and bring to a boil over medium high heat. Cook, stirring, until wine evaporates, about 3 minutes. Stir in cream, basil sprigs, and bunches of chives and bring to a boil. Simmer over medium heat until cream thickens, about 15 minutes. Strain sauce into another saucepan through a fine-mesh sieve.

PREPARE THE "SPAGHETTI": In a large pot, steam the carrot strips until just tender, about 3 minutes. Remove from pot and rinse under cold water; drain carrots very well.

Melt butter in a very large skillet. Add zucchini and carrot strips and cook over medium high heat, tossing gently, until tender and heated through, about 3 minutes. Add thyme and season to taste with salt and pepper.

TO SERVE: Reheat sauce over medium heat. Roll carrot and zucchini "spaghetti" on a large fork to form little nests. Place 4 of these nests on each of 4 large dinner plates. Place 2 green and 2 black olives on each serving. Spoon chopped tomato onto center of each plate and sprinkle with chopped basil.

Stir snipped chives into sauce and pour into a sauceboat to be passed separately. Serve immediately. *Makes 4 servings.*

NOTE: The sauce can also be spooned onto the plates before the nests of vegetable pasta are added. You will need a mandoline to slice the carrots and zucchini into the long, thin spaghetti-like strips called for here. If you like, the vegetables can be sliced and the sauce can be prepared in advance.

BUT DRAMATIC FARE. INTERESTINGLY, THE CARROT, WHICH WAS IN FACT BORN IN GAUL, HAS ONLY GAINED ITS LOVELY REDDISH-ORANGE COLOR OVER THE COURSE OF CENTURIES; IT WAS ORIGINALLY AS PALE AS THE TURNIP, AND ITS HEART WAS HARD AND WOODY.

STUFFED MORELS
MORILLES FARCIES

THE FIRST VINE LEAVES BEGIN TO APPEAR UNDER THE AIN BRIDGE IN THE FOOTHILLS OF BUGEY. IN THIS RECIPE, MORELS OF THE REGION ARE FILLED WITH A VEGETABLE STUFFING, AND SERVED WITH A CREAM SAUCE ON TRIANGLES OF TOAST.

12 LARGE FRESH MORELS
    SALT AND FRESHLY GROUND PEPPER
    LEMON JUICE
1 CUP UNSALTED BUTTER
1 MEDIUM CARROT, PEELED AND VERY
    FINELY CHOPPED
1 RIB CELERY FROM THE HEART, PEELED
    AND MINCED
2 SHALLOTS, MINCED

⅔ CUP PORT WINE
½ CUP HEAVY CREAM
2 TABLESPOONS FINE FRESH BREAD
    CRUMBS
1 EGG YOLK
4 SLICES OF WHITE BREAD, CRUSTS
    REMOVED
    MINCED PARSLEY

PREPARE THE MORELS: Wash morels very gently but thoroughly in cold water to rid them of sand and grit. Cut off stems and set aside. Make a ¼-inch slit in side of morels, if necessary, to ensure that any sand trapped inside has been rinsed away.

In a medium saucepan, bring 4 cups water to a boil. Add salt, 1 tablespoon lemon juice, and 1 tablespoon butter. When water returns to a boil, add morels and reserved stems and boil for 1 minute. Drain well in a colander. Set morels aside and chop stems very fine.

PREPARE THE STUFFING: Melt 2 tablespoons butter in a medium skillet. Add reserved morel stems, carrot, celery, and half of the chopped shallots. Cook, stirring, over medium heat until vegetables are soft, about 2 minutes. Add ⅓ cup port and simmer until only 1 tablespoon remains, about 4 minutes. Stir in 2 tablespoons cream and bread crumbs and remove from the heat. Stir in the egg yolk. (The mixture will be quite soft.) Season to taste with salt and pepper.

Transfer stuffing to a small pastry bag fitted with a ¼-inch round or star tip. Pipe stuffing into morels until filled. Melt 3 tablespoons butter in a medium skillet and add morels and remaining chopped shallots. Cover and cook over medium heat for 2 minutes. Uncover and add remaining ⅓ cup port and 6 tablespoons cream. Continue cooking, stirring morels gently and frequently basting with cooking liquid, until sauce thickens slightly, about 3 minutes. Remove from heat and set aside. (The recipe can be prepared ahead to this point.)

TO SERVE: Cut each slice of bread diagonally into 4 triangles. Melt 6 tablespoons butter in a large skillet over medium heat. Add bread and fry until golden brown, about 3 minutes per side. Remove croutons and drain on paper towels.

Reheat morels in their sauce. Using a small spatula, place 3 morels on each of 4 plates. Set sauce over low heat and whisk in remaining 4 tablespoons of butter, 1 tablespoon at a time. Strain sauce through a fine-mesh sieve and pour over stuffed morels. Garnish each serving with 4 croutons, sprinkle with minced parsley, and serve immediately. *Makes 4 servings.*

THREE VEGETABLE MOUSSES IN LEEK ASPIC
TROIS MOUSSES PRINTANIERES EN GELEE DE POIREAUX

4 LEEKS, TRIMMED AND WELL-WASHED	1 POUND YOUNG CARROTS, TRIMMED,
SALT	PEELED, AND SLICED
4½ TEASPOONS UNFLAVORED GELATIN	1 POUND SHELLED PEAS
1 SPRIG OF TARRAGON	6 TABLESPOONS CREME FRAICHE
FRESHLY GROUND PEPPER	RED WINE VINEGAR
1 SMALL CAULIFLOWER, CUT INTO	
FLORETS	

PREPARE THE LEEK ASPIC: Cut dark green portion from leeks and set aside. Tie leeks into a bundle with string. In a medium saucepan, combine 5 cups water, salt, the bundle of leeks, and leek greens. Bring to a boil over high heat. Reduce heat to medium high and simmer until bundled leeks are just tender when pierced, about 12 minutes. Remove bundled leeks and continue cooking leek greens over medium low heat for another 15 minutes to flavor liquid. Refresh bundled leeks under cold water; drain very well, discard strings, and let leeks cool. Cover leeks with plastic wrap and refrigerate until time to assemble the dish.

In a small bowl, soften gelatin in ¼ cup water for about 5 minutes. When leek broth is done, add tarragon and set aside for 30 seconds. Strain liquid through a fine-mesh strainer set over another saucepan. Stir in softened gelatin and bring the liquid to a boil, stirring frequently. Remove from heat and season to taste with salt and pepper. Let cool slightly. Cover and refrigerate until just beginning to set.

MAKE THE VEGETABLE MOUSSES: Bring a medium saucepan of salted water to a boil. Add cauliflower florets and cook until very tender but not soft or mushy, about 10 minutes. Remove cauliflower with a slotted spoon and refresh under cold water. Drain very well, then wrap cauliflower in a kitchen towel and squeeze to extract as much moisture as possible. Puree cauliflower in a food processor, scraping down sides of bowl every 10 seconds, until very smooth. Strain puree through a fine-mesh sieve set over a bowl and set aside. Repeat this cooking, refreshing, draining, squeezing, pureeing, and straining procedure with carrots and peas, cooking carrots for about 10 minutes, depending on their size, and cooking peas for about 15 minutes.

Stir ¼ cup cool but still fluid aspic into each puree. Stir 2 tablespoons crème fraîche into each. Season purees to taste with vinegar, salt, and pepper, cover with plastic wrap and refrigerate overnight.

ASSEMBLE THE DISH: Melt remaining leek aspic over medium heat. Pour into a bowl set in a bowl of ice water and stir frequently to prevent aspic from setting at bottom of bowl. When the aspic is cool, ladle a thin, even layer onto 4 large dinner plates and refrigerate until completely set. Using 2 soup spoons, mold each mousse into 4 even ovals and place decoratively in center of aspic-covered plates.

Slice white portion of reserved leeks ⅓-inch-thick and cut rounds in half. Decorate purees with leek pieces. Then, using a spoon or a very soft brush, cover each oval of mousse and piece of leek with a thin layer of barely set aspic. (If the aspic has set up by this point, simply remelt slightly and pour back into bowl. Stir until cool and just beginning to thicken up again.) Refrigerate plates until aspic is completely set. If you like, cover purees with another thin layer of aspic. Refrigerate until serving time. *Makes 4 servings*.

LEEKS ARE RESERVED FOR A SPECIAL ASPIC TO COAT THE THREE VEGETABLE MOUSSES—CARROT, CAULIFLOWER, AND PEA—IN THIS SOPHISTICATED BUT REFRESHING DISH. TO EMBELLISH THE PRESENTATION FURTHER, GARNISH EACH MOUSSE WITH ITS RESPECTIVE VEGETABLE (TINY BABY CARROTS WITH TOPS, TINY CAULIFLOWER FLORETS, AND PEAS, ALL COOKED UNTIL TENDER); FINALLY, COAT EACH MOUSSE IN ASPIC. EARLY CARROTS, SUCH AS THOSE USED IN THIS RECIPE, ARE SOLD IN SMALL BUNCHES AND NEED NOT BE PEELED BUT SIMPLY BRUSHED; THEY CAN BE SERVED LEAVING AN INCH OR TWO OF GREENS.

PUFF PASTRY WITH BROCCOLI MOUSSE, ASPARAGUS, AND MORELS

FEUILLETE DE MOUSSE DE BROCCOLIS AUX POINTES D'ASPERGES ET AUX MORILLES

2	POUNDS BROCCOLI, CUT INTO FLORETS	3	TABLESPOONS UNSALTED BUTTER
1¼	CUPS CREME FRAICHE	1	LARGE SHALLOT, MINCED
	SALT AND FRESHLY GROUND PEPPER	24	ASPARAGUS SPEARS
	WINE VINEGAR	6	OUNCES PUFF PASTRY, THAWED IF
	OLIVE OIL		FROZEN
1	POUND FRESH MORELS, PREFERABLY	2	EGG YOLKS
	SMALL, BLACK, POINTED ONES		

PREPARE THE BROCCOLI MOUSSE: Cook broccoli florets in a large pot of boiling salted water until very soft, about 13 minutes. Drain and refresh under cold water. Drain again, then wrap broccoli in a kitchen towel and squeeze to extract as much moisture as possible. Transfer to a food processor and puree, scraping down sides every 15 seconds, until very smooth. Transfer puree to a saucepan and warm over medium heat. Stir in enough crème fraîche to give mousse a soft, but not runny consistency, about 3 tablespoons. (The amount of crème fraîche will be determined by consistency of puree.) Season with salt, pepper, vinegar, and oil to taste.

PREPARE THE MORELS: Cut stems from morels and discard. Rinse mushrooms gently but thoroughly to remove any grit. Dry on paper towels. Melt 2 tablespoons butter in a medium skillet and add shallot. Cook over medium heat, stirring, until translucent, about 2 minutes. Add morels and ¼ cup water, cover, and cook for 5 minutes. Uncover, season lightly with salt, and stir in ¾ cup crème fraîche. Bring to a boil over high heat; remove from heat and set aside.

PREPARE THE ASPARAGUS: Cut asparagus tips 2 inches long. (Reserve remaining asparagus for another use.) Cook asparagus tips in boiling salted water until just tender, about 5 minutes. Drain and refresh under cold water. Transfer to paper towels to drain completely.

PREPARE THE PUFF PASTRY: Preheat oven to 400 degrees. Roll out pastry ⅛-inch-thick. Using a sharp knife, cut out four 5-by-2-inch rectangles. Place pastry rectangles on a moistened heavy baking sheet. Beat one egg yolk in a small bowl. Brush pastry with beaten yolk. Using a fork, score an attractive design on pastry. Bake rectangles until puffed and golden brown, about 15 minutes. (The recipe can be prepared to this point in advance.)

TO SERVE: Reheat broccoli mousse over medium heat. In a medium skillet, rewarm asparagus tips in remaining 1 tablespoon butter. In a small bowl, blend remaining egg yolk with remaining crème fraîche (4 to 5 tablespoons). Reheat morels over medium heat and stir in egg yolk/ crème fraîche mixture. Cook until sauce is thickened and warmed through, about 2 minutes; do not boil. Reheat puff pastry rectangles if desired.

Using 2 large spoons, shape broccoli mousse into large ovals and place in center of 4 large serving plates. Arrange asparagus tips and morels attractively on plates. Spoon morel cream over asparagus and top mousse with a puff pastry rectangle. Serve hot. *Makes 4 servings.*

Broccoli mousses are served topped with puff pastry. Fresh asparagus tips and fresh morels complete the dish. The combination of morels and asparagus may be traditional, but it is too good to pass up merely for the sake of some newer innovation. Spring is the season to enjoy this marriage of tastes, so savor it while you can because the season never lasts long enough.

RED RADISH SOUP WITH TAPIOCA
TAPIOCA DE RADIS ROSES AUX FANES

It may be impossible to conceive of a spring meal without radishes as a starter. Originally from China, the radish has found a favored place in French cuisine during the past four centuries. Radishes eaten raw with butter are a perennial favorite, but they are also delicious served with a sauce of FROMAGE BLANC. Split in

four, without fully separating the "petals," and placed in a bowl of water with ice cubes, radishes will open up like flowers. The leafy tops of red radishes are also put to use in this delightful spring soup (pictured on pages 52–53), served garnished with radish slices.

1	LARGE BUNCH OF RED RADISHES WITH LEAFY TOPS	2½ TO 3 TABLESPOONS INSTANT TAPIOCA
1	SMALL LEEK, WELL-WASHED AND FINELY CHOPPED	2 TABLESPOONS UNSALTED BUTTER SALT AND FRESHLY GROUND PEPPER
		6 TABLESPOONS HEAVY CREAM

Trim roots and cut off any wilted leaves from radishes. Rinse radishes and leafy tops very well. Holding on to tops, slice radishes ⅛-inch-thick. Coarsely chop tops and any trimmings.

Cook radish slices in a medium saucepan of boiling salted water until just tender, 2 to 3 minutes. Drain, refresh under cold water, and drain again. Set aside 28 of the prettiest slices to garnish soup.

In a large saucepan, bring 6 cups salted water to a boil. Add leek and simmer over medium high heat for 5 minutes. Add chopped radish tops and any trimmings, as well as remaining radish slices. Boil over high heat for 7 minutes. (Longer cooking will dull color of leaves.) Transfer soup to a blender and puree until very smooth. Strain soup through a fine-mesh strainer into a saucepan.

Bring soup to a boil over high heat. Whisking constantly, sprinkle in tapioca. Reduce heat to low and cook, whisking constantly, for 6 minutes. Whisk in butter until thoroughly blended. Season to taste with salt and pepper.

TO SERVE: Ladle soup into 4 soup plates and drizzle 1½ tablespoons of the cream over each serving. Float 7 reserved radish slices on top of each and serve immediately. *Makes 4 servings.*

NOTE: To give this soup additional body, stir in 2 well-beaten eggs. For a richer consistency, you could also stir additional cream into the soup before ladling it into plates.

Once you've added the tapioca, be sure to stir constantly—it has a tendency to coagulate. This soup cannot be prepared well in advance.

SORREL SOUP WITH FRESH CHEESE QUENELLES
SOUPE D'OSEILLE AUX QUENELLES DE FROMAGE BLANC

QUENELLES
⅔ CUP MILK
3½ TABLESPOONS UNSALTED BUTTER
¾ CUP ALL-PURPOSE FLOUR
1 EGG
½ CUP RICOTTA CHEESE
½ TEASPOON SALT
¼ TEASPOON FRESHLY GROUND PEPPER

SOUP
1 POUND POTATOES
½ POUND FRESH SORREL, WELL-WASHED
  AND LARGE STEMS REMOVED
1 LARGE LEEK, WELL-WASHED AND SLICED
¼ CUP HEAVY CREAM
  SALT AND FRESHLY GROUND PEPPER
  FRESH CHERVIL LEAVES FOR GARNISH

PREPARE THE QUENELLES: In a medium saucepan, bring the milk and 1½ tablespoons butter to a boil. All at once, add flour and stir vigorously with a wooden spoon until blended. (The mixture will be extremely thick.) Cook over medium heat, stirring constantly, until very dry, about 2 minutes. Remove from heat. Add egg and immediately beat it into the mixture until thoroughly incorporated. Let cool slightly.

Melt remaining 2 tablespoons butter in a small pan. Add ricotta and melted butter to the quenelle mixture and stir until thoroughly blended. Transfer dough to a bowl and season with the salt and pepper. Beat with an electric mixer until smooth and light, about 3 minutes. Cover with plastic wrap and refrigerate for at least 8 hours or overnight.

PREPARE THE SOUP: Peel and rinse potatoes. Cut into small chunks. Shred sorrel leaves. Place potatoes, sorrel, and leek in a large saucepan and add 6 cups water. Bring to a boil over high heat. Reduce heat to medium and simmer until potatoes are extremely tender, about 15 minutes. Transfer vegetables and cooking liquid to a blender and puree until very smooth. Strain soup through a fine-mesh sieve into a saucepan. Add cream and season to taste with salt and pepper.

TO SERVE: Fill a large, wide casserole with water and bring to a boil. Reduce heat to medium or medium high, so that water simmers gently. Using 2 tablespoons, mold quenelle mixture into ovals and drop into simmering water. Cook, without crowding, until fluffy, about 3 minutes per side. With a slotted spoon, transfer quenelles to a towel to drain. Repeat quenelle making and poaching procedure until all the mixture has been used.

Bring soup to a boil. Ladle into 4 rimmed soup plates. Arrange the quenelles decoratively in the soup in a star pattern and sprinkle each serving with fresh chervil leaves. *Makes 4 servings.*

QUENELLES MADE WITH FRESH RICOTTA CHEESE ARE SERVED WITH THIS RICH SORREL SOUP. SET ON A TABLE IN THE GARDEN OF MY NEIGHBOR, MONSIEUR CONVERT, THIS SOUP WAS CREATED FOR MY FRIEND LOUIS CHEVENET D'HURIGNY, WHO LIVES NEAR MACON AND CREATES SUPERB GOAT CHEESE. A DISTANT COUSIN OF SPINACH, SORREL APPEARS IN THE MARKET-

PLACE IN MARCH AND MUST BE EATEN PROMPTLY. IT IS OFTEN BLENDED WITH SPINACH TO REDUCE ITS ACIDITY. ONCE USED AS LITTLE MORE THAN A GARNISH, SORREL HAS GAINED A PLACE IN IMAGINATIVE DISHES CREATED BY THOSE INTERESTED IN A NATURAL CUISINE.

JACQUES MAXIMIN'S ASPARAGUS CHARLOTTE
CHARLOTTE AUX POINTES D'ASPERGES ET PETIT CAVIAR DE JACQUES MAXIMIN

AT THE MARKET IN CHATILLON SUR CHAL-ARONNE, ASPARAGUS COMES IN EVERY SIZE AND COLOR: THE WHITE, WHICH IS CUT AS SOON AS IT COMES UP FROM THE EARTH; THE VIOLET, WHICH IS ALLOWED TO GROW SEVERAL INCHES ABOVE THE GROUND BEFORE CUTTING; AND THE GREEN. I MUST THANK THE TALENTED JACQUES MAXIMIN FOR INTRODUCING ME TO THIS SPLENDID AND UNFORGETTABLE ASPARAGUS CHARLOTTE, FEATURING WHOLE STEMS OF ASPARAGUS AND SERVED WITH CAVIAR. ONE CAN FIND CYLINDRICAL POTS ESPECIALLY MADE FOR COOKING ASPARAGUS UPRIGHT, TIPS IN THE AIR. AT THE MOMENT OF

SERVING, ASPARAGUS SHOULD BE PLACED ON A FOLDED NAPKIN IN ORDER TO ABSORB THE EXCESS COOKING WATER.

48	MEDIUM-SIZE, VERY STRAIGHT ASPARAGUS SPEARS	SALT AND FRESHLY GROUND PEPPER
1	SMALL BUNCH OF CHERVIL, LEAVES FINELY CHOPPED	1 SMALL HEAD OF CHICORY, YELLOW LEAVES ONLY
	JUICE OF 1 LEMON	3 HARD-COOKED EGGS
2	TABLESPOONS CREME FRAICHE	1½ OUNCES SEVRUGA CAVIAR

Snap tough, woody stems from asparagus and peel stalks. Cook asparagus in a large pot of boiling water until just tender, about 7 minutes. Drain and refresh immediately under cold water; drain again. Cut asparagus tips into even 2-inch lengths and set aside. Cut remaining stalks into fine julienne and place in a bowl. Add chopped chervil and lemon juice to stalks to taste. Stir in the crème fraîche and season with salt and pepper; toss gently.

Measure out 2 packed cups of yellow leaves from heart of chicory. Cut leaves into fine shreds.

Halve hard-cooked eggs and separate whites from yolks. Sieve whites and yolks separately.

ASSEMBLE THE CHARLOTTES: Place a 4-inch round flan ring or biscuit cutter in the center of each of 4 plates. Stand asparagus, tips up, around inner rim of rings to form a tight circle. Divide shredded chicory among center of rings and press down well with the back of a small fork to form a flat bed. Cover with a layer of asparagus julienne. Top julienne with a layer of sieved yolks, followed by a layer of sieved whites. (The asparagus charlottes can be prepared up to 6 hours ahead. Cover carefully with plastic and chill until serving time.)

TO SERVE: Spoon caviar onto sieved egg whites and gently smooth top without crushing caviar. Carefully remove flan rings with one hand while steadying asparagus with the other. *Makes 4 servings.*

NOTE: When serving, transport the charlottes to the table carefully because the asparagus have a tendency to tip over.

CREAM OF BROCCOLI AND WATERCRESS WITH SALSIFY DUCHESSE
CREME DE BROCCOLIS ET CRESSON A LA DUCHESSE DE SALSIFIS

THE SOUP IS PHOTOGRAPHED IN THE WOODS OF BEOST AT THE FOOT OF AN OAK, WHILE ON ALL SIDES NATURE REAWAKENS WITH THE SPRING. ONE OF THE HERBS WHICH REAPPEARS IN THE SPRINGTIME IS WATERCRESS, HERE COMBINED WITH BROCCOLI IN A CREAMED PUREE. THIS HERB, WITH ITS SLIGHTLY BITING TASTE, IS ONE OF THE MOST ANCIENT, SINCE HISTORIANS RECOUNT THAT CHARLEMAGNE GREW IT IN HIS GARDEN OVER A THOUSAND YEARS AGO.

SALSIFY DUCHESSE
2 TABLESPOONS ALL-PURPOSE FLOUR
1 LEMON, HALVED
2 POUNDS SALSIFY, SCRUBBED AND RINSED
1 WHOLE EGG
2 EGG YOLKS
2 TABLESPOONS HEAVY CREAM
SALT AND FRESHLY GROUND PEPPER

SOUP
2¼ POUNDS BROCCOLI
2 LARGE BUNCHES OF WATERCRESS, LARGE STEMS REMOVED
3 TABLESPOONS UNSALTED BUTTER
SALT AND FRESHLY GROUND PEPPER
1¾ CUPS PLUS 2 TABLESPOONS HEAVY CREAM

PREPARE THE SALSIFY DUCHESSE: Fill a medium saucepan with water and whisk in flour. Squeeze juice from lemon halves into water and add lemon. Peel salsify and cut into 1½-inch pieces. Add pieces to saucepan as you go. Bring the salsify to a boil over medium heat and simmer until tender, about 35 minutes. Drain, rinse well, and drain again.

Place salsify in a food processor and puree, scraping down sides, until very smooth. Strain puree through a fine-mesh strainer into a saucepan. Cook puree over medium high heat, stirring constantly, until very dry, about 15 minutes. Remove from heat and let cool for 1 minute. Stir in whole egg, then egg yolks, then heavy cream, stirring well between additions. Season to taste with salt and pepper.

Scrape salsify mixture into a pastry bag fitted with a star tip and pipe little ovals or strips onto a nonstick baking sheet. Set aside at room temperature.

PREPARE THE SOUP: Slice off broccoli florets and set aside 2 cups. Peel stems and cut into small pieces. Finely chop watercress.

In a large casserole, melt butter over medium heat. Add watercress and cook, stirring, until wilted, about 3 minutes. Add pieces of broccoli stems, along with enough water to barely cover. Season with ⅛ teaspoon each of salt and pepper and cook until broccoli is tender, about 10 minutes. Transfer vegetables and cooking liquid to a blender and puree until very smooth. Strain soup through a fine-mesh strainer into a saucepan. Stir in heavy cream and bring to a simmer over medium heat. Season to taste with salt and pepper. If soup is too thick, thin it out with a little water or cream. (The recipe can be prepared ahead to this point.)

TO SERVE: Preheat oven to 500 degrees. Bake salsify duchesse on top rack of oven until well-browned on the ridges, about 10 minutes. Cook reserved broccoli florets in boiling salted water until just tender, about 4 minutes. Drain well. Reheat soup.

Ladle soup into 6 shallow soup plates. Arrange broccoli florets and salsify duchesse on each serving in a decorative fashion. Serve immediately. *Makes 6 servings.*

LITTLE STUFFED CABBAGES
PETITS CHOUX FARCIS

TWO STUFFED CABBAGES, STILL IN THE PAN, SIT COOLING ON AN OLD BURGUNDIAN TILE. FRESH YOUNG SPINACH IS USED IN THE STUFFING; AND ALTHOUGH SPINACH CAN BE FOUND THROUGHOUT THE YEAR, IT IS BEST IN THE SPRING, WHEN ITS LEAVES ARE SMALL AND TENDER. WHILE SPINACH HAS A REPUTATION FOR BEING EXTREMELY IRON RICH, THANKS TO ITS

WORLD-RENOWNED PROPAGANDIST, POPEYE THE SAILOR, ALL HORTICULTURISTS WILL EXPLAIN THAT OTHER VEGETABLES, NOTABLY LETTUCE, CONTAIN MORE IRON.

1	MEDIUM GREEN CABBAGE	1	CUP DRIED FRESH BREAD CRUMBS
½	CUP RICE	½	CUP HEAVY CREAM
8	TABLESPOONS UNSALTED BUTTER	1	HARD-COOKED EGG, COARSELY
2	ONIONS		CHOPPED
½	POUND YOUNG SPINACH, STEMMED,	3	CARROTS, SLICED INTO THIN ROUNDS
	WELL-WASHED, DRAINED, AND	2	SPRIGS OF FRESH THYME
	COARSELY CHOPPED	1	BAY LEAF
	SALT AND FRESHLY GROUND PEPPER	½	CUP DRY WHITE WINE
	FRESHLY GRATED NUTMEG		

PREPARE THE CABBAGE: Separate cabbage leaves without tearing. (If necessary, immerse head of cabbage in boiling water for a few seconds to soften leaves.) With a sharp knife, shave off any large protruding ribs to make them flush with the rest of the leaf. Blanch cabbage leaves in boiling water until tender, about 6 minutes. Drain and refresh under cold water. Transfer leaves to paper towels to drain.

PREPARE THE STUFFING: Place the rice in a saucepan with water to cover by 3 inches. Bring to a boil over high heat and cook until tender, about 12 minutes. Drain well and set aside.

Meanwhile, melt 1½ tablespoons butter in a large skillet. Chop 1 onion and add to skillet. Sauté over medium high heat until translucent, about 3 minutes. Add spinach and cook, stirring, until completely wilted, about 2 minutes. Season with salt and pepper. Stir in bread crumbs and 3 tablespoons cream. Remove from heat and add reserved rice and chopped egg. Stir to thoroughly combine and season to taste with salt, pepper, and nutmeg. Let cool slightly.

STUFF AND COOK THE CABBAGE: Using your hands, roll the rice mixture into 8 balls of equal size. Wrap each ball of stuffing in cabbage leaves to enclose it completely. Try to save greenest leaves for covering balls. To give cabbage rolls a nice, even, compact shape, place in a kitchen towel and, holding cabbage with one hand, twist towel with the other to squeeze cabbage into a round ball. When all cabbages have been shaped, set aside.

Preheat oven to 375 degrees. Slice remaining onion. In a buttered shallow baking dish or casserole, make a bed of sliced onion and carrots. Add thyme and bay leaf and place the cabbages on top of vegetables. (The recipe can be prepared ahead to this point.) Add wine and ½ cup water to dish and bake, basting frequently with cooking liquid to prevent drying out, until cabbages are shiny, about 25 minutes. Remove cabbages from baking dish and keep warm in oven while you prepare sauce.

PREPARE THE SAUCE: Strain cooking liquid into a saucepan; discard solids. Bring to a boil and cook until reduced to ½ cup, about 2 minutes. Add remaining 5 tablespoons heavy cream and boil until slightly reduced, about 2 minutes more. Reduce heat to medium and whisk in remaining 6½ tablespoons butter, 1 tablespoon at a time. Season sauce with salt and pepper to taste.

TO SERVE: Place 2 stuffed cabbages on each of 4 plates and pour sauce over and around them. *Makes 4 servings.*

POOR MAN'S ASPARAGUS
ASPERGE DU PAUVRE

4	LARGE LEEKS	1 GREEN ONION OR SMALL SPRING
8	PRETTY CELERY LEAVES	ONION GREEN, THINLY SLICED
3	OUNCES BELUGA CAVIAR	

Cut off and discard dark green leaves from leeks. Starting at light green end, halve leeks lengthwise, cutting only 1 inch into white portion. Rinse very carefully to remove all sand and grit. Tie leeks into a tight bundle with kitchen string and cook in boiling salted water until just tender, about 10 minutes. Drain and immediately refresh under cold water. Drain well. Untie leeks and drain very well on paper towels.

If necessary, slit leeks a little further into white portion to enable you to separate the 2 halves (joined at the top) to form a *V*. Place each leek on a small plate and slide 2 celery leaves under the white portion of each. Place a small mound of caviar in the center of each *V*. Garnish with sliced green onion. *Makes 4 servings.*

Poor man's asparagus is not asparagus at all, but the simple and elegant leek. Here tender leek stems are slit in a V, garnished with celery leaves, and embellished with caviar to make a dramatic dish fit for a king. The leek is a vegetable that demands a meticulous washing before use, even if in cooking we have become accustomed to eating mainly the white part and reserving the green leaves for soups and purees.

SPRING VEGETABLES VINAIGRETTE
VINAIGRETTE TIEDE DE JEUNES LEGUMES A LA CORIANDRE ET AU GROS SEL

VEGETABLES

DEPENDING ON WHAT THE GREENGROCER HAS TO OFFER, CHOOSE A VARIED ASSORTMENT OF VEGETABLES FOR THE NUMBER OF PEOPLE YOU INTEND TO SERVE.

ASPARAGUS TIPS, CUT 2-INCHES LONG

BABY LEEKS, WELL-WASHED AND DARK GREEN PORTION REMOVED

CELERY RIBS FROM THE HEART, PEELED AND CUT INTO 2-INCH LENGTHS

BABY CARROTS WITH TOPS, PEELED AND TOPS TRIMMED

SMALL RED RADISHES WITH TOPS, TOPS TRIMMED

SMALL ARTICHOKE BOTTOMS

SMALL SPRING ONIONS, TOPS AND ROOTS TRIMMED

FRESHLY SHELLED PEAS

BABY TURNIPS WITH TOPS, TOPS TRIMMED

UNSALTED BUTTER

VINAIGRETTE AND GARNISH

SHERRY VINEGAR

AGED WINE VINEGAR

SALT AND FRESHLY GROUND PEPPER

OLIVE OIL

GRAPESEED OIL

SMALL CORIANDER LEAVES, SLIVERED

FRESH TARRAGON LEAVES, SLIVERED

LEMON JUICE

CHIVES

SMALL CHERVIL SPRIGS

YOUNG WATERCRESS SPRIGS

COARSE SEA SALT

TOMATOES, PEELED, SEEDED, AND CUT INTO SMALL DICE

YOUNG FAVA BEANS, BLANCHED AND SKINNED

ANY OTHER YOUNG VEGETABLES OF CHOICE, PEELED AND/OR TRIMMED AS NECESSARY

Select an assortment of the very freshest vegetables you can find. Take into account your personal taste, as well as the color and shape of the vegetables in order to ensure an attractive presentation.

COOK THE VEGETABLES: Cook asparagus, leeks, and celery separately in boiling salted water until just tender. Drain and refresh each vegetable under cold water and drain very well. For carrots, radishes, artichoke bottoms, spring onions, peas, and turnips, stew lightly in butter over medium heat until hot, then add a little water, cover tightly and cook until tender. (All vegetables must be cooked separately since each requires a different cooking time.) Set vegetables aside.

PREPARE THE VINAIGRETTE: Prepare a vinaigrette by combining vinegars with salt and pepper. Whisk in oils, balancing flavor to your taste, until dressing emulsifies. Stir in slivered coriander and tarragon and season to taste with lemon juice.

TO SERVE: Just before serving, reheat all vegetables in a steamer, including tomatoes and fava beans, if using. Alternatively, reheat vegetables in melted butter in a large skillet until heated through but not browned. Drain vegetables and arrange them attractively on serving plates. Spoon some of the vinaigrette over each serving and sprinkle with chives and/or chervil and additional coriander, if you like.

Toss the watercress with vinaigrette and place sprigs around each plate as a border. Sprinkle each serving with coarse salt. Serve at room temperature—I think that that's when the flavors are best.

WHAT BETTER WAY TO CELEBRATE THE ABUNDANCE OF A SPRING HARVEST THAN WITH THIS SPICY VEGETABLE VINAIGRETTE? PICK WHAT-EVER VEGETABLES SEEM FRESHEST—ASPARAGUS, RED RADISHES, BABY LEEKS, BABY CARROTS, AR-TICHOKES. TO TAKE FULL ADVANTAGE OF A NATURAL CUISINE, YOU MUST KNOW HOW TO SELECT AND USE PRODUCTS AT THE BEST MOMENT, THE HEIGHT OF FRESHNESS. THIS SIMPLE AND SATISFYING DISH BURSTS WITH SPRINGTIME LIFE.

CREAM OF WATERCRESS SOUP WITH FROG LEGS
CRESSONMERE AUX GRENOUILLES

1 BUNCH WATERCRESS (ABOUT ¼ POUND)
6 TABLESPOONS UNSALTED BUTTER
4 TO 5 MEDIUM POTATOES (ABOUT 1 POUND), PEELED AND QUARTERED

SALT AND FRESHLY GROUND PEPPER
1½ POUNDS FROG LEGS
¼ CUP CREME FRAICHE

Wash and drain watercress. Remove large, tough stems. Coarsely chop. Melt 2 tablespoons butter in a large sauté pan over low heat. Add watercress and cook, without coloring, until soft, about 5 minutes. Add potatoes and boiling water to cover. Season with salt and pepper. Simmer, uncovered, until potatoes are cooked, about 30 minutes.

Melt remaining 4 tablespoons butter in a large skillet over medium high heat. Add frog legs and season with salt and pepper. Cook, covered, without browning for 10 minutes. Take off heat and let cool slightly. Remove meat from bones and keep warm in a covered bowl. Drain off cooking liquid and pour into watercress soup.

Place soup in a food processor and puree, about 30 seconds. Pass through a fine-mesh sieve into a medium saucepan. Add crème fraîche; adjust seasonings. Keep warm.

TO SERVE: Place meat from frog legs in bottom of a soup tureen. Heat soup until very hot but not boiling and pour into tureen. Garnish with several leaves of bright green watercress, if desired. *Makes 4 servings*.

NOTE: The watercress can be replaced with chervil, if desired, or a mixture of the two.

A DISH OF CREAM OF WATERCRESS SOUP WITH FROGS' LEGS SITS NESTLED ON THE BANKS OF THE RIVER THAT COULD BE ITS INSPIRATION—ANOTHER SPRINGTIME COMBINATION OF COLOR AND TASTE. THERE ARE FOUR GREAT VARIETIES OF WATERCRESS; THE MOST COMMON IS *CRESSON A FONTAINE*, WHICH GROWS RIGHT IN THE WATER AND HAS A FLAVOR REMINISCENT OF MUSTARD. IN FRANCE ONE STILL FINDS GARDEN CRESS, WHICH IS ESPECIALLY APPRECIATED IN SOUPS AND PUREES, WHICH ONE MAKES BY ADDING POTATOES OR SPLIT PEAS. WATERCRESS IS ALSO AN EXCELLENT GARNISH FOR GRILLED MEATS.

MUSSELS WITH HERBED BROTH AND VEGETABLES
MARINIERE D'AZUR AUX LEGUMES

COURT BOUILLON
2   CUPS DRY WHITE WINE
2   CARROTS, WASHED AND CUT INTO
     1-INCH PIECES
1   MEDIUM ONION, PEELED AND
     QUARTERED
1   RIB CELERY, WASHED AND CUT INTO
     1-INCH SLICES
1   CLOVE GARLIC
1   BOUQUET GARNI
1   TABLESPOON COARSE SEA SALT
5   TO 6 BLACK PEPPERCORNS, CRUSHED
BROTH
¼   CUP OLIVE OIL
3   SHALLOTS, FINELY CHOPPED
1   CLOVE GARLIC, FINELY CHOPPED
2   TEASPOONS TOMATO PASTE
1   TEASPOON FRESH THYME FLOWERS,
     PULVERIZED IN A SPICE GRINDER
1   BAY LEAF, PULVERIZED IN A SPICE
     GRINDER

4   TABLESPOONS UNSALTED BUTTER, CUT
     INTO SMALL PIECES
2   TABLESPOONS CREME FRAICHE
1   TABLESPOON CHOPPED TARRAGON
1   TABLESPOON CHOPPED BASIL
1   TABLESPOON FINELY CHOPPED CHIVES
     PINCH OF THREAD SAFFRON
     SALT AND FRESHLY GROUND PEPPER
MUSSELS AND VEGETABLES
3   POUNDS MUSSELS, SCRUBBED CLEAN
4   SMALL RED-SKINNED POTATOES (ABOUT
     ¾ POUND)
1   MEDIUM ZUCCHINI
1   RIB CELERY
1   EGGPLANT
1   TOMATO
1   TO 2 CUPS OLIVE OIL
     COOKED SNOW PEAS FOR GARNISH
     SEVERAL SAFFRON THREADS FOR
     GARNISH

ALL THE SAVORY ELEMENTS OF THE SEA-SHORE COMBINE WITH A SPRING MARKET'S FRESH-EST HERBS AND VEGETABLES TO GIVE CHARACTER TO THIS FLAVORFUL DISH. IT IS A DISH I'M PARTICULARLY FOND OF, AND IT ADDS A SPICY SOUTHERN ACCENT TO THE SEASON.

PREPARE THE COURT BOUILLON: In a large, nonreactive pot, combine wine and 2 cups water. Add vegetables and seasonings. Bring to a boil and simmer over medium heat for 30 minutes. Strain through a fine-mesh sieve; reserve court bouillon.

PREPARE THE BROTH: Heat oil in a large saucepan over low heat. Add shallots and garlic and cook until soft, about 5 minutes. Add tomato paste. Pour in 2 cups of reserved court bouillon. Stir in ground thyme and bay leaf. Bring to a boil over high heat. Boil for 10 minutes.

Whisk in pieces of butter, one by one. Stir in crème fraîche. Add fresh herbs and saffron. Season with salt and pepper. Add more crème fraîche if a thinner broth is desired. Keep warm

PREPARE THE MUSSELS AND VEGETABLES: Place mussels in a large non-reactive pot with 1 cup of reserved court bouillon. (Add water, if necessary, to completely cover bottom of pot.) Cook, covered, over medium high heat until mussels open, about 10 minutes. Remove mussels to a bowl with a slotted spoon. Keep warm.

Strain cooking liquid through a fine-mesh sieve lined with a doubled layer of dampened cheesecloth. Add to reserved broth.

Cut potatoes and zucchini into uniform pieces about the size of a garlic clove. Cut celery into thin slices. Cut eggplant and tomato into ½-inch cubes, leaving on some of the skins. Cook vegetables separately in olive oil to desired degree of doneness. Season each well and drain on paper towels. Keep warm.

ASSEMBLE THE DISH: Add cooked vegetables to reserved broth. Bring to a simmer over low heat. Ladle broth into 4 shallow individual soup plates. Place mussels on top. Garnish with snow peas and several threads of saffron. Serve immediately. *Makes 4 servings.*

FRESH SPINACH WITH SKILLET-ROASTED SALMON
BRANCHES D'EPINARDS A LA QUEUE DE SAUMON ROTIE FLEUR DE SEL

THE PRIZE OF A FISHERMAN'S NET, A SALMON FILLET BASKS IN A RAY OF SUNLIGHT AS IT SITS ON A BED OF FRESH SPRING SPINACH. THE FLAVOR OF THE SPINACH, A VEGETABLE WHICH ORIGINALLY CAME TO FRANCE FROM PERSIA, IS ENHANCED BY ITS SEASONING OF NUTMEG. WHEN SPINACH FIRST ARRIVED IN FRANCE NEARLY NINE HUNDRED YEARS AGO, IT BARELY RESEMBLED THAT WHICH WE BUY TODAY AND WAS MOSTLY USED FOR MAKING POULTICES TO HEAL LIVER AND STOMACH AILMENTS.

BLACK PEPPERCORNS

FOUR 6-OUNCE BONELESS SALMON FILLETS, WITH SKIN, PREFERABLY CUT FROM THE TAIL END

10 TABLESPOONS UNSALTED BUTTER

1 TABLESPOON OLIVE OIL

1¾ POUNDS FRESH SPINACH, WELL-WASHED AND LARGE STEMS REMOVED

SALT AND FRESHLY GROUND PEPPER

FRESHLY GRATED NUTMEG

COARSE SEA SALT

Press a few black peppercorns into each salmon fillet. Heat 4 tablespoons butter with oil in a large heavy-bottomed skillet over medium heat. Add salmon fillets, skin side down, and cook, without turning, until color of fish changes and surface is no longer opaque, about 18 minutes. (The salmon cooks from the bottom up.)

While the salmon is roasting, prepare spinach. Melt 4 tablespoons butter in a large enameled pot. Add spinach and sprinkle with salt, pepper, and nutmeg. Cook, covered, over medium high heat, for 30 seconds. Uncover and continue to cook, stirring frequently, until spinach wilts and liquid in pot evaporates, about 8 minutes. Add remaining 2 tablespoons butter and toss gently to coat spinach. Season with salt and pepper to taste.

TO SERVE: Place spinach on a large, heated serving platter. Place salmon on spinach, skin side down, and sprinkle each fillet with coarse sea salt. *Makes 4 servings.*

NOTE: The cooking time for the salmon will vary, depending on the thickness of the fillets. If properly cooked, this simple and natural salmon preparation does not require any sauce.

SPRING FRUITS

S TRAWBERRIES AND CHERRIES ARE THE FIRST
FRUITS TO ARRIVE IN SPRING MARKETS AND,
ALONG WITH THE FLOWERING OF THE ORCHARDS
AFTER THE LONG WINTER, ARE THE HARBINGERS
OF THE PLENTIFUL HARVEST YET TO COME. ENJOY
THESE EARLY FRUITS WHILE YOU CAN, SINCE THEIR
SEASON DOES NOT LAST LONG—STRAWBERRY
SEASON IS ONLY FROM MID-APRIL UNTIL THE END
OF JUNE, AND THE CHERRY SEASON IS EVEN
SHORTER.

LEMON VERBENA ICE CREAM WITH LIGHT CHERRIES

BIGARREAUX AU JUS DE CERISES NOIRES ET A LA VERVEINE GLACEE

ICE CREAM

2	CUPS MILK
½	VANILLA BEAN, SPLIT
1⅔	OUNCES FRESH LEMON VERBENA LEAVES, COARSELY CHOPPED
4	EGG YOLKS
⅔	CUP GRANULATED SUGAR

CHERRIES AND JUICE

1	POUND DARK CHERRIES, SUCH AS BING OR LAMBERT
	POWDERED SUGAR
	LEMON JUICE
1	POUND LIGHT CHERRIES, SUCH AS ROYAL ANNE OR RAINIER
	FRESH LEMON VERBENA, BASIL, OR MINT LEAVES FOR GARNISH

PREPARE THE ICE CREAM: In a medium saucepan, scald milk with vanilla bean and verbena leaves. Meanwhile, beat egg yolks with granulated sugar until pale in color and thick enough to leave a ribbon trail when whisk is lifted. Gradually whisk in hot milk and whisk until thoroughly blended.

Return mixture to saucepan and cook over medium heat, stirring constantly with a wooden spoon and scraping bottom and edges of pan, until custard is thick enough to lightly coat the spoon, about 6 minutes. (Do not let custard boil or egg yolks will curdle.) Strain custard through a fine-mesh strainer set over a heatproof bowl. Let cool slightly. Cover and refrigerate until well-chilled. Pour mixture into an ice cream maker and freeze according to manufacturer's instructions. Pack finished ice cream into a container and keep frozen until serving time.

PREPARE THE CHERRIES AND JUICE: Place dark cherries in a food processor and puree until smooth. Strain cherry juice through a very fine strainer set over a bowl, pressing hard on solids to extract all juice. Whisk in powdered sugar and lemon juice to taste. Cover and refrigerate until serving time.

Very shortly before serving, halve light cherries and remove pits.

TO SERVE: Pour some dark cherry juice into 4 dessert bowls. Place a large scoop of lemon verbena ice cream in each bowl and surround with pitted light cherries. Garnish with verbena, basil, or mint leaves and serve immediately. *Makes 4 servings.*

NOTE: I recommend wearing rubber gloves when handling dark cherries because the juice stains the fingers. If you like, you can add a little Verveine (verbena liqueur) to the ice cream for a stronger flavor.

THIS DESSERT COMBINES LIGHT, FIRM-FLESHED CHERRIES WITH THE JUICE OF DARKER FRUIT, A COMBINATION WHICH IS SET OFF BY THE TANG OF FRESH LEMON VERBENA ICE CREAM. IN THE BEGINNING OF MAY THE FIRST CHERRIES ARRIVE FROM THE VAR AND PYRENEES-ORIENTALES. THEN COME THOSE FROM THE RHONE VALLEY AND FROM THE WHOLE SOUTHEAST, PRINCIPAL

REGIONS FOR THE HARVEST OF *BIGARREAUX*, THOSE LARGE CRIMSON CHERRIES WHICH REPRESENT EIGHTY PERCENT OF FRENCH PRODUCTION.

RHUBARB COMPOTE WITH *STRAWBERRIES* AND CANDIED LEMON ZEST
COMPOTE DE RHUBARBE AUX FRAISES ET ZESTES CONFITS

THE COMBINATION OF STRAWBERRIES AND RHUBARB IS A PERENNIAL FAVORITE, AND THIS DELIGHTFUL COMPOTE SITS AMIDST A SPRING GARDEN, LIT BY THE FIRST RAYS OF THE SUN. STRAWBERRIES ARE A FRAGILE FRUIT WHICH DO NOT KEEP WELL AND SHOULD BE CHOSEN WELL-COLORED, FIRM AND SHINY. THEY SHOULD BE WASHED RAPIDLY WITHOUT SOAKING.

1 POUND RHUBARB STALKS, TRIMMED, PEELED, AND CUT INTO 1-INCH LENGTHS	1 VANILLA BEAN, SPLIT LENGTHWISE
3 CUPS SUGAR SYRUP	2 TABLESPOONS FINELY JULIENNED LEMON ZEST
	1 PINT STRAWBERRIES

Place rhubarb in a nonreactive medium saucepan and add enough sugar syrup to cover it by half. Add vanilla bean, cover, and cook over medium heat, without stirring, until tender, about 5 minutes. Transfer compote to a heatproof glass bowl. Add a little more syrup, if necessary, and refrigerate until cool.

While rhubarb chills, blanch julienned lemon zest in boiling water for 30 seconds. Drain, refresh under cold water, and blanch again in fresh boiling water for 30 seconds. Drain and refresh again. (This blanching process removes bitterness.) Bring any remaining syrup to a boil in a small heavy saucepan. Add blanched zests and simmer in syrup over medium high heat until lightly candied, about 10 minutes. Drain zests well. Place on a small plate and separate strands with a fork.

TO SERVE: Quickly rinse and dry strawberries. Remove hulls. Halve strawberries lengthwise and use to decorate the compote. Sprinkle rhubarb with candied zests and serve immediately. *Makes 4 servings.*

NOTE: Once assembled, this dessert should be served immediately, before the strawberries fade.

CHOOSE THE MELONS CAREFULLY FOR THIS SIMPLE BUT EXCELLENT DESSERT. THE LIGHT CHERRIES, WHICH ACCOMPANY THE MELON BALLS, COULD BE REPLACED BY OTHER RED FRUITS SUCH AS WILD STRAWBERRIES.

MUSCAT-MACERATED MELON WITH LIGHT CHERRIES
NAGE DE MELON ET BIGARREAUX AU VIN DE MUSCAT

2 SMALL RIPE CANTALOUPES OR OTHER MUSK MELONS	½ POUND LIGHT-COLORED CHERRIES, SUCH AS ROYAL ANNE OR RAINIER
2 TABLESPOONS SUGAR	FRESH MINT LEAVES FOR GARNISH
½ BOTTLE MUSCAT WINE	

Cut melons in half with a sharp nonreactive knife. Scoop out seeds and membranes. Using a medium melon baller, scoop out melon balls. Place balls in a medium bowl and sprinkle with 1 tablespoon sugar. Toss well, taste, and add the remaining 1 tablespoon sugar only if necessary. Stir in Muscat, cover with plastic wrap and let macerate in the refrigerator for about 2 hours. Meanwhile, halve cherries and remove pits.

TO SERVE: Divide melon balls and their liquid among 4 serving bowls or coupes. Add halved cherries in a decorative pattern and garnish with mint leaves. *Makes 4 servings.*

NOTE: If you like, you can halve the melons by making saw-toothed cuts all the way around and then serve the macerated melon inside.

PINEAPPLE FRITTERS WITH MACERATED KIWI FRUIT
FRITES D'ANANAS A LA SALADE VERTE

THIS DESSERT (PICTURED ON PAGE 76) OFFERS AN ORIGINAL TWIST TO OLD FAVORITES—FRENCH FRIES AND GREEN SALAD. HERE, AN ARRANGEMENT OF BRILLIANT GREEN KIWI SLICES IS SERVED SURROUNDED BY THE SURPRISING AND AMUSING PINEAPPLE FRITTERS THAT COULD EASILY BE MISTAKEN FOR FRENCH FRIES.

KIWI FRUIT AND SYRUP
1¼ CUPS SUGAR
    JUICE OF 1 LEMON
4 KIWI FRUITS, PEELED AND SLICED
    ¼-INCH-THICK
    KIRSCH OR OTHER *EAU-DE-VIE*
    (OPTIONAL)
BATTER
1¾ CUPS ALL-PURPOSE FLOUR
1 CUP BEER

2 WHOLE EGGS, LIGHTLY BEATEN
2 TABLESPOONS FLAVORLESS VEGETABLE
    OIL
½ TEASPOON SALT
3 EGG WHITES
FRITTERS
1 PINEAPPLE, PEELED, QUARTERED
    LENGTHWISE, AND CORED
    OIL FOR DEEP FRYING

PREPARE THE SYRUP: In a small saucepan, combine sugar and 1¼ cups water. Bring to a boil over medium high heat, stirring occasionally with a wooden spoon. With a damp pastry brush, wipe down any sugar crystals that accumulate in pan. When syrup boils, remove from heat. Stir in lemon juice. Strain syrup into medium bowl and refrigerate until chilled.

When the syrup is cold, add kiwi slices. Stir in kirsch or other *eau-de-vie* to taste, if you like. Cover and refrigerate until serving time.

PREPARE THE FRITTERS: Sift flour into a large bowl. Make a well in the center and add beer, beaten eggs, oil, and salt; stir well to combine. Gradually stir in flour and whisk until batter is smooth. Beat egg whites until stiff peaks form. Fold into batter until thoroughly incorporated. Cover and refrigerate batter.

Preheat oven to 300 degrees. Cut pineapple quarters into thin sticks about 2-by-¼-by-¼-inches, to resemble French fries. Drain pineapple sticks on paper towels.

Heat oil in a deep-fat fryer or deep saucepan until it reaches 365 degrees. One by one, dip each pineapple stick into batter and deep fry, in batches, turning once, until golden brown, about 1½ minutes. Transfer to paper towels to drain. Keep the pineapple "fries" warm in the oven while you fry the remainder.

TO SERVE: Drain kiwi slices and arrange in the center of 4 dessert plates. Surround with pineapple "fries" and served immediately. *Makes 4 servings.*

MEDLEY OF EXOTIC FRUITS
CAPRICE EXOTIQUE

MANGO
BANANAS
PINEAPPLE
KIWI FRUITS
PAPAYA
BLOOD ORANGES
FRESH LYCHEES

PASSION FRUIT COULIS
2 POUNDS FRESH PASSION FRUITS
LEMON JUICE
SUGAR
FRESH MINT LEAVES FOR GARNISH

THIS SIMPLE DESSERT SHOULD APPEAL TO THOSE WHO ARE FOND OF EXOTIC TASTES. IT ALSO CALLS ON YOUR IMAGINATION AND YOUR FLAIR FOR THE DRAMATIC WHEN CHOOSING THE FRUITS AND ARRANGING EACH SERVING ARTISTICALLY.

For this dessert, select whichever fruits are most to your liking. Aim for a good assortment which will serve 4 people. Most important, choose fruits that are at the peak of ripeness—not overripe, but just right. Peel the fruits and remove any pits or seeds. Slice the fruits as attractively as possible. Place the fruits on a large plate, cover with plastic wrap and refrigerate for at least 2 hours.

PREPARE THE PASSION FRUIT COULIS: Halve passion fruits and scoop all pulp and seeds into a fine-mesh strainer set over a bowl. Strain out all juice, pressing on seeds to extract as much liquid as possible. Stir in lemon juice and sugar to taste. Cover and refrigerate until serving time. (The fruits and the passion fruit *coulis* can be prepared the morning before you plan to serve the dessert.)

TO SERVE: Artistically arrange the fruits on 4 serving plates, keeping color and form in mind. Sprinkle each serving with the passion fruit *coulis* and garnish with fresh mint leaves. Pass any remaining *coulis* separately in a small sauceboat. *Makes 4 servings.*

CARAMELIZED RICE PUDDING WITH PEACHES AND CHERRIES
GATEAU DE RIZ AUX PECHES ET CERISES

ANOTHER SPRINGTIME TREAT. HERE THE RICH, TENDER TASTE OF WHITE AND YELLOW PEACHES IS COMPLEMENTED BY CHERRIES. IN ADDITION TO ANNOUNCING THE FRUIT SEASON, CHERRIES HAVE MULTIPLE USES IN PASTRY AND COOKING. TARTES, CLAFOUTIS, BLACK FOREST CAKES, AND FLANS ARE AMONG THE MANY POSSIBILITIES. CHERRIES MAY ALSO SERVE AS AN ACCOMPANIMENT TO GAME AND DUCK, AND IN ALSACE THEY ARE THE BASE OF A HIGHLY ORIGINAL SOUP.

4	CUPS SUGAR SYRUP	1	CUP ROUND OR SHORT-GRAIN RICE (UNTREATED)
2	YELLOW PEACHES		
2	WHITE PEACHES	4	EGG YOLKS
1⅔	CUPS SUGAR	4	TABLESPOONS UNSALTED BUTTER, CUT INTO PIECES AND SOFTENED
3½	CUPS MILK		
2	VANILLA BEANS, SPLIT LENGTHWISE	½	POUND SWEET OR SOUR CHERRIES, PITTED

In a medium saucepan, bring sugar syrup to a simmer. Add peaches and poach over medium heat until just tender, 7 to 10 minutes. Remove peaches with a slotted spoon. When cool enough to handle, peel peaches and return them to cooled syrup.

Place 1 cup sugar in a small heavy-bottomed saucepan. Measure out ⅓ cup peach poaching liquid and add to sugar, stirring to completely moisten. Bring to a boil over medium high heat without stirring. Cook sugar, swirling pan from time to time, until it turns a light brown caramel, 5 to 7 minutes. Remove from heat and pour half the caramel into a 4- to 4½-cup charlotte mold. Quickly rotate mold to coat bottom and sides with caramel. Pour any excess caramel back into pan. Add 6 tablespoons water to saucepan and whisk constantly to dissolve caramel slightly and form a light, syrupy sauce. If caramel is already too firm, set pan over medium heat and stir until dissolved. Set sauce aside.

In a medium saucepan, bring milk to a boil with vanilla beans. Add rice, reduce heat, and simmer over medium heat, stirring from time to time, until rice is quite tender, about 15 minutes.

While rice is cooking, combine egg yolks with remaining ⅔ cup sugar in a medium bowl. Whisk until light and thoroughly blended.

When rice is cooked, remove from heat and remove vanilla beans. Using the back of a knife, scrape tiny vanilla seeds from pod and add to rice. Stir in softened butter, a few pieces at a time. Then add yolk/sugar mixture and stir gently with a wooden spoon until well combined. Pour rice mixture into caramelized mold and refrigerate for at least 4 hours or overnight until set. (If refrigerating overnight, cover pudding with foil.)

TO SERVE: Dip charlotte mold in very hot water for about 15 seconds to soften caramel. Using a long, flexible knife, scrape around inner rim of mold to loosen pudding, then unmold it onto a serving platter.

Drain peaches. Halve them and remove pits. Cut into quarters. Arrange peaches, alternating yellow and white slices, around rice pudding. Garnish with cherries. Pour some of the caramel sauce around fruit and pour remainder into a sauceboat to be passed separately. *Makes 4 servings.*

NOTE: Apricots or other fruits would work equally as well in this recipe. The caramel sauce called for above could also be replaced by a crème anglaise or a *coulis*. If the caramel sauce firms up on standing, simply reheat it and whisk in a little additional water until the desired consistency is reached.

FLOATING ISLANDS
WITH CARAMELIZED RASPBERRIES
BLANC EN NEIGE AUX FRAMBOISES DEGUISEES

IN THIS INTERPRETATION OF A CLASSIC DESSERT, THE TART RASPBERRIES, ENCASED IN THEIR COATING OF CARAMEL, ENHANCE THE PRESENTATION AND PROVIDE AN ADDITIONAL CONTRAST OF FLAVORS AND TEXTURES. IF YOU LIKE, MAKE ONLY ONE LARGE MERINGUE PER SERVING, AND DECORATE IT WITH SEVERAL RASPBERRIES.

1¼ CUPS PLUS 1 TABLESPOON SUGAR
1   TABLESPOON LIGHT CORN SYRUP
24 LARGE RED RASPBERRIES
8   EGG WHITES

PINCH OF SALT
2   CUPS CREME ANGLAISE, MADE WITH
    EXTRA VANILLA (SEE APPENDIX)

Lightly oil a baking sheet; set aside. In a small stainless-steel saucepan or copper pot, combine 1¼ cups sugar, corn syrup and ⅓ cup water; mix well with a wooden spoon. Bring to a boil over high heat, then reduce heat to medium high and cook until sugar becomes a light caramel, about 12 minutes. Watch carefully during the last 5 minutes of cooking and brush down any sugar crystals that accumulate on the sides of the pan with a damp pastry brush. When caramel is ready, set bottom of saucepan in cold water to stop the cooking. Remove the pan from water. Using a fork, dip raspberries into caramel, one by one, turning to coat completely. Transfer coated berries to oiled baking sheet to cool and harden.

Fill a large, wide casserole with water and bring to a simmer. Meanwhile, in a large stainless-steel bowl, beat egg whites with salt until soft peaks form. Add remaining 1 tablespoon sugar and continue beating until stiff. Using 2 soup spoons, shape meringue into ovals and place in simmering water. Poach until just firm, about 45 seconds per side. Using a wire skimmer, transfer poached meringues to paper towels to drain. Repeat with remaining meringue until all is shaped and poached.

TO SERVE: Pour ½ cup crème anglaise onto each of 4 shallow-rimmed dessert plates. Arrange meringues in a star pattern on custard and garnish each with a raspberry. Serve immediately. *Makes 4 servings.*

STRAWBERRY-VANILLA CHARLOTTE WITH STRAWBERRIES

CHARLOTTE VANILLE-FRAISE A LA FRAISE

VANILLA BAVARIAN

2   TEASPOONS UNFLAVORED GELATIN
1   CUP PLUS 2 TABLESPOONS MILK
1   VANILLA BEAN, SPLIT
3   EGG YOLKS
⅓   CUP GRANULATED SUGAR
1¼ CUPS HEAVY CREAM

STRAWBERRY BAVARIAN

1   POUND RIPE STRAWBERRIES, RINSED
     AND HULLED
1¼ CUPS POWDERED SUGAR, SIFTED
4   TEASPOONS UNFLAVORED GELATIN
2½ CUPS HEAVY CREAM
     LEMON JUICE

LADYFINGERS

5   EGGS, SEPARATED AND AT ROOM
     TEMPERATURE
⅔   CUP PLUS ¼ CUP GRANULATED SUGAR
1   CUP ALL-PURPOSE FLOUR, SIFTED
     POWDERED SUGAR

GARNISH

¾   POUND RIPE STRAWBERRIES, RINSED,
     HULLED, AND SLICED LENGTHWISE
     WHIPPED CREAM
     MINT LEAVES
     STRAWBERRY *COULIS* (SEE APPENDIX)

PREPARE THE VANILLA BAVARIAN: In a small bowl, soften gelatin in 2 tablespoons milk. Place remaining 1 cup milk and vanilla bean in a heavy-bottomed saucepan and bring to a boil. Remove from heat.

Meanwhile, beat egg yolks with sugar until the mixture is very light and thick. Whisk in hot milk, then return mixture to the saucepan. Cook over medium heat, stirring constantly with a wooden spoon, until mixture thickens enough to coat the back of the spoon and a clear trail is left when a finger is drawn across. Remove from heat and stir in softened gelatin. Let cool, then strain into a bowl; cover and refrigerate. When mixture is cold, beat heavy cream until soft peaks form. Fold whipped cream into bavarian mixture until blended. Cover and refrigerate.

PREPARE THE STRAWBERRY BAVARIAN: Puree strawberries in a food processor. Strain puree through a fine-mesh strainer into a bowl and whisk in powdered sugar. Set bowl over a pan of simmering water and sprinkle gelatin over puree; as puree warms, the gelatin will dissolve. Once the gelatin dissolves, remove bowl from heat. Cover and refrigerate until cold.

Whip cream until soft peaks form. Fold chilled puree into cream until blended. Stir in lemon juice to taste; cover and refrigerate.

PREPARE THE LADYFINGERS: Preheat oven to 375 degrees. Butter and flour a large, heavy baking sheet.

In a large bowl, beat egg yolks with ⅔ cup granulated sugar until mixture is very pale and forms a ribbon on the surface when whisk or beaters are lifted, about 5 minutes. In another bowl, beat egg whites until stiff. Beat in remaining ¼ cup granulated sugar.

Sift flour over egg yolk mixture and fold in gently. Fold in one-third of egg whites until thoroughly incorporated, then fold in remaining egg whites.

Spoon batter into a large pastry bag fitted with a ¾- to 1-inch round tip. Pipe even strips of batter onto baking sheet, making them about 4 inches long and leaving 1½ inches between them. Sift powdered sugar over. Bake until ladyfingers are lightly browned and sugar begins to form little beads on the surface, 8 to 10 minutes. Transfer ladyfingers to a rack to cool.

ASSEMBLE THE CHARLOTTE: Line sides of a 9- or 9½-cup soufflé dish, charlotte mold, or bowl with ladyfingers, flat sides facing in. Trim sides as necessary, so they fit snugly. Spoon vanilla bavarian into ladyfinger-lined mold and refrigerate until cold and set, about 1½ hours. Fill mold with strawberry bavarian and smooth surface. Refrigerate for 4 hours. If ladyfingers extend further than bavarian mixture, trim them. (The charlotte can be prepared ahead to this point.)

TO SERVE: Dip bottom of mold into hot water for 10 seconds, or until you can feel charlotte twist slightly in mold. Place a serving plate over mold and invert charlotte onto plate. Decorate top of charlotte with sliced strawberries by arranging them in circles, completely covering surface of charlotte. Scoop whipped cream into a pastry bag fitted with a medium star tip and pipe cream in the center of charlotte. Arrange strawberries in a flower pattern in the cream. Garnish with mint leaves and serve *coulis* separately in a sauceboat. *Makes 8 to 10 servings.*

NOTE: This same recipe can be used to make individual charlottes as well. When you are getting ready to pipe out the ladyfingers, keep in mind the size of your mold and try to pipe them to fit. Instead of the strawberry *coulis*, you could serve a raspberry *coulis* or a crème anglaise.

A SEASONAL SPLENDOR THAT WILL SERVE WONDERFULLY ON FESTIVE OCCASIONS, THIS DESSERT TAKES FULL ADVANTAGE OF THE STRAW-BERRY'S VERSATILITY. HISTORIANS RECOUNT THAT LOUIS XIV DEMANDED STRAWBERRIES ON HIS TABLE BY THE END OF MARCH, WHICH INSPIRED THE AGRONOMIST JEAN LA QUINTINIE TO GROW THEM UNDER SHELTER IN HOTHOUSES. SINCE ROMAN TIMES, PEOPLE HAVE STRONGLY BELIEVED IN THE STRAWBERRY'S THERAPEUTIC POWERS; ONE EIGHTEENTH-CENTURY PHILOSOPHER, WHO DIED A CENTENARIAN, EVEN ATTRIBUTED HIS LONGEV-ITY TO THE REGULAR CONSUMPTION OF SEVERAL BOWLS OF STRAWBERRIES.

LAYERED MARJOLAINE WITH RED BERRIES
MARJOLAINE FEUILLETEE AUX FRUITS ROUGES

MARJOLAINE

⅓ CUP FINELY GROUND BLANCHED
    ALMONDS
½ CUP POWDERED SUGAR
1 TABLESPOON ALL-PURPOSE FLOUR
3 EGG WHITES, AT ROOM TEMPERATURE
2½ TABLESPOONS GRANULATED SUGAR
2 TEASPOONS MELTED BUTTER, COOLED
    SLIGHTLY

ASSEMBLY

½ CUP CREME FRAICHE
1 CUP PASTRY CREAM (SEE APPENDIX)
½ POUND FRESH RASPBERRIES OR
    STRAWBERRIES, HULLED AND
    QUARTERED
    POWDERED SUGAR, FOR SPRINKLING
1 CUP RASPBERRY *COULIS* (SEE APPENDIX)

PREPARE THE MARJOLAINE: Preheat oven to 325 degrees. Butter two baking sheets. Using a 5-inch round cookie cutter as a guide, score four well-spaced rounds on each sheet.

In a bowl, sift together ground almonds, powdered sugar, and flour. In another bowl, beat egg whites until soft peaks form. Add granulated sugar and continue beating until stiff peaks form. Lightly fold sifted dry ingredients into beaten whites, and fold in melted butter until thoroughly combined.

Spoon marjolaine batter into the center of each round, dividing evenly. Use a flat spatula to spread batter evenly to scored rims. Bake rounds until lightly browned all over, about 15 minutes. Carefully transfer to a rack and let cool completely. (These marjolaine rounds can be prepared in advance and stored in an airtight container. If they do become soggy, re-crisp them in a warm oven for 2 to 3 minutes before assembling the dessert.)

ASSEMBLE THE DESSERT: Beat crème fraîche until stiff. Fold into pastry cream until no streaks remain. Spoon mixture into a pastry bag fitted with a ¾-inch round tip. Pipe a little bit of cream onto the center of 4 large dessert plates. Place a marjolaine round on top of cream.

Pipe an even layer of cream over each round and top with berries. Cover berries with another layer of cream. Sift powdered sugar over remaining 4 marjolaines on rack and carefully place them on top of the cream-covered berries. Drizzle raspberry *coulis* around each stacked marjolaine, if you like, and serve immediately. *Makes 4 servings.*

NOTE: This dessert should be served as soon as possible after assembly so that the marjolaine wafers remain a crisp contrast to the smooth cream and fresh berries. To decorate the sugared tops of the marjolaine, heat a trussing needle over a gas flame and score in a decorative pattern. And, instead of piping, the cream can be spread over the marjolaines and berries with a spoon or a small flat spatula.

NESTLED IN ITS BASKET AND SURROUNDED BY SPRAYS OF WHITE LILACS, THIS MARJOLAINE (PICTURED ON PAGES 86–87) CAN MAKE YOU MELT WITH DELIGHT AT ITS DIZZYING COMBINATION OF CREAM AND FRESH RASPBERRIES. BOTH SWEET AND ACID AT THE SAME TIME, RASPBERRIES ARE EXTREMELY FRAGILE. THIS FRAGRANT, PURPLISH RED FRUIT MUST BE EATEN VERY RIPE. IT MAY BE EATEN PLAIN OR WITH SUGAR OR CREAM, BUT RASPBERRIES ARE ALSO EXCELLENT MACERATED IN A SUGARY RED WINE OR IN CHAMPAGNE.

PINK GRAPEFRUIT MERINGUES WITH HAZELNUTS
SURPRISE DE PAMPLEMOUSSE ROSE MERINGUE AUX NOISETTES

THIS DRAMATIC DESSERT, ITS SNOWY TOP DUSTED WITH CONFECTIONER'S SUGAR, ECHOES THE CASCADES OF WHITE BLOSSOMS ON THE APPLE TREES AND MAKES A FITTING SPRINGTIME SHOWPIECE. ITS COMBINATION OF RED CURRANT JUICE AND GRAPEFRUIT OFFERS AN UNUSUAL BLEND OF FRUIT TASTES.

3   LARGE AND 2 SMALLER PINK GRAPEFRUITS
2   TABLESPOONS RED CURRANT JELLY OR SEEDLESS RASPBERRY JAM
3   EGG WHITES
¾   CUP POWDERED SUGAR, PLUS ADDITIONAL FOR SPRINKLING WHOLE HAZELNUTS, WALNUT HALVES, OR COARSELY CHOPPED NUTS FOR GARNISH

Peel 3 large grapefruits with a sharp knife, cutting off all of bitter white pith. Cut in between membranes to release sections into a bowl. If sections are large, cut them in half or in thirds.

Halve remaining 2 smaller grapefruits, using a straight or saw-toothed cut; separate halves. Juice grapefruits on an electric juicer, taking great care not to damage their shape or edges. Strain juice through a fine-mesh strainer into a bowl and stir in the currant jelly until smooth. Using a teaspoon and your fingers, remove all flesh and membranes from grapefruit halves, leaving empty shells. (The recipe can be prepared ahead to this point.)

Preheat oven to 450 degrees. Place grapefruit shells on a baking sheet. (Cut a thin slice off bottoms, if necessary, to steady the shells.) Fill shells with grapefruit sections and spoon currant jelly mixture over fruit.

In a large bowl, beat egg whites until firm peaks form. Add sugar and continue beating until meringue is stiff and glossy. Scoop meringue into a pastry bag fitted with a medium star tip and pipe decoratively over grapefruits. (Make sure to cover sections completely with meringue and to cover shell rims.) Arrange whole nuts on meringue, or sprinkle with coarsely chopped nuts. Dust meringue lightly with additional sugar and bake for 4 minutes, or until meringue is golden and set. Serve immediately. *Makes 4 servings.*

NOTE: Serve these grapefruits in rimmed dessert plates or shallow bowls to catch the grapefruit and red currant juice.

S U M

M   E   R

SUMMER VEGETABLES

*S*UMMER, THE SEASON OF BALMY SKIES AND
LUSH GREENERY, IS ALSO THE TIME OF ABUN-
DANCE IN GARDENS AND ORCHARDS. FRUIT AND
VEGETABLE CROPS ARE NOW AT THEIR PEAK, AND
MARKET STALLS, OVERFLOWING WITH MAGNIFI-
CENT, RIPE PRODUCE, OFFER US SPECTACULAR
SYMPHONIES OF COLOR.

CELERY ROOT AND GOAT CHEESE PROFITEROLES WITH FRESH TOMATO SAUCE
PROFITEROLES AU CELERI, AU FROMAGE DE CHEVRE, ET AU SUC DE TOMATE

THESE PROFITEROLES WOULD DELIGHT LOUIS CHEVENET, KING OF GOAT CHEESE. IN HIS CAVE (SEE PAGE 98), FORMERLY AN ANCIENT WATER RESERVOIR AT HURIGNY IN THE REGION OF MACON, HE PRODUCES BOTH SOFT, FRESH GOAT CHEESE AND THE KIND THAT MUST BE CAREFULLY AGED. THIS RECIPE ALSO CALLS FOR A SAUCE MADE FROM TOMATOES, THE FRUIT-VEGETABLE

WHOSE SCARLET COLOR BLAZES BRIGHTLY AMID ALL THE OTHER VEGETABLES OF THE SUMMER MARKET.

PROFITEROLES
3½ TABLESPOONS UNSALTED BUTTER
1¾ TEASPOONS SUGAR
    PINCH OF SALT
⅔ CUP ALL-PURPOSE FLOUR, SIFTED
3 EGGS, AT ROOM TEMPERATURE
PUREE
⅔ POUND CELERY ROOT (CELERIAC), PEELED AND CUT INTO 1-INCH CHUNKS
6 OUNCES FRESH GOAT CHEESE, AT ROOM TEMPERATURE
    SALT AND FRESHLY GROUND PEPPER

TOMATO SAUCE
2 LARGE RIPE TOMATOES, CORED
1 TABLESPOON OLIVE OIL
1 TEASPOON WINE VINEGAR
    SALT AND FRESHLY GROUND PEPPER
CHIVE GLAZE
2 LARGE BUNCHES OF CHIVES, RINSED, DRIED, AND FINELY CHOPPED
1½ TEASPOONS OLIVE OIL
1 TEASPOON RED WINE VINEGAR
    SALT AND FRESHLY GROUND PEPPER

PREPARE THE PROFITEROLES: Preheat oven to 450 degrees. In a medium saucepan, bring butter, sugar, salt, and ⅔ cup water to a boil. Immediately add flour and stir briskly with a wooden spoon to form a soft dough. Continue stirring over medium heat for 2 minutes to dry out dough. Off heat, add 1 egg and beat until completely absorbed into dough. Add remaining 2 eggs, one at a time, beating well after each addition.

Butter and lightly flour a baking sheet. Spoon *choux* dough into a pastry bag fitted with a 1-inch round tip. On baking sheet, pipe out 16 evenly spaced mounds of equal size. Bake *choux* for 10 minutes, reduce temperature to 350 degrees and continue baking until *choux* are golden brown all over and dry, about 20 minutes longer. Transfer puffs to a rack to cool. Slice each one horizontally in half to allow steam to escape and prevent them from getting soggy.

PREPARE THE PUREE: Place celery root in a medium saucepan with salted water to cover by 2 inches. Bring to a boil and cook over medium high heat until very soft, about 25 minutes. Drain celery root and refresh under cold water. Drain very well and squeeze to extract any excess moisture. Puree celery root in a food processor. Strain puree through a fine-mesh strainer. In a bowl, mash goat cheese until smooth. Add celery root puree and stir until well blended. Season with salt and pepper to taste. Cover and refrigerate until chilled.

PREPARE THE TOMATO SAUCE: Quarter tomatoes and puree in a food processor until smooth. Add the olive oil and vinegar and puree until blended. Strain through a fine-mesh strainer into a bowl; season to taste with salt and pepper. Cover and refrigerate until serving time.

PREPARE THE CHIVE GLAZE: In a blender or mini food processor, puree chives with the oil and vinegar. Strain puree through a fine-mesh sieve and season to taste with salt and pepper.

TO SERVE: Using a teaspoon or a pastry bag fitted with a ½-inch round tip, fill bottom half of *choux* puffs with celery root and goat cheese puree. Dip the *choux* tops in chive glaze to coat, then place on top of puree. Pour tomato sauce onto 4 serving plates and set 4 filled profiteroles on each. Serve immediately so that *choux* remain crisp. *Makes 4 servings.*

NOTE: Another method for filling the profiteroles is to pierce the *choux* puffs on the underside and then insert the pastry bag and pipe in the filling. This recipe can also be served hot. Simply fill the profiteroles and place them on a baking sheet. Bake them in a 300 degree oven for 2 to 3 minutes. Remember to warm the tomato sauce if you will be serving them hot. All of the elements of this recipe can be prepared in advance. If the *choux* puffs become soft, simply recrisp them in a hot oven for 1 minute.

TERRINE OF AVOCADO AND LEEKS
TERRINE D'AVOCATS ET DE POIREAUX

6	TO 8 LEEKS (ABOUT 2½ POUNDS)	2	ENVELOPES (2 TABLESPOONS)
3	MEDIUM AVOCADOS, PEELED AND PITS		UNFLAVORED GELATIN
	REMOVED	⅔	CUP HEAVY CREAM
	SALT AND FRESHLY GROUND PEPPER	1	CUP VINAIGRETTE
	JUICE OF 1 LEMON		

Trim and clean leeks. Cut off the green part and discard. Plunge white part of leeks into boiling salted water. Cook over medium high heat until tender, about 15 minutes. Refresh under cold running water. Drain and pat dry.

Place avocado pulp in a food processor and puree until smooth, about 30 seconds. Season with salt and pepper. Add lemon juice and process quickly to blend.

In a medium mixing bowl, sprinkle gelatin over ⅓ cup cold water. Let soften, without stirring, for 10 minutes. In a small saucepan, heat cream over low heat until almost simmering. Let cook slightly, then pour into dissolved gelatin. Mix well and pass through a fine-mesh strainer to remove any lumps.

Blend together avocado and cream mixtures. Set aside, but do not refrigerate.

Generously butter an 8½-inch-long terrine mold or loaf pan. Line bottom and sides with parchment paper, allowing the ends to hang over top edge of terrine.

Spread a ¼-inch-thick layer of avocado mixture over the bottom of terrine. Cut leeks lengthwise in half and arrange over avocado layer. Season with salt and pepper. Cover with a thin layer of avocado mixture. Refrigerate to set slightly, about 10 minutes. Remove and completely fill terrine with remaining avocado mixture.

Cover the top with the overhanging parchment paper, folding to avoid any exposure to air. Cover and refrigerate for 24 hours.

TO SERVE: Carefully cut slices from terrine with a sharp, thin-bladed knife dipped in hot water. Grind fresh pepper over the top and serve with a vinaigrette (flavored with chopped truffles or chopped herbs, if desired). *Makes 8 servings*.

THEY MAY BE CALLED "POOR MAN'S ASPARAGUS," BUT LEEKS SERVED WITH A MUSTARDY VINAIGRETTE AND SPRINKLED WITH THE YOLK OF A HARD-BOILED EGG PASSED THROUGH A SIEVE IS A DISH WHICH NEVER DISHONORED ANY MAN. THIS TERRINE, WHICH COMBINES LAYERS OF AN AVOCADO MIXTURE WITH LAYERS OF LEEKS, SHOULD ALSO BE SERVED WITH A GOOD MUS-

TARDY VINAIGRETTE. THE AVOCADO HAS BEEN EATEN IN FRANCE FOR BARELY THIRTY YEARS, BUT CONTEMPORARY COOKS HAVE UNDERSTOOD THE INTEREST THAT THEY COULD ATTRACT WITH THIS TROPICAL PEAR-SHAPED FRUIT, A NATIVE OF MEXICO.

RATATOUILLE PROVENCAL
RATATOUILLE COMME EN PROVENCE

RATATOUILLE, THAT GREAT CLASSIC OF PROVENCAL CUISINE, IS A TRUE SUMMER DISH, COMBINING ALL THE WARM, GENEROUS FLAVORS OF THE SEASON AND A VIRTUAL CATALOGUE OF SUMMER VEGETABLES: EGGPLANT, ZUCCHINI, PEPPERS, ONION, AND TOMATO. THE EGGPLANT, LIKE ITS COUSINS THE TOMATO AND ZUCCHINI, IS A MEMBER OF THE *CUCURBITACEAE* FAMILY; IT

COMES FROM INDIA, WHILE THE TOMATO AND THE ZUCCHINI ORIGINATED IN THE NEW WORLD. THE TOMATO AND THE EGGPLANT WERE LONG GROWN FOR THEIR ORNAMENTAL QUALITIES; IN BOTH CASES IT WAS THE PEOPLE OF THE SOUTH WHO INITIATED THE CONSUMPTION OF THESE VEGETABLES IN FRANCE.

ABOUT ⅔ CUP VEGETABLE OIL
1   ONION, CHOPPED
4   CLOVES GARLIC, FINELY CHOPPED
1   POUND RIPE TOMATOES, PEELED, SEEDED, AND CHOPPED
1   TEASPOON TOMATO PASTE
    BOUQUET GARNI MADE WITH PARSLEY, CELERY, ROSEMARY, THYME, BAY LEAF, AND MARJORAM

SALT AND FRESHLY GROUND PEPPER
1   POUND ZUCCHINI
¾   POUND EGGPLANT, CUT INTO 1-INCH CUBES
1   LARGE RED BELL PEPPER, CORED, SEEDED, DERIBBED, AND CUT INTO 1-INCH SQUARES
1½ TABLESPOONS OLIVE OIL
1½ TABLESPOONS CHOPPED PARSLEY

Heat 2 tablespoons vegetable oil in a large, heavy-bottomed non-reactive skillet over medium heat. Add onion and sauté until lightly browned, 3 to 4 minutes. Add half of the chopped garlic, the tomatoes, tomato paste, and bouquet garni. Season with salt and pepper and cook over medium heat, stirring frequently, until liquid evaporates and mixture is quite thick, about 8 minutes. Remove from heat.

Meanwhile, use a swivel vegetable peeler to remove thin strips of skin from zucchini. Cut zucchini into 1-inch cubes. Heat 2½ tablespoons of vegetable oil in a large skillet, add zucchini and sauté over medium high heat until tender, about 6 minutes. Drain zucchini in a colander.

Add 3½ tablespoons vegetable oil to skillet. When the oil is hot, add eggplant and sauté until tender and lightly browned, about 10 minutes. Drain eggplant.

Heat remaining 2 tablespoons vegetable oil in skillet. Add red pepper squares and cook over medium heat, tossing frequently, until softened, about 7 minutes. Drain pepper well.

Preheat oven to 425 degrees. In an ovenproof casserole with a lid, combine zucchini, eggplant, red pepper, and tomato mixture. Stir gently to combine, but take care not to crush vegetables. Cover tightly and bake ratatouille for 15 minutes. Remove and discard bouquet garni. (The recipe can be prepared ahead to this point.)

TO SERVE: Heat olive oil in a small skillet. Add the remaining chopped garlic and the parsley and cook over medium heat until very fragrant, about 45 seconds. (Don't let garlic brown.) Add to ratatouille and serve. *Makes 4 servings.*

NOTE: Ratatouille can be served cold, as an hors d'oeuvre. It can also be reheated, and is even better the next day. For a more elegant presentation, the ratatouille can be served in hollowed-out fried eggplants, or surrounded by fried onion slices and deep-fried parsley. Lastly, the mixture can be molded in a nonreactive bowl and turned out just before serving.

CLUSTERS OF LEEKS WITH BEET VINAIGRETTE
GRAPPE DE POIREAUX A LA VINAIGRETTE DE BETTERAVE ROUGE

8 TO 12 MEDIUM LEEKS (ACCORDING TO
      SIZE)
   SALT
1 MEDIUM BEET (ABOUT ¼ POUND),
      COOKED AND PEELED
1 TABLESPOON RED WINE VINEGAR

2 TEASPOONS DIJON MUSTARD
      FRESHLY GROUND PEPPER
1 CUP VEGETABLE OIL
4 LEAVES OF CELERY OR 4 GRAPE VINE
      LEAVES FOR DECORATION

Choose long, straight leeks. Wash and trim, removing green parts (reserve for soup). Tie the white part of leeks into neat, tight bundles using heavy-duty kitchen string. Place in a large pot and cover with cold water. Add a pinch of salt. Bring to a boil and cook for 10 to 15 minutes, or until tender but still slightly firm. Refresh under cold water and drain on paper towels.

Cut beet into small pieces. Place in a food processor with vinegar and puree, scraping down sides as necessary. Pass through a fine-mesh sieve into a nonreactive bowl, pressing slightly with a rubber spatula to retrieve juice but not pulp.

Mix beet juice with mustard. Add salt and pepper to taste. Blend well. Pour in oil, drop by drop, whisking constantly to emulsify.

Cut leeks into ¾-inch rounds. On 4 individual serving plates, make a design of leek rounds in the form of grape clusters. Pour red vinaigrette sauce on or around each cluster. Decorate with the celery or grape vine leaves, lightly brushed with oil. *Makes 4 servings.*

HERE IS A SIMPLE RECIPE, FRESH AND ORIGINAL IN ITS PRESENTATION, COMBINING LEEKS WITH A BEET VINAIGRETTE. BEETS, WHICH CAN BE EATEN RAW AND GRATED OR COOKED AND COLD WITH A SPICY SEASONING, HAVE TWO DIFFERENT FORMS: SMALL AND ROUND OR VERY ELONGATED. IN ADDITION, THERE ARE TWO OTHER VARIETIES, THE ONE DESTINED FOR CATTLE FODDER, PICTURED HERE LOADED ON A CART RETURNING FROM THE MARKET NEAR LOUHANS, AND THE *BETTERAVE SUCRIERE*, USED IN EUROPE TO PRODUCE SUGAR.

BATTER-FRIED THIN GREEN BEANS
PETITE FRITURE D'HARICOTS VERTS

A DEVOTED NATURE LOVER, THE RECENTLY RETIRED MONSIEUR "LE GEORGES" DELIVERS FRESH SUMMER VEGETABLES FROM HIS GARDEN TO ME EVERY DAY. AMONG THE BOUNTY WILL OFTEN BE FRESH GREEN BEANS SUCH AS THOSE USED IN THIS RECIPE. ONE SHOULD NOT BE AFRAID TO DISPLAY A CERTAIN CHAUVINISM BY CLAIMING THAT THE TASTIEST GREEN BEANS ARE THOSE HARVESTED IN FRANCE FROM MAY THROUGH SEPTEMBER. THE IDEA OF GROWING THIS NATIVE OF THE ANDES IN ORDER TO EAT ITS POD CAME TO FRANCE FROM ITALY BARELY TWO CENTURIES AGO. IF WE ONCE HESITATED TO IMITATE OUR

NEIGHBORS, WE HAVE RAPIDLY MADE UP FOR LOST TIME SINCE THEN.

HARICOTS VERTS

1   POUND THIN *HARICOTS VERTS* (FRENCH GREEN BEANS), TRIMMED
1   TABLESPOON OLIVE OIL
2   TEASPOONS LEMON JUICE
    SALT AND FRESHLY GROUND PEPPER
1   TABLESPOON CHOPPED PARSLEY
1   TABLESPOON CHOPPED CHERVIL

BATTER

2   EGGS, SEPARATED
¾   CUP BEER
2   TABLESPOONS VEGETABLE OIL
½   TEASPOON SALT
1   CUP ALL-PURPOSE FLOUR
4   CUPS LIGHT VEGETABLE OIL FOR DEEP-FRYING
3   LEMONS, QUARTERED

PREPARE THE HARICOTS VERT: Blanch green beans in boiling salted water for 1½ minutes; they should remain quite crisp. Drain and refresh beans under cold water. Drain again and dry very well on paper towels.

In a large bowl, combine olive oil, lemon juice, salt, pepper, parsley, and chervil. Add beans and toss well to coat; set aside.

PREPARE THE BATTER: In a medium bowl, whisk together egg yolks, beer, vegetable oil, and salt. Stir in flour until batter is smooth. Beat egg whites until stiff. Fold whites into batter until thoroughly incorporated.

In a deep-fryer, heat oil until the surface begins to shimmer. One by one, dip green beans in batter and fry in hot oil until lightly browned all over, about 20 seconds. Drain on paper towels. Keep each batch warm in oven while you fry remainder. Salt beans lightly and mound them on 4 serving plates. Serve immediately, with lemon quarters. *Makes 4 servings.*

PROCEDURE FOR SUCCESSFUL SALAD PREPARATION
POUR REUSSIR UNE BONNE SALADE

Salads—compositions of herbaceous plants or vegetables—are generally seasoned with oil, vinegar or lemon, and salt and pepper. Often they include other aromatic ingredients such as mustard, shallots, garlic, spices, or fresh herbs.

This refreshing dish, which can be presented either simply tossed in a bowl or elaborately composed on a plate, may be combined with ingredients other than leafy greens, depending on the location, season, taste, and imagination.

The success of a salad depends upon a harmonious final combination and on the care given to the preparation of the various elements—to the mastery of the seasoning; to the taste and savoir-faire evident in the final assembly, whether it be very simple or very rich and elaborate.

Personally, I prefer a simple balance between the different ingredients. Too much diversity can only be harmful to the balance of the dish and thus to its flavor. That is why throughout the book I recommend combinations in which the individual components are complementary in regard to their flavors, textures, and visual appeal.

SUCCESSFUL PREPARATION OF SALAD GREENS
POUR UN BON TRAITEMENT DES SALADES VERTES

Always treat the salad greens with great care and attention while preparing them, while washing, seasoning, and assembling. It is particularly important to drain and dry the salad greens properly and thoroughly so that the excess moisture doesn't prevent the dressing from clinging to the greens.

Remember to add the salad dressing just before serving and never in advance.

Make sure to toss the salad in a large enough bowl so that the greens are not bruised.

For vinaigrette, the ratio of vinegar to oil should be 1 to 3. Salt, freshly ground pepper, and mustard (as well as any herbs or spices you care to add) should be added to taste. Whisk the seasonings into the vinegar before adding the oil gradually, whisking to make the emulsion.

It is a good idea to add a pinch of salt to the still unseasoned salad immediately before seasoning; it is also a good idea to trickle a bit of aged wine vinegar into the dressing at the very last minute.

In general, I would recommend adding finely chopped fresh herbs such as chives and chervil to the salad after it has been seasoned; however, such herbs as tarragon may be added to the vinaigrette beforehand to obtain a delicate maceration.

WHILE RABELAIS BROUGHT THE FIRST LETTUCE SEEDS FROM ITALY, AND THE PLANT ORIGINATED IN ASIA, IT WAS A FRENCHMAN WHO INVENTED THE "SEASONED" SALAD. THE CHEVALIER D'ALBIGNAC, AN EMIGRE FROM THE FRENCH REVOLUTION, MADE A FORTUNE IN LONDON INTRODUCING THE ENGLISH TO GREEN SALADS, WHICH HE SEASONED BEFORE THEIR EYES

WITH ANY AMOUNT OF VINAIGRETTE AND OTHER ASSORTED INGREDIENTS. FLANKED BY A SERVANT WHO CARRIED HIS ACCESSORIES IN A BEAUTIFUL MAHOGANY CASE, THE CHEVALIER MADE A CIRCUIT OF GREAT RESTAURANTS AND PRIVATE HOMES IN NEED OF HIS SERVICES AT THE SALAD HOUR.

Use a light hand with flavored oils. Hazelnut and walnut particularly tend to produce very strong flavors, so it is best to mix them with more neutral oils. I recommend using olive oil and would suggest also mixing it with other oils such as peanut, soya, corn, or rapeseed.

Wine vinegar can also be combined with other complementary vinegars such as sherry vinegar. The vinegar may in fact be replaced with lemon juice.

As an ancient maxim says, in order to successfully prepare a salad, it takes four people:

A SAGE WHO WILL WISELY RATION THE SALT, PEPPER, AND MUSTARD
A MISER WHO WILL PARSIMONIOUSLY DEAL OUT THE VINEGAR
A LAVISH (MAN) WHO WILL GIVE FORTH IN ABUNDANCE THE OIL, PRECIOUS LUBRICANT
AND THE MASTERPIECE WILL BE COMPLETED BY A CRAZY MAN WHO WILL WHIP THE WHOLE INTO A FLAVORFUL EMULSION ENVELOPING THE LEAVES OF OUR SALAD.

It seems that while nothing appears simpler than preparing a salad, it can be said that the care and attention given to its preparation ranks the savoir-faire and talent of the salad chef equal to that of a rôtisserie chef as he perfectly roasts a simple cut of meat.

SOME THOUGHTS ON MAYONNAISE
PROPOS SUR LES SALADES DE LEGUMES

Vegetable salads, whether raw or cooked, are generally seasoned with a vinaigrette or, more frequently, with mayonnaise. Mayonnaise is a simple, cold, emulsified sauce made with egg yolks, oil, mustard, vinegar, salt, and pepper.

This legendary, multipurpose sauce really deserves more credit than it is generally given. The simple, classic mayonnaise plays a major role as a binding and flavoring agent. It is also the mother sauce for most of the cold white sauces. When properly prepared, with judiciously selected ingredients and a little imagination, mayonnaise offers unlimited possibilities. For example, depending on the intended use of the sauce, mayonnaise can be thinned out with flavorful liquids such as truffle juice, anis, or white wine that has been simmered with aromatics for half an hour. Mayonnaise can also be flavored with vegetable purees such as watercress, tomato, or sweet bell pepper. The myriad possible additions to enhance the character of the sauce include pickles, capers, shallots, garlic, anchovies, caviar, shrimp, truffles, chopped or snipped herbs such as tarragon, chervil, or chives; spices such as saffron, curry, and paprika; or even fruit juices such as lemon or orange.

MY SUGGESTIONS FOR MAYONNAISE
MON CONSEIL

1   LARGE EGG YOLK, AT ROOM
    TEMPERATURE
½   TEASPOON DIJON MUSTARD, AT ROOM
    TEMPERATURE

SALT AND FRESHLY GROUND PEPPER
⅔   CUP OIL, AT ROOM TEMPERATURE
VINEGAR OR LEMON JUICE

To begin, make sure all ingredients are at same temperature. In a medium bowl, whisk egg yolk with mustard. Season with salt and pepper. Begin whisking in oil, a few drops at a time. As mayonnaise thickens, add oil in a thin stream, whisking briskly. When mayonnaise becomes very thick, whisk in 1 tablespoon vinegar or lemon juice to thin it slightly. Continue whisking in oil until all has been incorporated. Whisk in additional vinegar or lemon juice to taste; season with salt and pepper. Keep the mayonnaise in a cool place but do not refrigerate. You should *not*, however, make mayonnaise well in advance of serving. *Makes about ¾ cup.*

NOTE: In order to stabilize the emulsion and to make mayonnaise less oily tasting, whisk in a few drops of hot water or vinegar. If the mayonnaise breaks while you are preparing it, spoon a little bit into another bowl, add ¼ teaspoon of mustard and whisk well, then whisk in mayonnaise and remaining oil, if any. In making mayonnaise, you should never use more than ¾ cup oil per large egg yolk.

CREAMED CUCUMBERS WITH CHIVES
EMINCE DE CONCOMBRE A LA CIBOULETTE

At Wednesday's market in Bourg-en-Bresse, small farmers gather to sell a few products from their gardens. Here, brightly colored, speckled dried beans are sold in an old cardboard sugar carton beside bunches of chives that can be used in this cucumber recipe. Cooked or raw, the cucumber remains a greatly appreciated part

of summer cooking. The cucumber has also long been known for its medicinal properties.

2	EUROPEAN CUCUMBERS, TRIMMED	1	CUP HEAVY CREAM
8	TABLESPOONS UNSALTED BUTTER		FRESHLY GROUND WHITE PEPPER
	PINCH OF SUGAR		PINCH OF PAPRIKA
	SALT	½	BUNCH OF CHIVES, FINELY CHOPPED

Peel 1 cucumber. Using a swivel vegetable peeler, cut lengthwise strips from both cucumbers to give them striped, scalloped edges when sliced. Cut the cucumbers into 1½-inch lengths. Using a small melon-ball cutter, scoop out seeds from center of each length. With a sharp knife, slice cucumbers ⅛-inch-thick.

Blanch cucumber slices in boiling salted water for 30 seconds. Drain and refresh under cold water. Drain very well on paper towels.

In a large skillet, melt 5 tablespoons butter over medium heat. Add cucumbers and season with the sugar and salt. Cook, tossing gently, until tender and glossy, about 5 minutes. Arrange cucumber slices, overlapping, in a heated rimmed serving dish.

Add cream to skillet and bring to a boil over high heat. Cook until slightly reduced and thickened, about 2 minutes. Season cream with salt and pepper to taste. Strain into a saucepan. Over low heat, whisk in remaining 3 tablespoons butter, 1 tablespoon at a time. Add paprika and spoon cream over cucumbers. Sprinkle with chives and serve hot. *Makes 4 servings.*

EGG CUP "POMME D'AMOUR"
COQUETIER POMME D'AMOUR

This recipe is an excellent accompaniment for apéritifs. A ceramic egg cup used for serving soft-cooked eggs is filled with layers of individual preparations, each complementary to the others in flavor and color.

PREPARE THE LAYERS: 1) Prepare a tomato *concassé* (peeled, seeded and coarsely chopped fresh tomatoes cooked over high heat until well reduced) flavored with shallots, fresh thyme, a thin trickle of vinegar, olive oil, cream, salt, and pepper.

2) Prepare eggs: put hard-cooked eggs in a food processor. Turn on and off several times to obtain a softened mixture (do not overmix or a sticky paste will form). Add mayonnaise and season with salt and pepper.

3) Prepare an olive spread (tapenade): carefully select and weigh large, healthy, pitted black olives. Add anchovy fillets in the amount of one-fifth of the total olive weight. Blend in some crushed garlic, a few capers, and chopped basil. Place this mixture in a food processor. With motor running, slowly add a stream of olive oil and process to obtain a smooth, well-aerated mixture.

ASSEMBLY: Using a teaspoon or one or two pastry bags, place a small amount of the olive spread in the bottom of each egg cup. Add a good-sized layer of tomato *concassé*. Top with a layer of the egg mixture. Lastly, add a thin layer of the olive spread on top of each egg cup. Decorate with sprigs of fresh parsley, a chervil leaf, or strip of tomato.

Chill the prepared egg cup until serving time. Serve with a small teaspoon. It should be recommended that guests plunge their spoons to the bottom of the dish in order to fully appreciate, with the eye as well as the palate, the simplicity and harmony of this dish.

EGG SELLERS AT THE MARKET IN BOURG COME TO BUY EGGS FROM OUR FAMOUS BRESSE HENS. THIS DELIGHTFUL RECIPE FEATURES THE PERFECTLY FLAVORED COMBINATION OF EGGS AND TOMATOES, SET OFF BY AN ACCENT OF "TAPENADE," OR OLIVE PASTE. IT IS SOMETIMES HARD TO BELIEVE THAT FOR THREE CENTURIES THE TOMATO WAS CONSIDERED POISONOUS AND

GROWN ONLY AS AN ORNAMENTAL PLANT, WHILE BEING FETED WITH SUCH CHARMING NAMES AS *POMME DE PEROU* (PERUVIAN APPLE) AND *POMME D'AMOUR* (LOVE APPLE).

VEGETABLE "VERMICELLI" WITH MACARONI AND LEMON BUTTER
VERMICELLE DE LEGUMES ET MACARONIS AU BEURRE DE CITRON

THE SMALL MALE AND FEMALE SQUASH BLOS-SOMS STILL CLING TO THESE ZUCCHINI FROM THE GARDEN OF MONSIEUR ROZIER OF ST. CYR SUR MENTHON NEAR VONNAS. M. ROZIER ALSO PRODUCES EXTRAORDINARY NEW POTATOES FOR ME. THE BEST ZUCCHINI SHOULD HAVE A FINE SKIN, AS THEY ARE THEN CRISP AND SWEET. ONE CAN MAKE TASTY PUREES WITH THEM, STEAM

THEM, OR QUITE SIMPLY MAKE A SALAD OF RAW ZUCCHINI CUT INTO THIN SLICES AND SEASONED WITH LEMON, OLIVE OIL, AND A BIT OF GARLIC.

1   LARGE CARROT, TRIMMED AND PEELED
1   SMALL CELERY ROOT (CELERIAC), TRIMMED AND PEELED
1   MEDIUM ZUCCHINI, TRIMMED
    GRATED ZEST AND STRAINED JUICE OF 1 LEMON
1   CUP HEAVY CREAM
10 TABLESPOONS UNSALTED BUTTER
    SALT AND FRESHLY GROUND PEPPER

1½ TABLESPOONS VEGETABLE OIL
1½ CUPS DRY MACARONI OR OTHER SMALL TUBULAR PASTA
    HERBS FOR GARNISH: ITALIAN FLAT-LEAF PARSLEY LEAVES, CHERVIL LEAVES, SNIPPED CHIVES, FRESH DILL (OPTIONAL)

Using a mandoline set on very finest julienne setting, shred carrot, celery root, and zucchini, keeping vegetables separated.

Blanch lemon zest in boiling water for 20 seconds. Drain well.

Place cream in a medium saucepan and boil over high heat for 2 minutes to reduce slightly. Reduce heat to medium and whisk in 8 tablespoons butter, 1 tablespoon at a time. Stir in the blanched lemon zest and lemon juice; season to taste with salt and pepper. Keep sauce warm over hot water while you cook macaroni and vegetables.

Bring a medium saucepan of salted water to a boil. Add oil and macaroni and cook until the pasta is *al dente*, about 7 minutes. Drain macaroni and return to saucepan. Add remaining 2 tablespoons butter and toss well to coat pasta; keep warm.

Bring another saucepan of salted water to a boil. Add carrot "vermicelli" and cook until just tender, about 1½ minutes. Remove with a slotted spoon and drain well. Repeat process with celery root, cooking for 1½ minutes, and zucchini, cooking for 45 seconds. Drain well.

TO SERVE: Mound macaroni in the center of 4 heated serving plates. Place individual mounds of each vegetable vermicelli around macaroni and spoon lemon butter over all. Sprinkle macaroni and vegetables with freshly ground pepper and garnish each plate with fresh herbs. *Makes 4 servings.*

NOTE: The vegetables, macaroni, and lemon butter can all be prepared in advance and reheated briefly before assembling the dish. Remember to drain the vegetables well before placing them on the plates.

EXTRA-FINE GREEN BEANS WITH FRESH TRUFFLES
BOUQUET D'HARICOTS VERTS AUX TRUFFES

THIS DISH CAN BE BRILLIANT IN ITS SIMPLICITY, DEPENDING FOR ITS SUCCESS ON THE QUALITY AND FRESHNESS OF THE BEANS. THE IDEAL TIME TO EAT GOOD GREEN BEANS IS DURING THE SUMMER, AND THE "STRING" OR "FRENCH" BEANS ARE THE FINEST. HARVESTED WHEN YOUNG, BEFORE THE STRINGY EDGE IS DEVELOPED, THEY ARE ELONGATED. LEARN TO COOK THE BEANS SO

THAT THEY REMAIN SLIGHTLY CRUNCHY; ALSO, COOK THEM WITHOUT A COVER TO PRESERVE THEIR LUMINOUS GREEN COLOR.

1	POUND *HARICOTS VERTS* (FRENCH GREEN BEANS), TRIMMED	SALT AND FRESHLY GROUND PEPPER
¾	CUP VINAIGRETTE	16 BIBB LETTUCE LEAVES
2	SHALLOTS, FINELY CHOPPED	1⅓ OUNCES FRESH TRUFFLE, CUT INTO THIN JULIENNE
1	TABLESPOON CREME FRAICHE	FRESH CHERVIL SPRIGS

Bring a large pot of salted water to a boil. Add green beans and cook until just tender, about 4 minutes after water returns to a boil. Test the beans during cooking—they should be neither crisp nor limp, but just tender to the bite. Drain beans and plunge them into a large bowl of ice water. Set aside until serving time.

Just before serving, drain beans well and dry thoroughly in a towel. Pour vinaigrette into a large bowl and whisk in shallots and crème fraîche. Add beans and toss gently but thoroughly to coat with dressing. Season with salt and pepper; toss again.

To SERVE: Arrange 4 lettuce leaves on each of 4 serving plates. Place a large bouquet of green beans in the center. Surround beans with the truffle julienne and garnish each serving with fresh chervil sprigs. *Makes 4 servings.*

NOTE: If you like, you can enhance the presentation of this festive first course with other fresh ingredients such as snipped chives, purslane, or diamonds of peeled tomato.

ZUCCHINI GRATIN
GRATIN DE COURGETTE A L'EPICE

Garlic and spices enhance the flavor of the zucchini in this recipe. Formerly, people ignored this vegetable, finding it bland and full of water because they ate zucchinis that were too big or too old. As with the green bean, this vegetable should be purchased when young and tender, and today is enjoyed for its melting flesh.

8	SMALL ZUCCHINI, WASHED, TRIMMED, AND SLICED ¼-INCH THICK		CURRY POWDER
4	CLOVES GARLIC, PEELED		POWDERED SAFFRON
	BOUQUET GARNI		FRESHLY GRATED NUTMEG
	SALT AND FRESHLY GROUND PEPPER		CAYENNE PEPPER
1	CUP CREME FRAICHE	¾	CUP GRATED GRUYERE CHEESE (OPTIONAL)

In a large pot of cold salted water, combine sliced zucchini, 3 garlic cloves, and bouquet garni. Bring to a boil and cook until zucchini is soft but still holds its shape, about 4 minutes. Drain zucchini and refresh under cold water. Place on paper towels to drain completely. (The zucchini can be prepared ahead. Cover and refrigerate.) Reserve garlic cloves.

Preheat oven to 450 degrees. Rub a medium gratin dish with remaining garlic clove and butter it lightly. Arrange zucchini slices in dish, seasoning each layer with salt and pepper. Finely chop reserved garlic cloves; sprinkle over zucchini.

In a bowl, whisk crème fraîche with a pinch of curry, saffron, nutmeg, and cayenne. Add salt to taste. Spread mixture evenly over zucchini and sprinkle with Gruyère, if using. Bake until bubbling and golden brown on top, about 15 minutes. *Makes 4 servings.*

NOTE: Make sure the zucchini slices are completely dry before layering them in the gratin dish.

NEST OF POTATOES WITH CAVIAR
NID DE POMME NOELLEUSE AU CAVIAR

4	TO 8 NEW POTATOES (ABOUT 1 POUND, DEPENDING ON SIZE)	½	BUNCH CHIVES, FINELY CHOPPED
2	TABLESPOONS BUTTER		SALT AND FRESHLY GROUND PEPPER
¾	CUP CREME FRAICHE	2	OUNCES CAVIAR

Select fairly even-sized new potatoes and scrub under cold water. Do not peel. Plunge into salted boiling water and cook for about 15 minutes, or until tender.

Refresh potatoes in cold water to stop cooking process. Slice off top of each potato.

Carefully scoop out some of potato pulp, leaving potato-lined shells. In a large bowl, mash potato pulp. Mix in butter, crème fraîche, chopped chives, salt, and pepper. Fill each potato three-fourths full with mashed mixture.

TO SERVE: Preheat oven to 350 degrees. Reheat stuffed potatoes for about 5 minutes. Just before serving, top with a generous portion of caviar. *Makes 4 servings.*

NOTE: This recipe may be served either as an entrée or as a side dish with fish *meunière.*

Simple, moist, and as rich as one wants to make it, this dish shows off the king of vegetables, the versatile potato, to advantage. While this tuber originated with the Incas, France celebrates the memory of the day—August 25, 1785—when the former military pharmacist, Antoine-Augustin Parmentier, offered a bouquet of potato flowers to Louis XVI and Marie Antoinette. His aim was to rehabilitate this vegetable, which until then suffered from a very bad reputation in France.

PIPERADE WITH POACHED EGGS IN RED WINE SAUCE
PIPERADE A L'OEUF POCHE VIGNERONNE

Here, the winning combination of egg and tomato is highlighted by the addition of sweet red peppers. The pepper, a native of South America, is indispensable to that specialty of the Pays Basque, *piperade*, a kind of fondue of sweet peppers and tomatoes, often mixed with scrambled eggs

OR AN OMELET, AND ACCOMPANIED BY A THICK SLICE OF BAYONNE HAM.

¼ CUP OLIVE OIL

2 ONIONS, CUT INTO ¼-INCH DICE

1 SMALL EGGPLANT, UNPEELED, CUT INTO ¼-INCH DICE

2 RED BELL PEPPERS, ROASTED, PEELED, SEEDED, AND CUT INTO ¼-INCH DICE

3 TOMATOES, PEELED, SEEDED, AND CUT INTO ¼-INCH DICE

   SALT AND FRESHLY GROUND PEPPER

3 TABLESPOONS UNSALTED BUTTER

1½ TEASPOONS LEMON JUICE

½ POUND MUSHROOMS, TRIMMED AND SLICED

2½ CUPS RED WINE FROM THE COTES DU RHONE

   BOUQUET GARNI MADE WITH PARSLEY STEMS, ½ BAY LEAF, THYME SPRIGS, 1 CLOVE GARLIC, AND SLICES OF ONION

4 VERY FRESH EGGS

2 TEASPOONS ALL-PURPOSE FLOUR

PREPARE THE PIPERADE: Heat olive oil in a large skillet. Add onions and cook over medium high heat, stirring frequently, until softened, about 5 minutes. Add eggplant and red peppers and cook, stirring, for 5 minutes longer. Stir in tomatoes and salt and pepper. Reduce heat to medium low and simmer vegetables, stirring occasionally, until very tender, about 20 minutes. Set piperade aside.

Melt 2 tablespoons butter in a medium skillet. Add lemon juice and mushrooms and sauté over high heat, tossing frequently until lightly browned, about 5 minutes. Season with salt and pepper and set aside.

In a small shallow, nonreactive saucepan, combine wine and bouquet garni and bring to a boil; boil for 5 minutes. Remove bouquet garni. Reduce heat to medium so that wine simmers gently. Carefully crack eggs into a glass or a cup, 1 at a time, and slide into the simmering wine. Poach eggs until whites are just set but yolks are still soft, about 5 minutes. Carefully remove eggs with a wire skimmer and transfer to a large bowl of warm water.

Strain the wine into a clean saucepan and boil until reduced by half, about 4 minutes. Meanwhile, in a small bowl, combine remaining 1 tablespoon butter with flour until a smooth paste forms. Little by little, whisk paste into wine to thicken it and form a sauce. Reduce heat to low and whisk until completely smooth. Add reserved mushrooms. Season sauce with salt and pepper to taste.

TO SERVE: Reheat piperade mixture. Carefully transfer eggs to paper towels to drain. Trim whites to give eggs a nice, even shape. Spoon piperade mixture onto 4 heated shallow serving plates and place a poached egg in the center. Spoon red wine sauce with mushrooms over eggs and serve immediately. *Makes 4 servings.*

NOTE: The piperade, eggs, and sauce can all be prepared in advance and reheated before serving. Place the poached eggs in a bowl of hot water for a minute to reheat them.

TOMATOES A LA JOEL ROBUCHON
FONDANT A LA TOMATE DE JOEL ROBUCHON

TOMATOES

6 TO 8 MEDIUM TOMATOES (ABOUT 2½ POUNDS), PEELED, SEEDED, AND CHOPPED

½ CUP TOMATO PASTE

3 MEDIUM RED BELL PEPPERS (ABOUT 1½ POUNDS), CORED, SEEDED, AND CHOPPED

1 RIB CELERY, PEELED AND CUT INTO ¼-INCH SLICES

SMALL PINCH OF THREAD SAFFRON

2 SPRIGS OF THYME

3 WHOLE LEAVES OF BASIL PLUS 2 LEAVES OF BASIL, CHOPPED

½ CLOVE GARLIC

1 TABLESPOON SUGAR

SALT AND FRESHLY GROUND PEPPER

1 TABLESPOON KETCHUP

2 TABLESPOONS TARRAGON LEAVES, CHOPPED

2 LEAVES FRESH BASIL, CHOPPED

DASH OF TABASCO SAUCE

1 ENVELOPE (1 TABLESPOON) UNFLAVORED GELATIN

⅔ CUP HEAVY CREAM

SAUCE

3 RIPE TOMATOES (ABOUT 1 POUND), PEELED, SEEDED, AND COARSELY CHOPPED

2 TABLESPOONS KETCHUP

¼ CUP TOMATO PASTE

SMALL PINCH OF SUGAR

¼ TEASPOON SALT

DASH OF TABASCO SAUCE

1 TEASPOON SHERRY VINEGAR

1 TABLESPOON OLIVE OIL

PREPARE THE TOMATOES: In a large nonreactive saucepan, combine tomatoes, tomato paste, peppers, celery, saffron, thyme, whole basil leaves, garlic, and sugar. Season with salt and pepper. Cook, stirring often, for 1 hour over medium high heat. Stir in ketchup, tarragon, chopped basil, and Tabasco sauce, Pass through a fine-mesh strainer. There will be about 2 cups of puree. Reduce over high heat if the amount of liquid exceeds this quantity.

Pour ¼ cup cold water into a large mixing bowl. Sprinkle gelatin over and let dissolve, undisturbed, for 10 minutes. Heat tomato puree until almost simmering. Stir into gelatin and mix well. Set aside to cool completely, but do not refrigerate.

Whip the cream until stiff. Add about ⅓ cup tomato puree and whisk in vigorously. Carefully fold in remaining puree. Refrigerate, covered, for at least 8 hours.

PREPARE THE SAUCE: Place all sauce ingredients except olive oil in a food processor and puree until smooth, about 30 seconds. With machine running, slowly dribble in olive oil; do not overprocess. Cover and refrigerate until ready to assemble the dish.

TO SERVE: Pour 1 tablespoon sauce in the center of 6 small serving plates. Tilt plate to spread sauce into a thin layer.

Using two spoons, form small oval shapes of cold tomato-cream mixture. Place three ovals on each plate. *Makes 6 servings.*

JOEL ROBUCHON FROM THE RESTAURANT JAMIN HAS ARTISTICALLY ARRANGED THIS PLATE, WHICH SHOWS OFF HIS IMMENSE TALENT AND EYE FOR PERFECTION, WHILE CELEBRATING THAT GLORY OF SUMMER GARDENS, THE TOMATO. IT IS SAID THAT NINE OUT OF TEN FRENCHMEN COULD NOT DO WITHOUT A TOMATO SALAD IN THE SUMMER; STILL, MANY DO NOT KNOW THAT IT IS BETTER TO

PEEL TOMATOES BEFORE SLICING, AND THAT IMMERSING THEM QUICKLY IN BOILING WATER FACILITATES PEELING. COOKED, TOMATOES NEED A PINCH OF SUGAR TO LESSEN THEIR ACIDITY.

TOMATO, RED PEPPER, AND OLIVE TART
TARTE ECARLATE A L'OLIVE NOIR

FRESH PRODUCE FROM THE KITCHEN GARDEN IS ON DISPLAY AT THE CHATEAU OF PONT DE VEYLE. THE SUN WARMS THIS COLORFUL TART, WHICH COMBINES TOMATOES, RED PEPPERS, AND OLIVES IN AN ARRAY OF SOUTHERN TASTES. THE TOMATO IS EXTREMELY VERSATILE; IN A SALAD IT GOES WELL WITH GARDEN HERBS; WITH GARLIC, ONION, AND SHALLOT; AND WITH OLIVES AND ANCHOVIES. CERTAIN PEOPLE, OF COURSE, PREFER THEIR TOMATOES COOKED—STUFFED *A LA PARI-SIENNE* (WITH A DICE OF TRUFFLES AND MUSH-ROOMS) OR SAUTEED *A LA PROVENCALE*.

⅔ POUND UNCOOKED BREAD DOUGH OR PIZZA DOUGH
2 TABLESPOONS OLIVE OIL
2 TABLESPOONS VEGETABLE OIL
3 SMALL ONIONS, FINELY CHOPPED
6 CLOVES GARLIC, MASHED AND PEELED
1 TABLESPOON TOMATO PASTE
1¼ POUNDS TOMATOES, PEELED, SEEDED, FINELY CHOPPED, AND WELL-DRAINED
SALT AND FRESHLY GROUND PEPPER
LARGE PINCH OF POWDERED SAFFRON

BOUQUET GARNI MADE WITH THYME SPRIGS, BAY LEAVES, PARSLEY STEMS, ½ RIB CELERY, AND 1 SPRIG OF TARRAGON
2 LARGE RED BELL PEPPERS
1 SPRIG OF THYME
1 BAY LEAF
1 EGG, BEATEN
¾ CUP IMPORTED BLACK OLIVES, PITTED, OR SMALL NICOISE OLIVES
PARSLEY SPRIGS OR AN OLIVE BRANCH FOR GARNISH

Roll out or stretch dough to form a 14-inch circle. Place dough in a lightly buttered, deep 12-inch springform pan and roll down edges to form a rim. Set dough aside to rise in a draft-free place for 1 hour.

Heat 1 tablespoon each olive and vegetable oils in a large skillet. Add onions and cook over medium high heat, stirring frequently until golden, about 10 minutes. Finely chop 2 garlic cloves and add to onions, along with tomato paste and chopped tomatoes. Season lightly with salt and pepper. Add saffron and bouquet garni. Cook over medium heat, stirring frequently, until most of the liquid evaporates and sauce is thick, about 20 minutes. Remove from heat.

Meanwhile, roast red peppers directly in a gas flame or under broiler, turning until charred all over. Place peppers in a bag to steam for 5 minutes; peel and remove cores, seeds, and veins.

Place the peppers in a medium skillet and add the remaining 1 tablespoon each olive and vegetable oils. Crush remaining 4 cloves garlic. Add to peppers along with thyme and bay leaf. Salt lightly and cook over medium low heat for 5 minutes.

Preheat oven to 475 degrees. Spread tomato mixture evenly over surface of dough. Drain red peppers and cut into thin strips. Arrange on tomato mixture to form a lattice pattern. Brush rim of dough with beaten egg. Bake tart until dough is cooked through, about 30 minutes. (Cover the tart with foil if the top begins to look dry.)

Remove tart from oven and carefully remove from pan. Brush surface lightly with olive oil to give it a nice sheen. Set tart on a large platter. Place an olive in the center of each lattice diamond. Surround tart with parsley sprigs or garnish platter with a small olive branch. *Makes 4 servings.*

NOTE: The tomato mixture and the red peppers can be prepared ahead.

DICED EGGPLANT AND TOMATO
WITH PEAS AND EGGS

BRUNOISE D'AUBERGINES, TOMATES, ET POIS A L'OEUF EN COCOTTE

3   TABLESPOONS OLIVE OIL
2   BABY EGGPLANTS, UNPEELED, CUT INTO
    ¼-INCH DICE
    SALT AND FRESHLY GROUND PEPPER
2   TABLESPOONS UNSALTED BUTTER,
    MELTED

2   TOMATOES, PEELED, SEEDED, AND CUT
    INTO ¼-INCH DICE
1¼ CUPS COOKED YOUNG PEAS
4   EXTRA-LARGE OR JUMBO EGGS

Heat oil in a medium skillet. Add diced eggplant and season with salt and pepper. Sauté over high heat, tossing frequently, until eggplant is lightly browned and tender, about 5 minutes. Spoon eggplant onto paper towels to drain.

Brush four 1-cup ramekins with melted butter. Sprinkle a little salt onto bottom of each one. Fill ramekins with diced eggplant, tomatoes, and peas; smooth top. Carefully crack 1 egg into each ramekin.

Place ramekins in a large skillet or sauté pan set over a burner. Add enough boiling water to skillet to reach halfway up sides of ramekins. Cover skillet and cook over medium high heat until egg whites are just set, about 8 minutes. Serve immediately. *Makes 4 servings.*

THE EGGPLANTS ARE IN BLOOM AT PONT DE VEYLE AND, WITH TOMATOES AND YOUNG PEAS, FORM A GARLAND OF SUMMER VEGETABLES COMPLEMENTING THE EGG IN THIS DISH. THIS RECIPE IS JUST ONE OF THE MANY HARMONIOUS WAYS OF COMBINING EGGS WITH FRESH VEGETABLES. SERVE THIS DISH WITH STRIPS OF WHITE BREAD FRIED IN BUTTER OR, IN THE SPRING, WITH COOKED ASPARAGUS TIPS.

A VARIETY OF STUFFED VEGETABLES
VARIATION SUR LES PETITS FARCIS

STUFFED ZUCCHINI
COURGETTES FARCIS

8	SMALL ZUCCHINI	1	EGG YOLK
	SALT AND FRESHLY GROUND PEPPER	6	TABLESPOONS DRY FRESH BREAD
3½	TABLESPOONS UNSALTED BUTTER		CRUMBS
1	SMALL WHITE ONION, FINELY CHOPPED	2	TABLESPOONS GRATED GRUYERE CHEESE
5	OUNCES MUSHROOMS, TRIMMED AND	1	TABLESPOON CHOPPED PARSLEY
	FINELY CHOPPED	1	TABLESPOON OLIVE OIL
1	CLOVE GARLIC, FINELY CHOPPED	1½	TABLESPOONS GRATED PARMESAN
1	TABLESPOON PEELED, SEEDED, AND		CHEESE
	CHOPPED TOMATO	4	TABLESPOONS UNSALTED BUTTER,
3	TABLESPOONS DRY WHITE WINE		MELTED
	QUATRE EPICES		

PREPARE THE ZUCCHINI: Cut off a thin, lengthwise strip from bottom of each zucchini so that it will sit flat. Trim ends. Hollow out zucchini: using tip of a small paring knife, score a deep rectangle in top of each zucchini, leaving at least a ¼-inch border all around for a sturdy shell. Make crosswise slits in rectangles and remove pieces with knife tip. Use a small melon ball cutter to scoop out more zucchini flesh, if necessary. Finely chop zucchini trimmings and set aside.

Blanch hollowed-out zucchini in a large pot of boiling salted water for 2 minutes. Drain and refresh under cold water. Dry the zucchini well. Place shells in a well-buttered baking dish, hollowed-side up. Sprinkle with salt and pepper; dot with 1½ tablespoons butter.

PREPARE THE STUFFING: Melt remaining 2 tablespoons butter in a medium skillet. Add onion and sauté over medium high heat, tossing, until softened, about 2 minutes. Add mushrooms and cook until most of their liquid evaporates. Stir in garlic, tomato, and wine. Reduce heat to medium and cook, stirring, for 2 minutes longer. Season with salt, pepper, and *quatre épices* to taste; remove from heat. Stir in egg yolk, 4 tablespoons bread crumbs, Gruyère, and parsley.

Preheat oven to 350 degrees. In a medium skillet, heat oil until smoking. Add chopped zucchini trimmings and sauté over medium high heat until softened, about 3 minutes. Sprinkle with salt. Stir zucchini into stuffing mixture.

Spoon stuffing into zucchini shells, mounding well. Sprinkle with remaining 2 tablespoons bread crumbs and Parmesan. Drizzle with melted butter. Bake until zucchini are tender and stuffing is very hot, about 40 minutes. *Makes 4 servings.*

NOTE: The zucchini can be prepared in advance and baked just before serving. If they have been refrigerated, allow 5 to 10 minutes more cooking time.

OPPOSITE, A FEAST OF STUFFED SUMMER VEGETABLES: ZUCCHINI, ONIONS, PEPPERS, CARROTS, EGGPLANT, AND, OF COURSE, POTATO.

Rich cheeses are produced at Brenod, in the region of Bugey (see opposite and following pages). The large wheels are set in a cave for ripening. The nutty taste of Gruyere is welcome in many of these stuffed vegetables.

STUFFED EGGPLANTS
AUBERGINES FARCIES

EGGPLANTS
4   SMALL EGGPLANTS (3 TO 3½ POUNDS)
½   CUP OLIVE OIL
     SALT AND FRESHLY GROUND PEPPER
5   TABLESPOONS UNSALTED BUTTER
2   SMALL ONIONS, FINELY CHOPPED
1   CUP LONG-GRAIN WHITE RICE
½   RED BELL PEPPER, PEELED, SEEDED, AND
        CUT INTO SMALL CUBES
2   CLOVES GARLIC, FINELY CHOPPED
1   TABLESPOON TOMATO PASTE

1   WHOLE EGG, BEATEN
½   CUP GRATED GRUYERE CHEESE
½   CUP COOKED GREEN PEAS
     SAUCE
2   CUPS HEAVY CREAM
1   CLOVE GARLIC, CUT IN HALF
     PINCH OF THREAD SAFFRON
     SALT AND FRESHLY GROUND PEPPER
2   EGG YOLKS
     PARSLEY SPRIGS FOR GARNISH

PREPARE THE EGGPLANTS: Wash and dry eggplants. Cut lengthwise in half. Do not peel. Cut around perimeter on cut side of eggplant halves, creating a ⅜-inch shell. Score interior flesh, but do not remove. Salt eggplant and invert on paper towels to drain for 1 hour.

Reserve 1 tablespoon olive oil. Pour remaining oil into a large sauté pan. Pat eggplants dry. Cook in oil, turning often over medium high heat, until soft, about 15 minutes. Work in batches, adding more oil if necessary. Take care not to break shells. Scoop out cooked flesh and season with salt and pepper; reserve. Arrange empty shells in a buttered baking dish.

Preheat oven to 400 degrees. Melt 2 tablespoons butter in a small ovenproof casserole with a tight-fitting lid. Add 1 chopped onion and cook until soft and translucent, about 3 minutes. Bring 1½ cups water to a boil. Add rice to onions and cook for 1 minute. Pour in boiling water, add a pinch of salt, and bring to a boil. Cover and bake in oven for 15 minutes. Remove and fluff with a fork. Stir in 1 tablespoon butter.

In a small heavy saucepan, combine red pepper dice, reserved 1 tablespoon olive oil, and 1 clove chopped garlic. Cook over medium high heat for 5 minutes. Season with salt.

Melt remaining 2 tablespoons butter in a large skillet. Add remaining chopped onion and remaining garlic clove; cook for 3 to 5 minutes, until onion is translucent, over medium heat. Stir in tomato paste. Cut eggplant pulp into cubes and add to skillet. Cook over medium high heat for 5 minutes. Scrape mixture into a large mixing bowl.

Gently fold in rice, red pepper, beaten egg, and a pinch of Gruyère. Stir in cooked green peas. Season with salt and pepper. Blend well without crushing vegetables.

Preheat oven to 475 degrees. Fill eggplant shells with vegetable mixture and sprinkle with remaining Gruyère. Bake for 10 minutes, until heated through. Preheat broiler. Quickly run under the broiler until cheese is lightly browned around edges.

PREPARE THE SAUCE: Place cream and garlic in a heavy saucepan. Bring to a boil and cook over medium high heat until reduced by half. Add saffron and season well with salt and pepper. At the last moment before serving, add egg yolks and heat through, but do not boil. Pass sauce through a fine-mesh strainer.

TO SERVE: Coat bottom of 4 individual serving plates with a small amount of sauce. Place eggplants in the center. Decorate with several threads of saffron or fresh parsley if desired. *Makes 4 servings.*

STUFFED POTATOES
POMMES DE TERRE FARCIES

¼ CUP DRIED FLAGEOLET BEANS, SOAKED OVERNIGHT AND DRAINED
1 SMALL ONION, STUDDED WITH 1 CLOVE
1 CARROT, PEELED AND HALVED
1 RIB CELERY, HALVED
1 SPRIG OF PARSLEY
3½ OUNCES YOUNG GREEN BEANS, TRIMMED
1½ TEASPOONS UNSALTED BUTTER
1½ TEASPOONS ALL-PURPOSE FLOUR
¼ CUP MILK

 SALT AND FRESHLY GROUND PEPPER
3 TABLESPOONS HEAVY CREAM
1 EGG YOLK
½ TEASPOON FINELY CHOPPED PARSLEY
½ TEASPOON FINELY CHOPPED CHERVIL
2 LARGE PINCHES OF POWDERED SAFFRON
4 LARGE BOILING POTATOES OR 8 SMALLER ONES
1¼ CUPS VEGETABLE STOCK
 MELTED UNSALTED BUTTER

Place flageolet beans in a medium saucepan with enough water to cover by 3 inches. Add onion, carrot, celery, and parsley sprig; bring to a boil. Cook over medium high heat until beans are tender, about 45 minutes. Drain beans; discard other vegetables and parsley.

Cook green beans in boiling salted water until just tender, about 5 minutes. Drain beans and refresh under cold water. Dry beans on paper towels; cut into ⅓-inch lengths.

Melt butter in a small saucepan. Whisk in flour and cook over medium high heat, whisking constantly, until foaming. Whisk in milk and cook, whisking constantly, until mixture thickens. Reduce heat to low and cook, whisking constantly, for 1½ minutes longer. Remove from heat. Season this very thick white sauce with salt and pepper.

In another small saucepan, boil cream until thickened slightly, about 1 minute. Add flageolets and green beans and toss to coat with cream. Stir in warm white sauce until thoroughly combined. Stir in egg yolk, parsley, and chervil. Season with salt and pepper to taste.

PREPARE THE POTATOES: Fill a saucepan just large enough to hold the potatoes with salted water. Add saffron. Meanwhile, peel potatoes. Cut a thin slice from the bottom of each so it will sit flat. Cut a ¾-inch slice from the top of each potato for a lid. Using a melon ball cutter, hollow out potatoes, leaving a ½-to ¾-inch shell.

Preheat oven to 450 degrees. Add potatoes and lids to saffron water and bring to a boil over medium high heat. Cook potatoes until yellow, about 10 minutes. Remove the potatoes and lids from water; drain well.

Place potatoes, hollowed-side up, in a well-buttered baking dish just large enough to hold them. Fill hollows with flageolet and green bean mixture; top with their respective lids. Add enough boiling vegetable stock to baking dish to reach halfway up sides of potatoes. Bake, basting frequently, until potatoes are tender and liquid in dish has evaporated, about 30 minutes. Remove from oven and brush each potato with melted butter before serving. *Makes 4 servings.*

STUFFED PEPPERS
POIVRONS FARCIS

STUFFING

½ CUP SHORT-GRAIN WHITE RICE

6 TABLESPOONS OLIVE OIL

1 BABY EGGPLANT, UNPEELED, CUT INTO ¼-INCH DICE

1 SMALL ZUCCHINI, UNPEELED, CUT INTO ¼-INCH DICE

½ GREEN BELL PEPPER, CUT INTO ¼-INCH DICE

1 VERY LARGE MUSHROOM, CUT INTO ¼-INCH DICE

1 COOKED ARTICHOKE BOTTOM, CUT INTO ¼-INCH DICE

1 TOMATO, PEELED, SEEDED, AND CUT INTO ¼-INCH DICE

1 SMALL ONION, PEELED AND CUT INTO ¼-INCH DICE

SALT AND FRESHLY GROUND PEPPER

PAPRIKA

1 HARD-COOKED EGG, PEELED AND CUT INTO ¼-INCH DICE

½ CUP COOKED YOUNG PEAS

2 TABLESPOONS UNSALTED BUTTER, MELTED

1 EGG

¾ CUP GRATED GRUYERE CHEESE

1 TEASPOON GRATED PARMESAN CHEESE

PEPPERS

4 LARGE RED BELL PEPPERS

1 ONION, SLICED

4 CLOVES GARLIC, PEELED AND CRUSHED

½ CUP OLIVE OIL

4 SPRIGS OF THYME

2 BAY LEAVES

SALT

PAPRIKA SAUCE

¼ CUP COOKED GREEN PEAS

PREPARE THE STUFFING: Cook rice in boiling salted water until the grains are tender, about 8 minutes. Drain and refresh under cold water; drain very well.

Heat olive oil in a large skillet. Add the diced eggplant, zucchini, green pepper, mushroom, artichoke, tomato, and onion; season with salt, pepper, and paprika. Cook over medium high heat, stirring frequently, until vegetables are tender, about 10 minutes. Drain in a colander and return mixture to skillet. Stir in the rice, hard-cooked egg, and peas. Fold in melted butter. Beat egg with Gruyère and Parmesan; fold into the vegetable mixture. Season with salt, pepper, and paprika to taste.

Using a sharp, flexible knife, cut around red pepper stems to release them. Remove the cores, ribs, and seeds from inside peppers. Reserve stems.

Preheat oven to 350 degrees. Butter a baking dish just large enough to hold peppers. Scatter onion and the garlic in dish.

Fill peppers with stuffing mixture, packing down well. Replace stems and set peppers on their sides in baking dish. Drizzle olive oil evenly over the peppers; add thyme and bay leaves. (The recipe can be prepared ahead to this point.) Bake peppers, turning them once halfway through the cooking period, until tender and filling is heated through, about 40 minutes.

Let peppers cool for about 10 minutes. Slice crosswise into 1¼-inch rings and place 1 on each of 4 serving plates. Stir the peas into the paprika sauce and serve peppers with the sauce. *Makes 4 servings.*

STUFFED CARROTS
CAROTTES FARCIS

4 VERY LARGE, LONG, STRAIGHT CARROTS, PEELED	4 TEASPOONS ALL-PURPOSE FLOUR
SALT	¾ CUP COOKED FRESH GREEN PEAS
1 TEASPOON SUGAR	4 TABLESPOONS UNSALTED BUTTER, MELTED
5½ TABLESPOONS UNSALTED BUTTER	**SERVING**
1 LARGE RIB CELERY, PEELED AND CUT INTO ⅛-INCH DICE	1 TABLESPOON FINELY DICED CELERY, COOKED UNTIL TENDER
1 SMALL TURNIP, PEELED AND CUT INTO ⅛-INCH DICE	1 TABLESPOON FINELY DICED CARROT, COOKED UNTIL TENDER
1 CUP MILK	1 TABLESPOON COOKED FRESH GREEN PEAS
1 SMALL BOUQUET GARNI	
FRESHLY GROUND PEPPER	1 CUP *BEURRE BLANC* (SEE APPENDIX)
1 SMALL ONION, FINELY CHOPPED	COOKED SNOW PEAS, CUT INTO
5 OUNCES MUSHROOMS, TRIMMED AND FINELY CHOPPED	DIAMONDS (OPTIONAL)
	CHERVIL SPRIGS (OPTIONAL)

PREPARE THE CARROTS: Using a swivel vegetable peeler, cut lengthwise strips from carrots to give carrots scalloped edges. Slice carrots into 1¼-inch cylinders. Using a small melon ball cutter, hollow out the center of each carrot cylinder. Reserve trimmings.

Stand carrots, hollowed-side up, in a large, well-buttered skillet. Pour in enough water to reach halfway up sides of carrots. Sprinkle lightly with salt and add sugar. Cut 2½ tablespoons of butter into small pieces and scatter evenly over carrots. Bring to a boil over high heat. Cover, reduce heat to medium, and simmer until carrots are tender and liquid evaporated, about 35 minutes.

PREPARE THE STUFFING: Dice enough of the carrot trimmings to measure 2 tablespoons. In a small saucepan, combine diced carrot, celery, turnip, and milk. Add the bouquet garni, season with salt and pepper, and bring to a boil over high heat. Reduce heat to medium and simmer until vegetables are just tender, about 5 minutes. Drain vegetables; reserve milk. Discard bouquet garni.

Preheat oven to 350 degrees. Melt remaining 3 tablespoons butter in a medium skillet. Add onion and cook over medium high heat, stirring, until softened, about 2 minutes. Stir in mushrooms and cook over high heat, stirring, until most of liquid has evaporated, about 5 minutes. Reduce heat to medium and stir in flour. Gradually add enough of reserved milk to make a thick sauce. Cook sauce for 1 minute. Stir in peas and cook for 2 minutes longer.

Puree vegetable mixture and strain through a fine-mesh strainer into a bowl. Stir in reserved cooked diced vegetables and season to taste with salt and pepper. With a small spoon, mound mixture in hollowed-out carrots. Drizzle with melted butter. Bake until heated through, about 25 minutes.

TO SERVE: Stir diced celery, carrot, and peas into Beurre Blanc. Spoon sauce onto 4 heated plates. Set stuffed carrots on sauce and garnish each serving, if you like, with snow pea diamonds and fresh chervil sprigs. *Makes 4 servings.*

NOTE: The carrots can be assembled in advance and baked just before serving.

THE PRINCIPLE OF MUSHROOM CULTIVATION, AS AT THIS CAVE IN JUJURIEUX, IS TYPICALLY FRENCH. HORSE MANURE IS SEEDED WITH SPAWN (THE FILAMENTS OF MYCELIUM), THEN REGULARLY WATERED. THE TWO TYPES OF CULTIVATED MUSHROOMS, WHITE AND BROWN, ARE SAID TO BE GOOD FOR SLIMMING AND HELP MAINTAIN A BALANCED DIET.

GLAZED VEGETABLES WITH GOLDEN RAISINS
CONFIT DE NAVETS, CAROTTES, ET PETITS OIGNONS AUX RAISINS BLONDES

DURING THE SUMMER IN VONNAS THE GERANIUMS TAKE OVER, THEIR BRIGHTLY COLORED FLOWERS BURSTING FROM THE STREETS, THE BRIDGES, THE RIVER BANKS, AND THE WINDOWS OF HOUSES—SOMETIMES IN THE BLUE, WHITE, AND RED OF FRANCE. THIS DISH COMBINES PEARL ONIONS WITH CARROTS AND TURNIPS IN A GLAZE. THE FRENCH HAVE ALWAYS BEEN GREAT EATERS

AND EXPERT GROWERS OF ONIONS OF ALL KINDS, AND DURING THE MIDDLE AGES EVERY GOOD HOSTESS OWED IT TO HERSELF TO OFFER A DISH OF ONIONS TO HER GUESTS.

½ CUP GOLDEN RAISINS
½ CUP PLUS 3 TABLESPOONS MUSCAT DE BEAUMES-DE-VENISE
20 PEARL ONIONS
6 MEDIUM TURNIPS, PEELED
6 LARGE CARROTS, PEELED
14 TABLESPOONS UNSALTED BUTTER
1 TABLESPOON SUGAR
1 SPRIG OF THYME
½ BAY LEAF
SALT
¼ CUP WHITE WINE VINEGAR
1½ TEASPOONS DRAINED GREEN PEPPERCORNS
3 TABLESPOONS LEMON JUICE
FRESHLY GROUND PEPPER

In a small bowl, combine raisins and ½ cup Muscat. Set aside to macerate at room temperature.

Drop onions into boiling water for 20 seconds to loosen skins. Drain and refresh under cold water. Peel onions and trim root ends, if necessary.

Using a small melon-ball cutter, scoop out balls from turnips and carrots. (The balls should be about the same size as the onions.)

Place vegetables in a large nonreactive skillet and add ½ inch water, 2 tablespoons butter, the sugar, thyme, bay leaf, and a good pinch of salt. Cover with a round of buttered parchment paper and cut a vent in the center of paper. Bring to a boil over high heat, reduce heat to medium, and cook until vegetables are just barely tender, about 5 minutes. Remove parchment paper. Increase heat to medium high and simmer, shaking skillet frequently, until water evaporates and pan juices begin to caramelize, about 10 minutes. Stir in vinegar and green peppercorns and reduce heat to low. Drain raisins and add to skillet; reserve soaking liquid. Toss vegetables well and divide among 4 porcelain cups or onto serving plates.

Return skillet to medium heat and deglaze with 2 tablespoons water, remaining 3 tablespoons of Muscat, and reserved raisin soaking liquid. Stir in the lemon juice. Whisk in remaining 12 tablespoons of butter, 1 tablespoon at a time, and season to taste with salt and pepper. Strain sauce and spoon over vegetables. Serve hot. *Makes 4 servings.*

NOTE: Baby carrots with tops could be used in this recipe in place of the carrot balls. You will need about 20 baby carrots.

HARLEQUIN TOMATOES
TOMATES ARLEQUINS

12	ITALIAN PLUM TOMATOES	4	TABLESPOONS UNSALTED BUTTER
	SALT AND FRESHLY GROUND PEPPER	1	LARGE WHITE ONION, CHOPPED
	SMALL PINCH OF SUGAR	½	CUP VEGETABLE STOCK
2	CUPS FRESH GREEN PEAS	2	TABLESPOONS CREME FRAICHE OR
1	MEDIUM CELERY ROOT (CELERIAC),		HEAVY CREAM
	PEELED AND TRIMMED		SEVERAL SPRIGS OF CHERVIL FOR
1	EGG WHITE		GARNISH
	CAYENNE PEPPER		THINLY SLICED RED AND GREEN PEPPERS
½	CUP HEAVY CREAM		FOR GARNISH (OPTIONAL)
	PAPRIKA		

Cut tomatoes at the stem end, about ¼ inch from top. Reserve tops. Carefully scoop out tomato pulp with a small spoon or melon ball cutter. Season the interior with salt, pepper, and a pinch of sugar. Turn upside down to drain on paper towels.

Plunge peas into a large amount of salted water and cook over high heat until tender, about 7 minutes. Rinse under cold running water. They should be bright green.

Place celery root in a medium saucepan; add cold water to cover and a pinch of salt. Bring to a boil over medium high heat and cook until tender, about 20 minutes. Drain well and set aside to cool.

Place celery root in a food processor and puree until smooth, about 30 seconds. Pass through a fine-mesh sieve into a nonreactive bowl. Add egg white and beat with a wooden spoon until incorporated. Season with salt and cayenne. Add cream, bit by bit, and beat until smooth. Finally stir in a pinch of paprika. Reserve ¼ cup peas. Fold remaining peas into celery root mixture. Cover and refrigerate for at least 2 hours.

Fill tomatoes with the celery root mixture. Replace tomato tops, pushing down slightly to secure. Reserve tomatoes.

Preheat oven to 325 degrees. Melt butter in a large ovenproof casserole. Add onions and cook, stirring, over medium high heat until translucent, about 5 minutes. Add a pinch of paprika and blend well.

Gently place filled tomatoes on top of onions in casserole. Pour in vegetable stock and bring to a simmer over medium high heat. Cover loosely with a piece of buttered foil. Bake until filling is poached, 10 to 15 minutes.

TO SERVE: Remove from oven and carefully lift out tomatoes with a slotted spoon. Keep warm. Reduce remaining cooking liquid by half over high heat. Add crème fraîche and boil until reduced by half. Pass through a fine-mesh strainer. Correct the seasonings.

Coat the bottom of each of 4 dinner plates with a small amount of sauce. Place 3 tomatoes in the center of each plate. Intersperse with sprigs of chervil and the reserved ¼ cup peas. Enhance the presentation with thin slices of peeled green and red peppers, if desired. *Makes 4 servings.*

I SET OUT THIS HARLEQUIN TOMATO AT LUNCHTIME ON THE BEACH OF MONSIEUR VACHERESSE, MY HORTICULTURALIST NEIGHBOR. WHILE SOME PREFER THEIR TOMATOES IN A SALAD, OTHERS WILL BE THE FIRST TO CRY, "HURRAY FOR STUFFED TOMATOES!" THIS FILLING, FOR ITALIAN PLUM TOMATOES, USES FRESH GREEN PEAS, ANOTHER OF FRANCE'S FAVORITE VEGETA-

BLES. MANY PEOPLE ARE OF THE SAME OPINION AS THE GASTRONOME GRIMOD DE LA REYNIERE, WHO MAINTAINED THAT GARDEN PEAS ARE "THE BEST AND THE MOST DELICATE OF VEGETABLES."

EGGPLANT QUENELLES WITH ZUCCHINI PETALS
QUENELLES D'AUBERGINES EN ECAILLES DE COURGETTES

½ CUP OLIVE OIL
1¾ POUNDS EGGPLANT, PEELED AND CUT
    INTO ½-INCH CUBES
    SALT AND FRESHLY GROUND PEPPER
5 LARGE ZUCCHINI, WELL-WASHED

1 TABLESPOON UNSALTED BUTTER
½ TEASPOON FRESH THYME
    VINAIGRETTE OR FRESH TOMATO *COULIS*
    (SEE APPENDIX)

Heat olive oil in a large skillet. Add eggplant cubes, season with salt and pepper, and cook over medium heat, stirring frequently, until softened, about 15 miutes. Drain eggplant. Place in a food processor and puree until smooth. Scrape eggplant into a bowl, season to taste with salt and pepper, and cover with foil to keep warm.

PREPARE THE ZUCCHINI PETALS: Using the tip of a vegetable peeler, carve small, oval-shaped petals from zucchini; they should be about the size of a nickel. Alternatively, use a paring knife to remove small ovals of zucchini skin with a thin portion of the green flesh attached.

Cook the zucchini petals in boiling salted water for 1 minute. Drain and refresh under cold water. Drain very well; pat dry on paper towels.

Melt butter in a medium skillet. Add the zucchini petals and toss gently to coat. Add thyme, season with salt and pepper, and toss well.

ASSEMBLE THE QUENELLES: Using 2 soup spoons, mold eggplant puree into even oval shapes and place 3 in the center of each of 4 plates in a flower petal configuration.

Cover eggplant quenelles with zucchini petals, overlapping slightly to cover puree completely.

Serve quenelles at room temperature, accompanied with Vinaigrette or a Fresh Tomato *Coulis* with a little vinegar added. *Makes 4 servings.*

A ROSE GARDEN BRIGHTENS AN OLD HOME AT CHATEAU-CHALON, A PRETTY, RESTORED VILLAGE IN THE JURA REGION, KNOWN FOR ITS WHITE WINES. THE EGGPLANT, ONCE GROWN SIMPLY AS DECORATION, NOW LENDS ITSELF TO MANY PREPARATIONS, INCLUDING THESE UNUSUAL QUENELLES. ITS PRINCIPAL VOCATION REMAINS AS AN ACCOMPANYING VEGETABLE, BUT IT MAY BE

SERVED SAUTÉED, IN SOUFFLES, OMELETS, PUREES, AU GRATIN, OR STUFFED. ONE MAY ALSO EAT IT RAW IN A SALAD WITH A TARRAGON VINAIGRETTE.

SALAD OF PLUCKED ARTICHOKES WITH PARSLEY
EFFEUILLEE DE COEUR D'ARTICHAUT AU PERSIL ET MESCLUN

On the Veyle River, just across from my kitchen, the lotuses grow. Here the pattern of artichoke leaves, laid out like petals on the plate, echoes the beauty of the lotus flower. The artichoke can be cooked with leaves intact. Pluck them off after cooking and neatly trim the bottom before filling them with the parsley mixture. Place the prettiest leaves in a crown around the filled artichoke bottom and place a piece of tomato on each leaf.

4 LARGE OR 8 SMALL ARTICHOKES
1 TABLESPOON ALL-PURPOSE FLOUR
   JUICE OF ½ LEMON
   SALT
1 POUND PARSLEY, EITHER CURLY, FLAT-LEAF, OR A COMBINATION OF BOTH
   FRESHLY GROUND PEPPER
1 TEASPOON RED WINE VINEGAR

2 TABLESPOONS HEAVY CREAM, LIGHTLY WHIPPED
1 POUND SALAD GREENS, CHOOSE ACCORDING TO MARKET AND SEASONAL AVAILABILITY
1 MEDIUM TOMATO, PEELED AND SEEDED
1 CUP VINAIGRETTE

Snap off stem and bottom of artichokes and place in a large stock pot; add cold water to cover. Add flour and lemon juice (this prevents discoloring). Season lightly with salt. Bring to a boil and cook over medium high heat until done, about 20 minutes. Set aside so artichokes can cool in liquid.

Strip leaves from parsley stems and wash. Plunge into salted boiling water. Bring back to a boil and cook rapidly for 10 minutes. Remove cooked parsley carefully with a slotted spoon. Place in a food processor and puree until smooth, about 30 seconds. Pass through a fine-mesh strainer into a bowl. Season with salt, pepper, and vinegar. Stir in cream. Adjust seasonings; cover and refrigerate until ready to use.

Wash the salad greens; wrap in paper towels to dry.

Pluck off leaves and neatly trim artichoke bottoms. Remove fibrous choke from each cooked artichoke. Fill with parsley mixture, mounding filling in the center.

Cut tomato into quarters and then into eighths.

To serve: Toss greens with Vinaigrette. Place filled artichoke hearts on top and decorate with tomato wedges. *Makes 4 servings.*

CROWN OF ARTICHOKE HEARTS WITH CREAMED FRESH GOAT CHEESE AND CHIVES

COROLLE D'ARTICHAUT A LA CREME DE CHEVRE FRAIS ET CIBOULETTE

8	ARTICHOKES	½	CUP CHOPPED FRESH CHIVES
	SALT	1	TABLESPOON RED WINE VINEGAR
	LEMON JUICE	2	TABLESPOONS OLIVE OIL
⅔	CUP (ABOUT ½ POUND) FRESH GOAT		FRESHLY GROUND PEPPER
	CHEESE	1	TOMATO, PEELED AND SEEDED
1½	CUPS HEAVY CREAM		(OPTIONAL)

Place artichokes in a large nonreactive pot and add cold water to cover. Add salt and bring to a boil. Cook until tender when pierced at the bottom with a knife tip, about 20 minutes. Refresh under cold water; drain well. Remove leaves. Cut out fibrous choke in center of each heart. Trim sides of artichoke bottom. Cut each heart into 8 equal pieces. Reserve on a plate; sprinkle with lemon juice to prevent discoloring.

In a large mixing bowl, crush fresh goat cheese with a fork. Slowly whisk in cream. Stir in chives, vinegar, and oil. Season with salt and pepper. Refrigerate for at least 1 hour.

Arrange sections of artichoke in the shape of a crown on 8 individual serving plates. Intersperse with sections of peeled tomato, if desired. Garnish center of each plate with a large spoonful of goat cheese. Decorate with additional snipped chives, if desired. *Makes 8 servings.*

WHILE SIMPLE TO PREPARE, THIS DISH IS NOTABLE FOR ITS BEAUTIFUL AND DRAMATIC PRESENTATION. THE SECTIONS OF ARTICHOKE ARE ARRANGED TO FORM A CROWN, INTERSPERSED WITH SECTIONS OF TOMATO AND GARNISHED WITH THE CREAMED GOAT CHEESE. THE *CAMUS* ARTICHOKE, THE MOST WIDELY GROWN VARIETY OF ARTICHOKE IN FRANCE, FILLS THE SHOPS AND

MARKETS FROM MAY TO OCTOBER. RECOGNIZED BY ITS GREAT ROUNDED HEAD AND BROAD SHORT LEAVES, IT IS PERFECT WHEN HEAVY AND FIRM; STIFF LEAVES ARE ALSO A SIGN OF GOOD CONDITION.

SUMMER VEGETABLE COMPOTE
COMPOTE ESTIVALE A LA CUILLER

3 MEDIUM EGGPLANTS (ABOUT 2 POUNDS)
4 TABLESPOONS OLIVE OIL
2 TABLESPOONS UNSALTED BUTTER
1 LARGE ONION, CHOPPED
2 CLOVES GARLIC, MINCED
SALT AND FRESHLY GROUND PEPPER
SEVERAL SPRIGS OF THYME

6 MEDIUM TOMATOES (ABOUT 2½ POUNDS), PEELED AND SEEDED
2 TABLESPOONS CREME FRAICHE
½ CUP VINAIGRETTE
CHERVIL SPRIGS OR SNIPPED CHIVES FOR GARNISH (OPTIONAL)
COARSE SEA SALT FOR GARNISH (OPTIONAL)

COLORFUL KITCHEN GARDENS FLOURISH AT THE FOOT OF THE OLD FORTIFICATION WALLS IN THE CITY OF CHATILLON SUR CHALARONNE. PART OF THE PLEASURE OF THIS SUMMER COMPOTE COMES FROM ITS ATTRACTIVE PRESENTATION: TOMATO "PETALS," GARNISHED WITH A VINAIGRETTE, ALTERNATE WITH EGGPLANT "QUENELLES" ON THE PLATE.

Preheat oven to 325 degrees. Halve eggplants lengthwise. Place, cut side up, in a lightly oiled baking dish and sprinkle with 2 tablespoons olive oil. Bake until tender, about 30 minutes. Scoop out flesh with a large spoon; discard shells. Finely chop pulp.

Heat remaining 2 tablespoons olive oil with the butter in a large sauté pan. Add the onion and garlic and cook over medium heat until soft, about 5 minutes. Add eggplant, salt, pepper, and thyme. Heat through, adjust seasonings; set aside.

Cut tomatoes into quarters. Cut away and discard tomato pulp with a sharp paring knife, leaving only a petal-shaped shell. Reserve 12 pretty petals for final presentation.

Cut remaining 12 tomato petals into large pieces and add to eggplant mixture along with crème fraîche. Cook over low heat for 5 minutes. Using two small spoons, form eggplant compote into 12 "quenelles" or small oval dumplings. Divide among 4 serving plates. Keep warm.

To serve: Place reserved tomato petals on an oiled baking sheet. Roast in 325 degree oven for 1 minute. Remove and arrange on plates between eggplant "quenelles."

Brush tomatoes with a small amount of vinaigrette. Garnish with snipped chives or sprigs of chervil and coarse sea salt, if desired. Serve hot or tepid. *Makes 4 servings.*

VEGETABLES AND BROTH MARC MENEAU
BOUILLON DE LEGUMES PARFUME SELON MARC MENEAU

Y FRIEND MARC MENEAU INSISTED ON PREPARING THIS FLAVORFUL VEGETABLE BOUILLON FOR THIS BOOK. FESTIVELY GARNISHED WITH FRESH VEGETABLES, IT IS SET ON A PATCH OF MOSS COVERING THE OLD BRIDGE IN THE GARDEN OF HIS FINE RESTAURANT, L'ESPERANCE, IN SAINT PERE SOUS VEZELAY. SHALLOTS, WHICH ARE USED TO SEASON THIS DISH, ARE A COUSIN OF THE

ONION BUT HAVE A MORE SUBTLE AROMA THAN OTHER MEMBERS OF THIS FAMILY. THE INDISPUTA-BLE QUEEN OF BORDELAIS CUISINE, THE SHALLOT HAS MADE FRANCE ITS FAVORED HOME IN EUROPE.

BROTH

6   MEDIUM CARROTS, CUT INTO 1-INCH LENGTHS
2   ONIONS, SLICED
1   LEEK, WHITE PART ONLY, WELL-WASHED, TRIMMED, AND CUT INTO 1-INCH SLICES
1   RIB CELERY, SLICED
3   SPRIGS OF PARSLEY
2   CLOVES GARLIC
2   SMALL SHALLOTS, SLICED
1   SPRIG OF FRESH THYME
1   BAY LEAF
10 PEPPERCORNS
1   TEASPOON SALT
1   TWO-LITER OR TWO-QUART MASON JAR, STERILIZED

VEGETABLES

2   CARROTS, PEELED AND TRIMMED INTO 2-INCH STICKS
2   SMALL TURNIPS, PEELED AND QUARTERED
1   SMALL ZUCCHINI, TRIMMED INTO 2-INCH PIECES
¼   POUND GREEN BEANS, STRINGS REMOVED AND CUT IN HALF CROSSWISE
4   CAULIFLOWER FLORETS, TRIMMED
1   MEDIUM TOMATO, PEELED, SEEDED, AND QUARTERED
    SALT AND FRESHLY GROUND PEPPER

PREPARE THE BROTH: Place vegetables and seasonings for broth in Mason jar. Add 4 cups water and hermetically seal. Place in a stockpot filled with boiling water, reduce heat and simmer for 3 hours. Let cool completely. Open jar and strain broth through a sieve lined with a layer of dampened cheesecloth; do not press on vegetables.

PREPARE THE VEGETABLES: Cook each vegetable separately in a small amount of broth until done but slightly crunchy. Let cool.

Distribute vegetables in individual shallow soup plates. Season broth with salt and pepper. Fill bowls. *Makes 4 servings.*

SQUASH BLOSSOM BEIGNETS WITH FRIED PARSLEY
BEIGNETS DE FLEURS DE COURGETTES AU PERSIL FRIT

BEIGNET BATTER
1   EGG
1   CUP ALL-PURPOSE FLOUR
    PINCH OF SALT
SQUASH BLOSSOM FILLING
1   ONION, THINLY SLICED
1   RED BELL PEPPER, CORED AND SEEDED
1   SMALL EGGPLANT, CUT INTO ½-INCH
    CUBES

2   TOMATOES, PEELED AND SEEDED
    OLIVE OIL
1   CLOVE GARLIC, MASHED
    SALT AND FRESHLY GROUND PEPPER
12 SQUASH BLOSSOMS, STEMS REMOVED
1   QUART VEGETABLE OIL
    ALL-PURPOSE FLOUR
1   BUNCH CURLY PARSLEY, WASHED AND
    COMPLETELY DRIED

PREPARE THE BATTER: In a medium mixing bowl, beat egg and 1 cup cold water with a fork. Gently stir in flour and salt. Set aside at room temperature for 1 hour.

PREPARE THE FILLING: Heat a small amount of olive oil in a sauté pan over medium heat. Add onion and cook until soft. Reserve. Repeat for red pepper, eggplant, and tomato. In a large nonreactive saucepan, combine cooked vegetables and garlic. Season with salt and pepper. Simmer over low heat for 15 minutes. Remove from heat and let "ratatouille" cool completely.

Using a pastry bag fitted with a ½-inch plain tip, fill squash blossoms with ratatouille. Close carefully.

Heat 3 inches vegetable oil in a large skillet to 350 degrees. Roll squash blossoms in flour and dip in batter. Fry in the hot oil for 3 to 5 minutes turning to brown evenly. Drain well on paper towels. Season with salt and pepper.

Just before serving, carefully add completely dry parsley to hot oil. Fry for only 10 to 15 seconds. Remove immediately and drain well.

Arrange *beignets* in a circle on a large serving platter. Mound fried parsley in the center. Serve immediately. *Makes 4 servings.*

WHEN SPEAKING OF THE ZUCCHINI, ONE MUST NOT FORGET THOSE TINY WONDERS OF THE CULINARY ART, ZUCCHINI BLOSSOMS, WHICH ARE OFTEN HARD TO COME BY OUTSIDE THE AREAS WHERE THE PLANTS ARE GROWN. THIS DELICATE AND ORIGINAL FOOD IS USUALLY PREPARED EITHER AS FRITTERS (THE FLOWERS ARE FIRST DIPPED IN A LIGHT BATTER) OR STUFFED AND BAKED. HERE,

THEY ARE STUFFED WITH A "RATATOUILLE" BEFORE FRYING—A MEDLEY OF SUMMER FLAVORS.

ZUCCHINI FLANS WITH SLICED ZUCCHINI AND SALMON CREAM

FLAN DE COURGETTE AUX COURGETTES A LA CREME DE SAUMON FUME

SALMON IS A WONDERFUL ADDITION TO THIS ZUCCHINI DISH, SINCE THE TASTES OF SALMON AND ZUCCHINI GO SO WELL TOGETHER. TO ENHANCE THE PRESENTATION OF THIS DISH, CUT TWELVE TINY TRIANGLES FROM THE SALMON BEFORE PREPARING THE SAUCE AND SET THEM ASIDE. JUST BEFORE SERVING, GENTLY HEAT THE SALMON TRIANGLES IN THE OVEN AND PLACE THEM DECORATIVELY BESIDE THE FLAN.

1¼ POUNDS ZUCCHINI, TRIMMED
1   LARGE LEEK, WHITE AND LIGHT GREEN, WELL-WASHED
¼   POUND POTATOES, PEELED
2   LARGE EGGS, BEATEN
2   CUPS HEAVY CREAM
SALT AND FRESHLY GROUND PEPPER
3½ OUNCES SMOKED SALMON, VERY THINLY SLICED
10 TABLESPOONS UNSALTED BUTTER
LEMON JUICE

PREPARE THE ZUCCHINI FLANS: Using a swivel vegetable peeler, remove lengthwise strips from 1 zucchini to form a striped pattern. With a sharp knife, slice that zucchini into 32 thin slices; set aside.

Bring a large pot of salted water to a boil. Cut leek and potatoes into thick slices. Add potatoes to pot and cook for 2 minutes. Add leek. Cut remaining zucchini into thick slices; add to pot. Cook vegetables for 6 minutes, or until the potatoes are tender. Drain and refresh vegetables under cold water. Drain very well. Wrap vegetables in a kitchen towel and twist towel at both ends to extract as much liquid as possible. (The vegetables must be very dry.)

Preheat oven to 375 degrees. Place vegetables in a food processor and puree. Strain puree through a fine-mesh sieve set over a bowl. Whisk in beaten eggs and 3 tablespoons cream. Season to taste with salt and pepper. Pour puree into 4 lightly buttered ¾-cup ramekins. Set ramekins in a hot water bath and bake until a knife inserted into the center of flans comes out clean, about 25 minutes.

PREPARE THE SALMON CREAM: Combine remaining cream with salmon in a medium saucepan. Bring to a boil over medium heat. Reduce heat to low and whisk in 8½ tablespoons butter, 1 tablespoon at a time. Add lemon juice to taste; season with salt and pepper. Strain sauce into another saucepan; keep warm.

Cook reserved zucchini slices in boiling salted water for 1 minute. Drain and refresh under cold water. Drain very well and pat dry on paper towels. Melt remaining 1½ tablespoons butter in a medium skillet. Add zucchini slices. Cook over medium heat, tossing, until tender and glazed, about 2 minutes. Drain well.

TO SERVE: Run a knife around rim of ramekins and unmold flans onto 4 serving plates. Spoon a thick ribbon of the salmon cream around base of flans; garnish each one with a small border of overlapping zucchini slices. *Makes 4 servings.*

NOTE: All of the elements in this recipe can be prepared ahead and reheated before serving.

BAKED CUCUMBERS *STUFFED WITH* COD MOUSSE
CONCOMBRE FARCI A LA MORUE FRAICHE

2   EUROPEAN CUCUMBERS, TRIMMED
½   POUND SKINLESS, BONELESS COD, CUT
        INTO CHUNKS
2   EGG WHITES, WELL-CHILLED
½   TEASPOON SALT
¼   TEASPOON PAPRIKA
     PINCH OF CAYENNE PEPPER
¾   CUP HEAVY CREAM, WELL-CHILLED

1   TEASPOON CHOPPED UNSALTED
        PISTACHIOS
     FRESHLY GROUND PEPPER
3   TABLESPOONS UNSALTED BUTTER,
        MELTED
1   CUP *BEURRE BATTU* (SEE APPENDIX),
        FLAVORED WITH CHOPPED FRESH
        HERBS OR PAPRIKA

Using a swivel vegetable peeler, remove alternating lengthwise strips of skin from cucumbers, leaving an attractive striped pattern. Cut cucumbers into 1½-inch pieces. Scoop out most of the seeds with a small melon-ball cutter, making cups that can hold stuffing. Blanch cucumbers in boiling salted water for 1½ minutes. Drain and refresh under very cold water or plunge into ice water. Drain well on paper towels.

Puree the cod in a food processor. With the machine running, add egg whites, salt, paprika, and cayenne. Pour in cream in a thin stream. When cream is incorporated, add pistachios and puree until just blended.

Preheat oven to 350 degrees. Place cucumber cups in a buttered baking dish just large enough to hold them. Season with salt and pepper. Using a spoon or pastry bag fitted with a round or star tip, fill cucumbers with cod mousse. Cover with buttered parchment paper. Bake for 15 minutes. Remove paper and bake until mousse browns lightly, about 10 minutes. Remove from oven and brush stuffed cucumbers with melted butter.

Divide cucumbers among 4 heated serving plates. Spoon *beurre battu* around them and pass remaining sauce separately in a sauceboat. Serve hot. *Makes 4 servings.*

THIS CUCUMBER STUFFED WITH COD MOUSSE OFFERS ANOTHER MARRIAGE OF ELEMENTS FROM THE GARDEN AND THE SEA. IF EATEN RAW, THE CUCUMBER SHOULD BE PEELED AND ITS JUICES EXTRACTED WITH SALT TO MAKE IT MORE DIGESTIBLE, TO REDUCE ITS "POCKET OF WATER," AND TO ALLEVIATE BITTERNESS. STEWED IN BUTTER, STUFFED, AU GRATIN, OR COOKED AND SERVED WITH A BECHAMEL SAUCE, THIS NATIVE OF THE HIMALAYAS IS A DELICATE ACCOMPANIMENT TO MEAT OR FISH. FOR A MORE ELABORATE PRESENTATION, GARNISH THE STUFFED CUCUMBERS WITH

TRIANGLES OF PEELED TOMATO, FRESH CHERVIL SPRIGS, AND TINY CUCUMBER BALLS STEWED IN BUTTER.

TOMATOES FILLED WITH CRAB
TOMATES A LA TOMATE ET AU CRABE

Serve these stuffed tomatoes as part of a large cold buffet or as the first course of an outdoor meal. Here they are set in the middle of the tomato plants of Monsieur "le Georges" in Chanon-Chatenay. Fragrant and tiny, cherry tomatoes may also be eaten as an aperitif, plain with salt. Tomatoes should be firm, fleshy, and shiny,

in which condition they may be kept for up to a week in the vegetable bin of the refrigerator.

24	CHERRY TOMATOES
	SALT AND FRESHLY GROUND PEPPER
2	TABLESPOONS RED WINE VINEGAR
4	LARGE RIPE TOMATOES (ABOUT 1¾ POUNDS), PEELED AND SEEDED
1	CUP CLASSIC MAYONNAISE
1	TABLESPOON DRY WHITE WINE
1	HARD-COOKED EGG, CHOPPED
1	TEASPOON CHOPPED FRESH TARRAGON
2	CUPS COOKED CRAB MEAT

Wash and rinse cherry tomatoes. Cut off tops at "shoulders" and gently scoop out pulp. Reserve tops, pulp, and seeds. Season tomato shells with salt and pepper. Sprinkle with vinegar and set aside for 1 hour. Invert to drain on paper towels until ready to fill.

Chop large tomatoes into chunks. Place in food processor along with reserved cherry tomato pulp and seeds. Process until liquid and smooth, about 30 seconds. Pass through a fine-mesh strainer. You will have about 2 cups.

Pour puree into a large nonreactive saucepan. Cook, stirring, over medium high heat until thick and syrupy and reduced to about ¾ cup. Season with salt and pepper. Refrigerate until ready to use.

In a bowl, mix mayonnaise with wine. Add egg and tarragon; fold in crab meat. Season with salt and pepper.

TO SERVE: Spoon a small amount of chilled tomato sauce into the bottom of each cherry tomato. Fill with crab mixture, and top with reserved tomato tops. *Makes 4 servings.*

LEEK AND TOMATO QUICHE WITH SALMON
QUICHE AU POIREAU, A LA TOMATE ET AU SAUMON

PASTRY

2   CUPS ALL-PURPOSE FLOUR

½   CUP UNSALTED BUTTER, SOFTENED
     SLIGHTLY AND CUT INTO BITS

1   EGG YOLK
     PINCH OF SALT

FILLING

1   POUND PLUM TOMATOES, PEELED
     SALT AND FRESHLY GROUND PEPPER

1   POUND LEEKS, DARK GREEN LEAVES
     REMOVED, WELL-WASHED AND FINELY
     CHOPPED

2½   TABLESPOONS UNSALTED BUTTER

⅓   CUP DRY WHITE WINE

1¼   CUPS HEAVY CREAM

1   CUP MILK

1   EGG

2   EGG YOLKS
     PAPRIKA

1   POUND SALMON FILLET OR ¾ POUND
     SMOKED SALMON, CUT INTO THIN
     SLICES
     SNIPPED CHIVES

PREPARE THE PASTRY: Sift flour into large bowl; make a well in the center. Add butter, egg yolk, salt, and ¼ cup water; mix with fingertips to blend. Gradually work in flour to form large crumbs. If dough seems dry, add a little more water, 1 tablespoon at a time. Gather dough together and place on a lightly floured work surface. Using the heel of your hand, press dough away from you to knead it gently and incorporate the butter. Gather dough into a disk and wrap in waxed paper or plastic. Chill for at least 30 minutes.

PREPARE THE FILLING: Preheat oven to 400 degrees. Slice tomatoes ⅓-inch-thick and place slices on a buttered nonreactive baking sheet. Bake tomatoes until dry but not browned, about 15 minutes. Season tomatoes with salt and pepper; set aside. Leave oven on.

On a lightly floured work surface, roll out pastry ¼-inch-thick. Fit dough into an 11-inch fluted tart pan with a 2-inch rim and a removable bottom. Line dough with parchment paper and fill with pie weights or dried beans. Bake shell for 15 minutes. Remove the paper and weights. Bake until edges are just beginning to brown and bottom is set, about 10 minutes. Set aside to cool slightly on a rack.

While tart shell bakes, blanch chopped leeks in boiling salted water for 30 seconds. Drain well and place leeks in a medium skillet. Add butter and cook over medium low heat, without browning, until leeks are soft, about 8 minutes. Add wine and simmer over medium heat for 2 minutes. Stir in ½ cup cream and simmer until thickened, about 4 minutes. Season with salt and pepper to taste. (The recipe can be prepared ahead to this point.)

ASSEMBLE THE QUICHE: Spread leek mixture in tart shell. In a bowl, whisk together remaining ¾ cup heavy cream, milk, whole egg, egg yolks, paprika, and salt and pepper to taste. Pour one-third of mixture over leeks and bake until just set, about 10 minutes. Remove from oven. Arrange salmon slices over quiche and top with oven-dried tomatoes. Pour remaining custard mixture over salmon and tomatoes and sprinkle with chives. Bake until set and lightly browned, about 15 minutes. Serve hot. *Makes 6 servings.*

THIS ORIGINAL QUICHE SITS IN THE MIDST OF WATER FLOWERS ON THE BANKS OF THE VEYLE RIVER. ONCE AGAIN, SALMON AND FRESH GARDEN VEGETABLES OFFER A DELIGHTFUL COMBINATION OF TASTES. THE LEEK IS A VERSATILE VEGETABLE, OFTEN ACCOMPANYING FISH AS WELL AS MEAT. IT IS THE INCONTESTABLE KING OF *FLAMICHE*, THE FAMOUS LEEK TART FROM PICARDY.

THIS VARIATION ON A LEEK TART TAKES FULL ADVANTAGE OF THE VEGETABLE'S VERSATILITY.

MICHEL GUERARD'S
TOMATO AND LOBSTER SALAD

SALADE DE TOMATES CONFITES AU HOMARD DE MICHEL GUERARD

GARNISH

3 LARGE TOMATOES (¾ TO 1¼ POUNDS)
  OLIVE OIL
  SEVERAL SPRIGS OF FRESH THYME
3 CLOVES GARLIC, FINELY CHOPPED
  PINCH OF SUGAR
  SALT AND FRESHLY GROUND PEPPER
½ POUND GREEN BEANS

LOBSTER

1 SMALL LOBSTER PREFERABLY FEMALE
  (ABOUT 1½ POUNDS)
2 QUARTS COURT BOUILLON (SEE
  MARINIERE D'AZUR AUX LEGUMES)
  SALT

SAUCE

1 EGG YOLK
½ TEASPOON DIJON MUSTARD
1 TEASPOON KETCHUP
1 TEASPOON LEMON JUICE
  SALT AND FRESHLY GROUND PEPPER
½ CUP VEGETABLE OIL
1 TEASPOON ARMAGNAC OR BRANDY
1 TABLESPOON CHOPPED TARRAGON
1 TABLESPOON CHOPPED CHERVIL PLUS
  SPRIGS FOR GARNISH

MICHEL GUERARD IS AN ARTIST WHO HAS DONE MUCH FOR THE ART OF MODERN COOKING. IT IS ONLY NATURAL, THEREFORE, THAT HIS SALAD OF COOKED TOMATOES AND LOBSTER BE IN-CLUDED IN THIS BOOK. THE FRESH GREEN BEANS ADD A CONTRAST IN TEXTURE AND ANOTHER ELEMENT OF COLOR TO THE PRESENTATION OF THIS DISH.

PREPARE THE GARNISH: Preheat oven to 250 degrees. Lightly brush a large baking dish with olive oil. Peel the tomatoes; cut in half crosswise. Remove seeds. Place on baking dish, cut sides up, and brush with olive oil. Season with thyme, garlic, sugar, salt, and pepper. Bake for 1½ hours. Let cool completely before assembling the salad; do not refrigerate.

Plunge the green beans into a pot of boiling salted water. Cook until tender. Refresh under cold water. Drain well.

PREPARE THE LOBSTER: Place lobster in a large nonreactive pot and pour in court bouillon. Add a pinch of salt. Bring to a boil and cook over high heat for 5 minutes. Remove to a bowl of cold water. Let cool completely.

Cut shell along the middle of the underside with kitchen scissors. If lobster is a female, scrape coral into a small mixing bowl; reserve for sauce. Gently pull off the tail. Pull back and gently remove the flesh. Cut into six medallions. Crack claws; remove meat. Keep all lobster meat tightly covered until ready to assemble the salad.

PREPARE THE SAUCE: In a small mixing bowl, whisk together egg yolk, mustard, ketchup, lemon juice, salt, and pepper. Pour in vegetable oil, drop by drop, beating constantly. Continue whisking until thickened and emulsified. Stir in Armagnac and chopped herbs. Add lobster eggs, if available. Cover and refrigerate.

ASSEMBLE THE SALAD: Place 3 tomato halves on each of 2 serving plates. Top each with a medallion of lobster. Arrange claw meat in the center. Surround tomatoes with cooked green beans. Top each lobster medallion with a spoonful of sauce. Decorate with sprigs of fresh chervil. Serve immediately. *Makes 2 servings.*

LADYBUG TOMATOES WITH OLIVES AND FRESH SARDINES

TOMATE EN COCCINELLE A L'OLIVE ET SARDINE FRAICHE

THE LADYBUG NESTLING AMONG THE LEAVES SYMBOLIZES THE ABUNDANCE OF NATURE AND IS A FITTING EMBLEM OF THE PHILOSOPHY BEHIND THIS BOOK. ONE LADYBUG TOMATO PER PERSON SHOULD SUFFICE IF THIS DISH IS TO BE SERVED AS A FIRST COURSE. IF ONLY WATERY, UNRIPE TOMATOES ARE AVAILABLE, DO NOT MAKE THIS DISH; HOWEVER, IF YOU CANNOT FIND ANY WATERCRESS, USE A MIXTURE OF PARSLEY AND CHERVIL INSTEAD.

LADYBUGS
OLIVE OIL
4 FRESH SARDINES
SALT AND FRESHLY GROUND PEPPER
12 TO 15 LARGE BLACK OLIVES, PITTED
10 BASIL LEAVES, CHOPPED
4 TABLESPOONS MAYONNAISE
1 TEASPOON RED WINE VINEGAR
3 EGGS, HARD-COOKED
4 LARGE RIPE TOMATOES, PEELED

SAUCE
1 BUNCH WATERCRESS (ABOUT ¼ POUND)
¾ CUP MAYONNAISE
1 TABLESPOON DRY WHITE WINE

ASSEMBLY
2 THIN SLICES OF TRUFFLE (OPTIONAL) OR BLACK OLIVES
SNIPPED CHIVES
SALT AND FRESHLY GROUND PEPPER

PREPARE THE LADYBUGS: Heat a small amount of olive oil in a medium skillet. Season sardines with salt and pepper. Cook over low heat for 5 to 7 minutes until firm, turning often. Do not dry out by overcooking. Transfer to a plate and gently remove the fillets. Discard skin and bones. Scrape off any bloody flesh with a sharp paring knife.

Place fillets in a food processor. Reserve 4 olives. Add remaining olives and chopped basil to bowl of processor and puree until smooth, about 30 seconds. Scrape down sides, if necessary; repeat procedure. Scrape into a bowl; stir in 2 tablespoons of mayonnaise and blend well. Season with salt, pepper, and 1 teaspoon each olive oil and vinegar. Set aside until ready to assemble the ladybug.

Shell eggs; place in a food processor and finely chop, turning machine on and off. Add remaining 2 tablespoons mayonnaise; process until blended and thick. Adjust the seasonings. Set aside.

Cut peeled tomatoes lengthwise into quarters. Remove pulp and seeds to make petals. Keep covered until ready to assemble dish.

PREPARE THE SAUCE: Strip leaves from watercress stems. Plunge into boiling water and cook over high heat for 2 minutes. Refresh under cold water; drain well. Place in a food processor and puree, about 30 seconds. Scrape into a small mixing bowl; add mayonnaise. Blend well. Thin with wine. Season well.

ASSEMBLE THE LADYBUG: Place a tomato petal on a large serving plate. Neatly coat with sardine mixture. Top with another tomato petal. Spread on a thin layer of egg mixture. Cover with one of the largest, nicest, and reddest tomato petals. (The layers of filling should not be too thick; in the end, the form should resemble the back of a ladybug.) Decorate with small black dots made by cutting out rounds from truffle slices to imitate the back of a ladybug. Use 1 reserved whole black olive for the head and points of chives for antennae. Continue making ladybugs, using all of the tomatoes and fillings. Carefully surround with watercress sauce to simulate a bed of greenery. Serve cold. *Makes 4 servings.*

EGGPLANT CAVIAR WRAPPED IN SMOKED SALMON
CAVIAR D'AUBERGINES EN PANNEQUET DE SAUMON FUME

THESE BUNDLES OF SALMON LIE NESTLED IN THE RICH GRASS OF NORMANDY, IN FRONT OF A MAGNIFICENT PARISH GARDEN. ONE MIGHT BE TEMPTED TO CALL THE EGGPLANT CAVIAR, USED HERE AS A FILLING, "THE CAVIAR OF THE POOR" IF IT WERE NOT SO TASTY. THE PRINCIPLE IS SIMPLE AND CONSISTS OF MIXING BAKED EGGPLANT PULP WITH TOMATO AND ONION, THEN WHISKING IN OLIVE OIL, AS WITH A MAYONNAISE. THE CAVIAR SHOULD BE REFRIGERATED AND CAN ALSO BE SERVED ON TOAST WITH ANCHOVY FILLETS, THIN SLICES OF ONION, AND QUARTERS OF HARD-BOILED EGG.

1½ POUNDS EGGPLANT
OLIVE OIL
SALT AND FRESHLY GROUND PEPPER
7 BRINE-CURED BLACK OLIVES, PITTED AND CHOPPED
1 CLOVE GARLIC, VERY FINELY CHOPPED

1½ TABLESPOONS SNIPPED CHIVES, PLUS MORE FOR GARNISH
12 THIN 2½-BY-4½-INCH SLICES OF SMOKED SALMON
1 SMALL HEAD OF OAK LEAF LETTUCE

Preheat oven to 400 degrees. Halve eggplants lengthwise and set, cut sides up, on a baking sheet. Brush surfaces with olive oil and sprinkle with salt and pepper. Bake eggplants until completely tender, about 35 minutes. (Baking time will vary depending on size of eggplants.) Let cool.

When eggplants are cool enough to handle, scrape flesh into a strainer; discard skins. Press on pulp to extract as much liquid as possible. Coarsely chop eggplant and place in a bowl. Stir in olives, garlic, 1½ tablespoons olive oil, and chives. Cover and refrigerate until cold, about 2 hours. (The eggplant caviar can be prepared ahead.)

Set salmon rectangles on a work surface and place a heaping tablespoon of eggplant in the center of each one. Roll salmon lengthwise around eggplant to form neat, evenly-filled cylinders. Smooth sides. (The rolls can be assembled up to 6 hours in advance; cover and refrigerate.)

TO SERVE: Place 3 salmon rolls on each of 4 serving plates. Slide a few lettuce leaves under rolls and garnish each serving with chives. Serve cold. *Makes 4 servings.*

TOMATO PETALS
FILLED WITH MUSHROOMS AND SNAILS
ROSACE DE TOMATE AUX CHAMPIGNONS, AUX NAVETS FONDANTS ET A L'ESCARGOT

TOMATOES AND FILLING

3	MEDIUM TOMATOES, PEELED
	SALT
12	LARGE SNAILS, RINSED AND DRAINED
¼	POUND MUSHROOMS, WASHED AND TRIMMED
	JUICE OF 1 LEMON
4	TABLESPOONS UNSALTED BUTTER
2	SHALLOTS, MINCED
1	CLOVE GARLIC, MINCED
1	TEASPOON DIJON MUSTARD
⅔	CUP CREME FRAICHE
1	TABLESPOON SNIPPED CHIVES
	FRESHLY GROUND PEPPER

TURNIPS

2	MEDIUM WHITE TURNIPS, PEELED
	SALT

HERB SAUCE

1	BUNCH PARSLEY
½	BUNCH WATERCRESS
1	SMALL BUNCH CHIVES
	SEVERAL SPRIGS FRESH CHERVIL
6	TABLESPOONS UNSALTED BUTTER, CUT INTO SMALL PIECES
2	TEASPOONS RED WINE VINEGAR
	SALT AND FRESHLY GROUND PEPPER

ASSEMBLY

	SALT AND FRESHLY GROUND PEPPER
	OLIVE OIL
2	TABLESPOONS UNSALTED BUTTER

PREPARE THE TOMATOES AND FILLING: Quarter tomatoes. Remove pulp and seeds, leaving petals of tomato flesh. Salt lightly and set aside to drain on paper towels.

Place snails in a food processor and pulse several times to coarsely chop. Do not remove.

Place mushrooms in a small saucepan. Add water to cover, lemon juice, and a pinch of salt. Bring to a boil, reduce heat, and simmer for 10 minutes. Drain well. Add to food processor and pulse several times to chop and blend with snails.

Melt butter in a medium skillet over medium heat. Add shallots and garlic and cook until soft, about 5 minutes. Add snails and mushrooms. Mix well and let dry out slightly over medium high heat, about 5 minutes. Add mustard and crème fraîche; reduce heat to medium low. Simmer for 5 minutes. Add chives and season with salt and pepper. Set filling aside.

PREPARE THE TURNIPS: Quarter turnips. Using a small paring knife, shape into neat, uniform pieces about the size of a large olive. Place in a small saucepan, add salt and cold water to cover; cook over high heat until soft, about 5 minutes. Refresh under cold running water and drain well. Set aside.

PREPARE THE HERB SAUCE: Wash herbs. Place in a medium saucepan and cover with cold water. Bring to a boil and cook over high heat for 3 minutes. Take off heat and allow to cool slightly in liquid.

Remove herbs with a slotted spoon. Place in a food processor and puree until smooth, about 30 seconds. Add a bit of the cooking liquid, if necessary, to make a thin, homogeneous sauce. Pour into a small saucepan and add pieces of butter, bit by bit, until completely incorporated. Season with vinegar, salt, and pepper. Keep warm.

ASSEMBLE THE DISH: Preheat oven to 325 degrees. Pour a small amount of herb sauce into the bottom of 4 shallow serving bowls. Using 2 soup spoons, form filling mixture into "quenelles" or small oval dumplings. Place 3 dumplings in a circle on top of herb sauce in the form of bicycle wheel spokes.

Place tomato petals in an oiled baking dish. Season with salt and pepper. Bake for 1 minute. Top "quenelles" with tomato petals. Brush to shine with olive oil.

Melt butter in a small skillet. Add turnips and heat through over high heat. Season with salt and pepper. Place neatly between tomato petals. Serve immediately. *Makes 4 servings.*

THIS IS ONE OF MY FAVORITE DISHES. THE PRESENTATION OF THE FILLED TOMATO PETALS CAN BE HEIGHTENED WITH A BIT OF COOKED TOMATO SAUCE IN THE CENTER OF THE PLATE AND LEAVES OF FRESH CHERVIL SPRINKLED AROUND THE SIDES. THE SNAIL AND MUSHROOM FILLING CAN BE REPLACED WITH A SIMILAR ONE BASED ON FISH OR SEAFOOD ACCORDING TO YOUR OWN INSPIRATION. CHERVIL, AN ELEGANT HERB WITH A SLIGHTLY ANISELIKE AROMA, WONDERFULLY PERFUMES SALADS AND IS INDISPENSABLE IN CERTAIN SAUCES. BECAUSE ITS AROMA IS VERY VOLATILE, IT IS BEST TO ADD THE CHERVIL LEAVES AT THE END OF COOKING WHEN IT ACCOMPANIES HOT DISHES.

SAUTEED EGGPLANT AND BAKED WHITING IN A BUTTER SAUCE

SAUTE D'AUBERGINES AUX GOUJONNETTES DE MERLAN

8 SMALL WHITING FILLETS, WITH THE SKIN LEFT ON

4 BABY EGGPLANTS

7 TABLESPOONS EXTRA-VIRGIN OLIVE OIL SALT AND FRESHLY GROUND PEPPER

2 SHALLOTS, FINELY CHOPPED

⅓ CUP DRY WHITE WINE

12 TABLESPOONS (¾ CUP) UNSALTED BUTTER, SOFTENED SLIGHTLY

⅛ TEASPOON CURRY POWDER, OR MORE TO TASTE

⅛ TEASPOON POWDERED SAFFRON, OR MORE TO TASTE

Cut whiting fillets diagonally into thick slices. Place, skin-side up, on a buttered baking sheet; refrigerate.

Slice eggplants into ½-inch-thick lengthwise strips. Cut strips into square or diamond shapes.

Heat olive oil in a large skillet. Add eggplant and season with salt and pepper. Sauté over medium high heat, tossing, until tender and lightly browned, about 8 minutes. Drain eggplant on paper towels and keep warm.

Preheat oven to 475 degrees. In a medium saucepan, combine shallots, wine, and 1 tablespoon water. Bring to a boil; simmer until almost all of liquid evaporates, about 2 minutes. Reduce heat to low and whisk in butter, 2 tablespoons at a time. Stir in the curry powder and saffron. Season to taste with salt and pepper. Strain sauce through a fine-mesh sieve; keep warm over hot water.

Season the whiting with salt and pepper and bake until just cooked through, about 4 minutes.

TO SERVE: Spoon sauce into 4 heated shallow soup plates. Arrange fish and eggplant decoratively on sauce and serve immediately. *Makes 4 servings.*

A GARDEN BORDERING ON THE WATER IN PONT DE VEYLE OVERFLOWS WITH BLOSSOMS. THIS DISH COMBINES DECORATIVELY ARRANGED EGGPLANT AND WHITING IN A SPICY BUTTER SAUCE. I PERSONALLY LIKE THE FLAVOR AND TEXTURE OF WHITING, DESPITE THE FACT THAT IT IS QUITE AN ORDINARY FISH. IF YOU WOULD PREFER TO PREPARE THIS RECIPE WITH ANOTHER FISH, SELECT A ROUND VARIETY SUCH AS BASS OR SALMON, AS OPPOSED TO A FLAT FISH SUCH AS SOLE OR TURBOT.

SUMMER FRUITS

We left the spring orchard scantily clad but full of hope for the harvest to come. Now, come summer, the fruits fulfill the promise of the blossoms, the trees and bushes bending under the weight of their colorful burdens. Berries provide the link between spring and summer. Raspberries, currants, black currants, blackberries, and bilberries appear in June and July, but, alas, have only a short season.

TERRINE OF PLUMS AND PEARS
POIRES ET PRUNES EN TERRINE

8	MEDIUM PEARS, PEELED, CORED, AND CUT IN HALF	3	ENVELOPES (3 TABLESPOONS) UNFLAVORED GELATIN
½	CUP SAUTERNES OR OTHER SWEET WHITE WINE	1	TABLESPOON BITTER ORANGE MARMALADE
2	TABLESPOONS POWDERED SUGAR JUICE OF 1 LEMON	10	TO 15 PLUMS (ABOUT 2 POUNDS), PEELED AND PITS REMOVED
		1	CUP THIN FRUIT *COULIS*

Place pears in a large saucepan and cover with cold water. Bring to a simmer over medium heat and cook until soft, 5 to 10 minutes depending on ripeness. Drain on paper towels. Place 8 pear halves in a food processor and puree until smooth, about 15 seconds. Reserve remaining pear halves.

In medium saucepan, combine pear puree with the Sauternes, sugar, and lemon juice. Remove one-third of mixture to a large mixing bowl. Sprinkle gelatin evenly over surface. Set aside to soften for 10 minutes. Meanwhile, bring remaining puree to a low simmer over medium heat. Pour over gelatin. Add marmalade and stir well. Set aside to cool completely.

When mixture is thick and syrupy, pour a ¼-inch-thick layer into an 8½-inch-long loaf pan. Refrigerate until slightly set, about 5 minutes. Cut remaining 8 pear halves into ⅛-inch-thick slices. Decoratively arrange some of slices over puree. Add another ¼-inch layer of puree and top with a layer of halved plums. Add layers of puree, pear slices, puree, remaining plums, and remaining puree. Cover with plastic and refrigerate overnight.

About 2 hours before serving, place terrine in freezer. Dip pan in hot water and unmold onto a large cutting surface. Carefully cut into 8 slices, using a thin-bladed, sharp knife dipped in hot water. Place each slice on an individual serving plate and surround with some of the thin fruit *coulis*. *Makes 4 servings.*

THIN FRUIT COULIS

Choose fresh fruit or berries such as raspberries, red currants, blackberries, or black currants. Place 2 or 3 cups fruit in a food processor and puree until smooth. Pour into a large mixing bowl. Sweeten to taste with powdered sugar. Add lemon juice to taste. Refrigerate for several hours. Thin out with soda water as necessary. The sauce should be very liquid but retain the flavor of fruit or berry.

To make this terrine, I gathered plums from the orchard of Antoine Riboud in Culoz, in the region known as "le Bugey." This dish became a souvenir of a pleasant summer trip during which I came to appreciate M. Riboud's culinary talents. The most highly esteemed and best known plums are the greengage or, in French, *Reine-Claude*,

which owe their name to the first wife of François I of France. They make excellent table fruits and are perfect for tarts, jams, and bottling in syrup.

MERINGUE AND SHERBET GOURMANDISE WITH RED FRUIT

GOURMANDISE GLACEE FREDERICK

My favorite dessert—a symphony of flavors dedicated to the glory of red fruit. Different variations on the theme are possible with various combinations of ice cream or sherbet, fruit, and vanilla cream; in all cases the pleasantly soft and crunchy consistency of the meringues gives a particular delicacy to this iced dessert. Here, red currants, which are predominantly used in jellies and jams, are the central fruit. Less sweet than the raspberry, but rich in vitamins and pectin, the

RED CURRANT CAN ALSO BE EATEN PLAIN (WITH SUGAR) OR IN TARTS OR FRUIT SALADS.

VANILLA CREAM
1 CUP MILK
1 VANILLA BEAN, HALVED LENGTHWISE
3 EGG YOLKS
½ CUP GRANULATED SUGAR
2 TABLESPOONS CORNSTARCH, SIFTED

SHERBET
1¼ CUPS GRANULATED SUGAR
1¼ CUPS SELTZER
2½ POUNDS RED CURRANTS, STEMS REMOVED
JUICE OF 2 LEMONS

MERINGUES
5 EGG WHITES, AT ROOM TEMPERATURE
½ CUP GRANULATED SUGAR
½ CUP POWDERED SUGAR

RED CURRANT SAUCE
1 POUND RED CURRANTS
1 CUP GRANULATED SUGAR
JUICE OF ½ LEMON

GARNISH
1½ PINTS WILD STRAWBERRIES OR FRESH RASPBERRIES OR A COMBINATION
MINT LEAVES OR SMALL CLUSTERS OF RED CURRANTS

PREPARE THE VANILLA CREAM: In a small saucepan, bring milk and vanilla bean to a boil over medium heat. Remove from heat, cover, and set aside to infuse for 15 minutes.

In a bowl, whisk egg yolks and sugar until light and creamy. Mix in cornstarch. Remove vanilla bean from milk. Add milk to yolks and stir well. Return to saucepan and cook, stirring constantly, over low heat until mixture comes to a boil.

Immediately pour into a bowl and let cool completely. Cover with plastic wrap placed directly on the surface; chill for at least 4 hours.

PREPARE THE SHERBET: In a small, heavy saucepan, combine sugar and soda water. Bring to a boil over medium heat without stirring. Remove from heat; let cool.

Place currants in a food processor and puree. Pass through a fine-mesh sieve set over a bowl to retrieve juice. Add lemon juice. Freeze in an ice cream maker following manufacturer's directions.

PREPARE THE MERINGUES: Preheat oven to 200 degrees. Place the egg whites in the bowl of an electric mixer. Beat until foamy. Add 2 tablespoons granulated sugar. Continue beating until soft peaks form. Combine remaining 6 tablespoons granulated sugar with the powdered sugar. Add to whites and beat until stiff and shiny.

Butter and lightly flour a large baking sheet. Using a pastry bag fitted with a ½-inch plain tip, make 16 uniform rounds about 3 inches in diameter. Bake until lightly browned, about 1½ hours. Cool completely.

PREPARE THE SAUCE: Place currants in a food processor and puree until smooth. Extract juice by straining through a fine-mesh seive set over a bowl. Stir in sugar and lemon juice. Refrigerate until ready to serve.

ASSEMBLE THE DESSERT: Spread chilled vanilla cream over half of the meringue rounds and arrange berries decoratively on top. Spread remaining meringues with sherbet. Pour currant sauce onto 8 dessert plates and place a sherbet-spread meringue on each. Top each one with a berry-topped meringue. Garnish with mint leaves and red currants and serve immediately. *Makes 8 servings.*

WHITE PEACHES IN CABERNET AND RASPBERRY SYRUP

BARBOTON DE PECHE DE VIGNE EN NAGE DE CASSIS ET CABERNET

In Vonnas, on an old grindstone that serves as a garden table, the mill Convert is reflected in the glass serving dish. This dessert uses white peaches, which represent less than one third of France's harvest, but are the tastiest, the most fragrant, and the most melting. Unfortunately, its fine skin makes the white peach extremely fragile

and it must be consumed quickly. This dish may also be prepared and assembled in advance so that the peaches macerate in the raspberry syrup for a few hours before serving. The marriage of flavors will then be all the more evident.

1½ cups Cabernet Sauvignon wine
1½ cups seltzer
½ cup sugar
2 strips of lemon zest
3 strips of orange zest
4 black peppercorns
  pinch of ground cinnamon
¾ pint fresh raspberries
8 ripe white peaches
  lemon juice (optional)

Combine wine and seltzer in a medium nonreactive saucepan. Add sugar, lemon and orange zests, peppercorns, and cinnamon and bring to a boil over high heat. Reduce heat to medium high and boil for 15 minutes. Remove from heat. Strain syrup and refrigerate until chilled.

Puree raspberries in a food processor. Strain puree into a bowl; set aside. When Cabernet syrup is cold, stir into raspberry puree.

To serve: Peel and stone peaches. If they are very ripe, they should peel easily without blanching. Cut into even slices and divide among 4 large round wine glasses. Taste wine syrup and add more sugar, lemon juice, or seltzer to taste. The syrup should be quite thin. Pour syrup over peaches and serve immediately. Here you have a harmonious marriage of fresh flavors. *Makes 4 servings*.

Note: The original version of this recipe calls for fresh black currants, which are often difficult to find in the United States. If you can obtain them, add ⅔ pound to the wine syrup to infuse for 5 minutes before straining. Press hard on berries when you strain them to extract as much juice as possible.

RED FRUIT JELLIES
PATE AUX FRUITS ROUGES

4   PINTS RIPE STRAWBERRIES, RINSED AND   ⅓   CUP PLUS 2½ CUPS SUGAR
        HULLED   2   TEASPOONS UNSALTED BUTTER
2   TABLESPOONS LIQUID PECTIN   GRANULATED SUGAR, FOR COATING

Puree strawberries in a food processor or blender. Strain puree through a fine-mesh stainless-steel strainer. You should have about 3½ cups strawberry juice.

In a small bowl, combine the pectin with ⅓ cup sugar; stir well to blend.

Combine strawberry juice, remaining 2½ cups sugar, and butter in a heavy medium saucepan. Bring to a boil over medium heat, whisking frequently to dissolve sugar. Whisk pectin and sugar mixture into the saucepan; whisk well to break up and dissolve pectin. Boil the mixture, stirring frequently, until it reaches 228 degrees on a candy thermometer, about 25 minutes.

While jelly mixture cooks, line bottom and sides of an 8-inch square baking pan with a sheet of parchment paper. When jelly reaches 228 degrees, immediately pour into prepared pan. Tap pan on a flat surface to even out jelly layer. Let cool completely, at least 2 hours. Do not refrigerate.

Invert jelly square onto a clean flat surface and carefully peel off parchment paper. Using a large sharp knife, cut the jelly into 1-inch square or diamond shapes.

Roll jellies in granulated sugar to coat completely. Store in an airtight container in a cool, dry place. *Makes about 48.*

MY SON ALEXANDRE LOVES THESE FRUIT JELLIES, WHICH CAN BE PREPARED WITH A VARIETY OF RED FRUITS SUCH AS BLUEBERRIES, RASPBERRIES OR RED CURRANTS, IN ADDITION TO THE STRAWBERRIES USED IN THIS RECIPE. THE PROPORTIONS DO NOT NEED TO BE CHANGED. IN ALL CASES YOU SHOULD START WITH TWO POUNDS OF FRESH

FRUIT. WHEN SERVING, GARNISH THE SUGAR-COATED JELLIES WITH FRESH FRUIT.

CHILLED WHITE PEACHES WITH RASPBERRY SAUCE AND BASIL

ROSACE DE PECHE BLANCHE GLACEE AU JUS DE FRAMBOISES ET AU BASILIC

RASPBERRY SAUCE
- ¾ PINT FRESH RASPBERRIES
- ¾ CUP POWDERED SUGAR
- SELTZER
- LEMON JUICE

PEACHES
- 4 LARGE, RIPE WHITE PEACHES
- LEMON JUICE (OPTIONAL)
- 1 SMALL BUNCH YOUNG BASIL FOR GARNISH

PREPARE THE RASPBERRY SAUCE: Toss raspberries and sugar in a bowl. Transfer to a large, fine-mesh stainless-steel strainer and press with the back of a small ladle into a bowl. Add a little seltzer, if necessary, to facilitate straining berries. Stir in lemon juice to taste and refrigerate sauce until serving time.

PREPARE THE PEACHES: Carefully peel peaches. If they are sufficiently ripe, they should peel easily without blanching. Cut each peach into 8 or 16 slices. If preparing the peaches in advance, place the slices in a bowl and toss with lemon juice. Cover and refrigerate until serving time.

TO SERVE: Pour cold raspberry sauce onto 4 large rimmed plates and arrange the peach slices decoratively on top. Garnish each serving with fresh basil sprigs and serve immediately. *Makes 4 servings.*

THIS REFRESHING DESSERT CAN BE EMBELLISHED WITH A SCOOP OF VANILLA OR BASIL ICE CREAM AND ALLOWS FOR A NUMBER OF ADAPTATIONS. THE RASPBERRY SAUCE CAN BE REPLACED BY ANOTHER RED FRUIT SAUCE, SUCH AS RED CURRANT. RIPE NECTARINES CAN ALSO TAKE THE PLACE OF THE WHITE PEACHES CALLED FOR. LIKE PEACHES, NECTARINES APPEAR IN WHITE- AND YELLOW-FLESHED VARIETIES, ALTHOUGH THE WHITE APPEARS BEFORE THE YELLOW.

THREE-PLUM SALAD WITH LEMON

TROIS PRUNES EN SALADE AU CITRON

- 1 POUND ITALIAN PRUNE PLUMS, HALVED AND PITTED
- 1 POUND GREENGAGE PLUMS, HALVED AND PITTED
- 1 POUND YELLOW OR RED PLUMS, HALVED AND PITTED
- ¾ CUP SUGAR
- 6 TABLESPOONS LEMON JUICE
- PLUM *EAU-DE-VIE* (OPTIONAL)

Cut pieces of plum in half if large. Place each type of plum in a separate bowl. Sprinkle ¼ cup sugar and 2 tablespoons lemon juice over plums in each bowl. Add a little plum *eau-de-vie*, if you like. Cover bowls with plastic and refrigerate for at least 3 hours.

TO SERVE: Drain all plums and combine in a large bowl; reserve liquid. Alternatively, arrange different plum varieties attractively on 4 large rimmed serving plates. Pour some of reserved liquid over plums and serve very cold. *Makes 4 servings.*

PLUMS, MORE PLUMS, AND LEMON MAKE A UNIQUE SALAD. CHOOSE AN ASSORTMENT OF THE BEST PLUMS AVAILABLE. THEY SHOULD BE PERFECTLY RIPE BUT NOT OVERRIPE. I LOVE TO MAKE THIS SIMPLE SALAD BECAUSE PLUMS, WHEN AT THEIR BEST, ARE ONE OF MY FAVORITE FRUITS. FREESTONE PLUMS (TECHNICALLY CALLED PRUNES) ARE IDEAL FOR THIS SALAD BECAUSE THEY ARE SO EASY TO PIT. IF THE KINDS LISTED ARE UNAVAILABLE, TRY TO FIND OTHER VARIETIES THAT WILL GIVE YOU A COLORFUL MIX.

APRICOT BAVARIANS WITH NECTARINES, PISTACHIOS, AND ALMONDS

BAVAROIS D'ABRICOT A LA PECHE NECTARINE, AUX AMANDES, ET PISTACHES VERTES

THIS IS AN UNUSUAL WAY TO SERVE APRICOTS. THE FIRST SUMMER FRUIT TO APPEAR IN THE MARKETS—WHOSE SEASON ONLY LASTS FOR SEVERAL WEEKS IN JUNE AND JULY—APRICOTS SHOULD BE BOUGHT PERFECTLY RIPE, FOR ONCE PICKED THEY STOP RIPENING. FOR AGES, OUR ANCESTORS ACCUSED THIS ORANGE-YELLOW FRUIT WITH A VELVETY SKIN AND SWEET, JUICY FLESH OF ALL POSSIBLE ILLS, BUT NOW IT HAS FOUND ITS PLACE AS AN ELEGANT SUMMER FRUIT.

18	LARGE RIPE APRICOTS, HALVED AND PITTED		LEMON JUICE
1	PACKAGE (1 TABLESPOON) UNFLAVORED GELATIN	5	RIPE NECTARINES
		1	OUNCE SLICED ALMONDS FOR GARNISH
1¼	CUPS SUGAR	1	OUNCE SHELLED UNSALTED PISTACHIOS FOR GARNISH
¾	CUP CREME FRAICHE		

Puree apricots in a food processor. Strain puree through a fine-mesh strainer into a bowl. Measure out 2 cups puree; cover and refrigerate remainder.

PREPARE THE BAVARIANS: In a small bowl, soften gelatin in 2 tablespoons cold water. Meanwhile, pour 2 cups apricot puree into a medium saucepan and add ½ cup sugar. Bring to a boil over medium heat, stirring to dissolve sugar. Whisk in softened gelatin; remove from heat. Continue whisking until gelatin is thoroughly melted and combined. Set aside to cool completely.

Beat crème fraîche until stiff. Fold into cooled apricot mixture. Spoon bavarian mixture into four 1-cup dariole molds or ramekins; smooth surfaces. Cover and refrigerate until set, at least 4 hours. (The bavarians can be prepared 1 day ahead.)

PREPARE THE SAUCE: Stir remaining ¾ cup sugar into remaining apricot puree. Whisk well to dissolve sugar; stir in lemon juice to taste. Refrigerate until serving time.

TO SERVE: Briefly dip molded bavarians into hot water. Run a thin knife around the edges to loosen. Unmold bavarians onto 4 dessert plates. Cut nectarines into ½-inch slices and arrange artistically on each side of the bavarians. Halve the pistachios and arrange them in a crown pattern on each bavarian. Spoon apricot sauce into the center of the crowns and on either side of the bavarians. Sprinkle sauce with sliced almonds and serve immediately. *Makes 4 servings.*

COLLAGE OF FRUIT PURÉES
FRAICHEUR D'ETE

WHITE PEACHES OR PEARS

RASPBERRIES AND RED CURRANTS

APRICOTS

KIWI FRUITS OR GREENGAGE PLUMS

BLACKBERRIES OR BING CHERRIES

SUGAR SYRUP (OPTIONAL)

SUGAR

LEMON JUICE

HEAVY CREAM

WARMED SLICES OF BRIOCHE

Depending on what is available at the market, choose a colorful assortment of ripe fruits, for example those listed above.

Puree fruits individually (or together if using a combination). Strain into individual bowls. (If using apricots or pears, poach lightly in sugar syrup and drain well before pureeing.) To each puree, add sugar and lemon juice to taste. Cover and refrigerate the purees until very cold, at least 2 hours.

TO SERVE: Chill shallow soup plates. Give each puree a good stir and pour each one into a small pitcher. Pour purees into soup plates in a decorative pattern, mingling colors as you wish. Pour a small pool of heavy cream into the center of each plate. Place a knife tip in the center of the pool of cream and draw it out to the rim of the plate to form spokelike stripes. Alternatively, swirl the cream into the purees with a knife. Serve immediately, with slices of warm brioche.

A LACE CURTAIN PROVIDES A BACKDROP FOR THIS BEAUTIFUL FRUIT MIXTURE. CHOOSE AN ASSORTMENT OF SUMMER FRUITS, COMBINING COLORS, TEXTURES, AND FLAVORS. BLACKBERRIES WOULD BE AN UNUSUAL ADDITION; THIS RED, ALMOST BLACK FRUIT WITH A FIRM CONSISTENCY OFTEN GROWS WILD ON BRAMBLES, ALTHOUGH IT HAS ALSO BEEN DOMESTICATED. IT IS MOST OFTEN USED IN STEWED FRUITS, JAMS, JELLIES, OR IN LIQUEUR. LIKE THE PEAR, IT IS A LATE SUMMER FRUIT.

PEAR GRATIN WITH SAUTERNES
AND CRUSHED PRALINE
GRATIN DE POIRES WILLIAM AU PRALIN ET AU SAUTERNES

THIS DELICATE GRATIN (PICTURED ON PAGE 186) SITS BENEATH THE COVERED BALCONY. WHILE THERE ARE OVER A HUNDRED VARIETIES OF PEAR, TWENTY OF WHICH ARE COMMERCIALIZED, THE FRENCH HAVE A WEAKNESS FOR THE MELTING, JUICY, SWEET, AND FRAGRANT FLESH OF THE WILLIAMS OR BARTLETT PEAR. IT WAS DISCOVERED BY AN ENGLISH NURSERYMAN, BUT FOR OVER A CENTURY AND A HALF ITS FAVORED HOME HAS BEEN THE MIDI. IT APPEARS IN LARGE QUANTITIES IN AUGUST AND SEPTEMBER AND IS THE IDEAL PEAR FOR SORBETS AS WELL AS THE SOURCE OF A MARVELOUSLY FRAGRANT BRANDY.

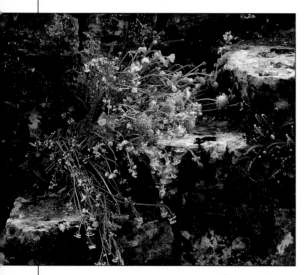

TO ADD A TOUCH OF COLOR TO THIS DESSERT, GARNISH EACH SERVING WITH WILD STRAWBERRIES AND A SMALL SPRIG OF FRESH MINT.

PEARS
4   RIPE BARTLETT PEARS, PEELED, HALVED, AND CORED
5   CUPS SUGAR SYRUP (SEE APPENDIX)
PRALINE
½   CUP GRANULATED SUGAR
½   VANILLA BEAN
¾   CUP TOASTED ALMONDS

SAUCE
4   EGG YOLKS
¼   CUP GRANULATED SUGAR
½   CUP CREME FRAICHE, BEATEN UNTIL STIFF
¼   CUP SAUTERNES
ASSEMBLY
4   SLICES OF SPONGE CAKE OR POUND CAKE
    POWDERED SUGAR

PREPARE THE PEARS: In a saucepan, poach pear halves in sugar syrup until tender, about 8 minutes. Remove from heat and let pears cool in syrup.

MAKE THE PRALINE: Lightly oil a baking sheet. In a small copper sugar pot or heavy-bottomed saucepan, combine sugar, vanilla bean, and 2 tablespoons water. Stir to moisten sugar. Cook over medium high heat, without stirring, until sugar becomes a golden brown caramel, about 7 minutes. Stir in almonds until completely coated, then pour mixture onto oiled sheet. When praline cools and hardens, break into chunks and place in a food processor. Process until the praline is finely ground. (The recipe can be prepared ahead to this point.)

PREPARE THE SAUCE: In a bowl, beat egg yolks with sugar until thick and light and mixture forms a ribbon on the surface when whisk is lifted. Gently fold in crème fraîche and Sauternes.

ASSEMBLE THE GRATIN: Preheat broiler. Place a slice of cake on each of 4 ovenproof serving plates. Drain pears well; slice lengthwise. Fan out pear slices on top of cake. Ladle the sauce over pears and cake and sprinkle first with praline and then with powdered sugar. Broil, as close to heat as possible, watching carefully until sauce browns lightly and sugar caramelizes, about 30 seconds. Serve immediately. *Makes 4 servings.*

NOTE: This dessert can also be prepared in a single gratin dish rather than in individual servings. The recipe makes considerably more praline then you will need, so save the rest for later in an airtight container.

PINK FLOATING ISLAND
ILE ROSE AU THE VERT

MERINGUES

8 EGG WHITES, AT ROOM TEMPERATURE
   SMALL PINCH OF SALT
1 CUP GRANULATED SUGAR
1 TABLESPOON CANDIED PINK ROSE
   PETALS, CRUSHED

GREEN TEA AND VANILLA CREAM

2 CUPS MILK
2 VANILLA BEANS

5 EGG YOLKS
¾ CUP GRANULATED SUGAR
2 TABLESPOONS GREEN TEA

GARNISH

½ POUND WILD STRAWBERRIES (FRAISES
   DES BOIS)
½ POUND FRESH RASPBERRIES
   SEVERAL LEAVES OF FRESH MINT

PREPARE THE MERINGUES: Preheat oven to 300 degrees. Generously butter four 1-cup molds. Dust with powdered sugar to coat bottoms and sides evenly.

In a bowl, beat egg whites with salt until soft peaks form. Gradually add granulated sugar and continue beating until stiff. Fold in crushed rose petals. Divide meringue among molds. Place molds in a deep baking dish and add hot water to reach halfway up sides of molds. Bake until meringues are consistency of sponge cake when lightly pressed with finger, 20 to 30 minutes. Remove molds from water bath and let cool.

PREPARE THE CREAM: In a nonreactive saucepan, bring milk and vanilla beans to a boil over medium high heat. Beat egg yolks with sugar in a nonreactive mixing bowl. Pour in boiling milk, mix well, and pour back into saucepan. Add tea. Stir over low heat until custard thickens and a finger drawn across the back of a spoon leaves a trail, 5 to 7 minutes. Pass custard through a fine-mesh strainer; let cool. Cover with plastic wrap placed directly on surface of custard and refrigerate for at least several hours.

TO SERVE: Unmold the meringues and place 1 in the center of each of 4 shallow dessert bowls. Garnish the tops with the wild strawberries and raspberries. Surround with the green tea and vanilla cream and decorate with mint leaves. *Makes 4 servings.*

NOTE: The green tea and vanilla sauce can be replaced with mint sauce or raspberry *coulis*.

WILD STRAWBERRIES, FRESH RASPBERRIES, AND MINT GARNISH THESE MERINGUE ISLANDS, SERVED WITH A REFRESHING AND UNUSUAL CREAM FLAVORED WITH GREEN TEA. MINT IS A HERB WHICH GOES WELL WITH FRESH FRUIT, PARTICULARLY RASPBERRIES. SOME PEOPLE CLAIM THAT THE FRENCH WORD *FRAMBOISE* (RASPBERRY) IS A CONTRACTION OF *FRAIS DE BOIS* (WILD

STRAWBERRY), ASSERTING THAT THE RASPBERRY FIRST GREW WILD IN THE ALPS OF THE DAUPHINE AND ON THE SLOPES OF THE MASSIF CENTRAL.

PINEAPPLE WITH RASPBERRY AND KIWI SAUCES AND PINEAPPLE SORBET

NAPOLITAINE D'ANANAS A L'ANANAS

THE FRESH AND GEOMETRIC PRESENTATION OF THIS DESSERT CONTRASTS WITH THE CASCADE OF BRIGHT PINK GERANIUM BLOSSOMS THAT FILL THE VILLAGE ALL SUMMER. RASPBERRIES, USED HERE IN A PUREE, ARE PART OF THE PREPARATION OF MANY PASTRIES; THEY MAKE DELICIOUS JELLIES AND JAMS, SYRUPS, AND *COULIS*; THEY FLAVOR ICE CREAM AND SORBETS; AND ARE USED TO MAKE AN INCOMPARABLY FINE *EAU DE VIE*.

1⅓ CUPS POWDERED SUGAR	1½ PINTS RASPBERRIES
2 LARGE RIPE PINEAPPLES	GRANULATED SUGAR
1½ TABLESPOONS LEMON JUICE	6 LARGE, RIPE KIWI FRUITS

Combine powdered sugar and 1¼ cups water in a saucepan and bring to a boil. Remove from heat and pour syrup into a heatproof bowl. Refrigerate until thoroughly chilled.

Using a stainless-steel knife, remove crown and base from both pineapples. Cut off skin, removing any "eyes" that remain in fruit. Slice 1 pineapple lengthwise, ⅓ inch thick. Cut slices into evenly-shaped 2-inch lengths. Discard core of pineapple; reserve any trimmings. Set aside 48 pineapple "sticks" in a bowl; cover and refrigerate until serving. (If you couldn't cut 48 nice sticks from one pineapple, cut a few of the same size from other one.)

Quarter remaining pineapple lengthwise; cut out and discard core. Cut pineapple into chunks and place in a food processor, along with all trimmings from first pineapple. Puree pineapple. Strain juice through a fine-mesh stainless steel strainer, pressing hard on the solids. Measure out 2 cups pineapple juice. (You may have to wait for a short while for the foam to rise to the surface, leaving the clear juice behind.)

Stir 2 cups pineapple juice and the lemon juice into cold sugar syrup. Pour mixture into an ice cream maker and freeze according to manufacturer's directions.

Puree raspberries in a food processor; strain into a bowl. Stir in granulated sugar to taste; cover and refrigerate. Puree kiwi fruits in a food processor. Strain puree into a bowl. Stir in granulated sugar to taste; cover and refrigerate. (All of the elements in this dessert can be prepared in advance.)

TO SERVE: Chill 6 large dessert plates. On one side of each plate, place 4 pineapple sticks end to end in a saw-toothed pattern. Repeat pattern on other side of each plate.

Pour kiwi and raspberry purees into pitchers. Pour kiwi puree into the center of each plate, between the pineapple sticks. Pour raspberry puree onto the plates on the other sides of pineapple sticks. Place a large scoop of pineapple sorbet atop the kiwi puree and serve immediately. *Makes 6 servings.*

A U T

U M N

AUTUMN VEGETABLES

IT IS AUTUMN AND SWEET CLUSTERS OF GRAPES WEIGH DOWN THE VINES; THE BARNS ARE FULL AND BASKETS OVERFLOW WITH A CORNUCOPIA OF FRUITS AND VEGETABLES. MUSHROOMS ARE HARVESTED FROM THE WOODS, CORN FROM THE FIELDS, AND IN THE GARDEN, THE LAST RIPE TOMATOES ARE PLUCKED BEFORE THE FROSTS.

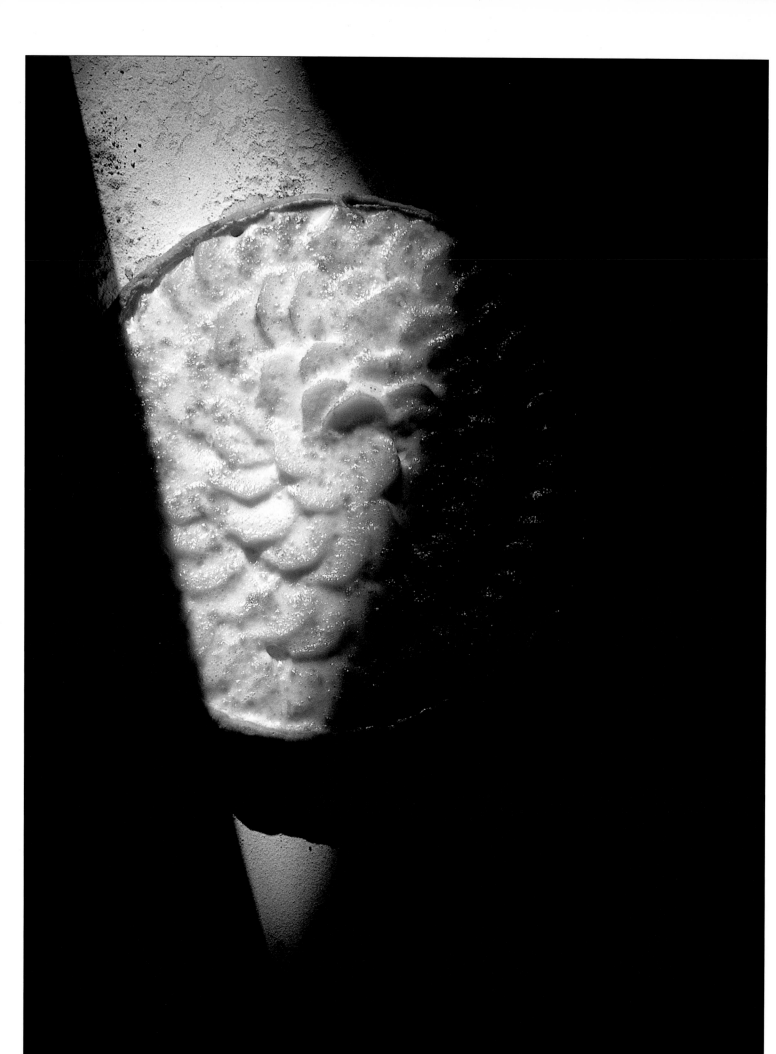

POTATO TART
TARTE AUX POMMES DE TERRE

PASTRY

2	CUPS ALL-PURPOSE FLOUR
½	CUP UNSALTED BUTTER
1	EGG YOLK
1	TEASPOON SALT

TOMATO CONCASSE

3	TABLESPOONS OLIVE OIL
2	SHALLOTS, MINCED
1	ONION, MINCED
8	MEDIUM TOMATOES, PEELED, SEEDED, AND CHOPPED
2	BAY LEAVES, CRUSHED
1	SPRIG OF THYME, OR 1 TEASPOON

A PINCH OF SUGAR

SALT AND FRESHLY GROUND PEPPER

POTATOES

8	YELLOW FLESH OR WAXY POTATOES
2	TABLESPOONS OIL OR BUTTER

ONIONS AND ASSEMBLY

½	CUP UNSALTED BUTTER
5	LARGE ONIONS, THINLY SLICED (ABOUT 6 CUPS)
	SALT AND FRESHLY GROUND PEPPER
1	CUP CREME FRAICHE, LIGHTLY WHIPPED
	FRESHLY GRATED NUTMEG

PREPARE THE PASTRY: Place flour on a smooth work surface, preferably marble. Make a well in the center and add butter, egg yolk, salt, and ¼ cup water. Mix with fingertips, incorporating flour little by little without overworking pastry. Divide pastry into 3 small pieces. Using the heel of the hand, rub each piece onto work surface, spreading dough thin. Combine pieces of dough into disk, cover, and refrigerate for 30 minutes.

Lightly dust work surface with flour. Roll out dough about ⅛-inch-thick and about 1 inch larger than the 11- or 12-inch tart pan you will be using. Center rolled out dough over the mold and gently press into place. Lightly crimp the edges. Refrigerate for at least 30 minutes.

PREPARE THE TOMATO CONCASSE: In a medium saucepan, heat olive oil over low heat. Add shallots and onion and sauté for 10 minutes, stirring often. Add tomatoes, bay leaves, thyme, sugar, salt, and pepper. Cook, uncovered, for 1 to 1½ hours over medium high heat, or until all liquid has evaporated. Set aside to cool.

PREPARE THE POTATOES: Preheat oven to 325 degrees. Peel and wash potatoes. With a small paring knife, carve potatoes into the shape and size of a large egg. Wash again and dry. Heat oil in an ovenproof casserole. Add potatoes and cook, turning often, over medium heat until lightly colored, about 10 minutes. When uniformly golden brown, place in the oven and roast until tender, 20 to 30 minutes. Set aside.

PREPARE THE ONIONS: Melt butter in a large saucepan. Add onions, season with salt and pepper, and sauté slowly, stirring often, for 20 to 30 minutes, or until soft and creamy. Set aside to cool slightly.

ASSEMBLE THE TART: Preheat oven to 425 degrees. Prick tart shell all over with a fork. Line with foil and fill with dried beans or aluminum baking weights. Bake for 10 to 15 minutes, until edges of pastry are set.

Remove foil and beans. Turn oven up to 500 degrees. Spread a layer of onions over bottom of tart. Top with a layer of tomato *concassé*. Thinly slice cooked potatoes and carefully arrange them in the tart shell, overlapping, as for an apple tart.

Season the whipped crème fraîche with salt, pepper, and nutmeg. Gently smooth over surface of tart and bake 6 to 7 minutes, until lightly browned. Serve warm. *Makes 4 servings.*

FERNS ARE TRANSFORMED INTO THEIR FALL COLORS WHILE A LAST, FURTIVE RAY OF SUNLIGHT CARESSES THE DELICATE SCALLOPED CIRCLES OF THIS JUST-BAKED POTATO TART. IN THE MONTH OF AUGUST, THE FIRST MATURE POTATOES ENTER THE MARKET AND REMAIN AVAILABLE UNTIL JUNE OF THE FOLLOWING YEAR. EVERYONE HAS BEEN DISCOMFORTED BY ALLYRIC SULFUR, THE SUBSTANCE WHICH MAKES ONE CRY WHEN PEELING ONIONS (WHICH ARE USED IN THIS TART). IT IS SIMPLE TO AVOID THIS BY FIRST PUTTING THE

ONIONS IN THE FREEZER FOR ABOUT TEN MINUTES OR BY PEELING THEM UNDER RUNNING WATER.

CHECKERBOARD OF EGGPLANT AND TOMATO
DAMIER D'AUBERGINE ET TOMATE MIMOSA

4	MEDIUM TOMATOES, PEELED AND QUARTERED	SALT AND FRESHLY GROUND PEPPER
		OLIVE OIL
4	SMALL EGGPLANTS, RINSED AND WIPED DRY	RED WINE VINEGAR
		2 HARD-COOKED EGGS

Cut out and reserve tomato seeds and pulp. Set tomato shells aside.

Place reserved seeds and pulp in a food processor and puree until smooth. Press through a fine-mesh strainer and set aside.

Preheat oven to 325 degrees. Place eggplants on individual squares of aluminum foil. Sprinkle with salt and pepper. Fold foil around eggplants and seal. In a baking dish, heat a small amount of olive oil. Add foil packages and bake until soft, about 30 minutes.

Remove eggplants from foil and halve lengthwise. Scrape out pulp, leaving a ⅛-inch-thick shell. Puree pulp in a food processor until smooth, about 1 minute. Remove to a bowl and set aside.

Cut tomato and eggplant shells into 1-inch diamond shapes. Arrange decoratively on 4 individual serving plates, alternating colors.

Season each puree with olive oil, vinegar, salt, and pepper to taste. Dribble equal amounts onto the sides of the checkerboard design.

Separate egg whites and yolks. Press each through a fine-mesh strainer. Use yellow and white colors alternately to complete plate decoration. *Makes 4 servings.*

THE TOMATOES THAT APPEAR TOWARD THE END OF THE SEASON ARE PERHAPS THOSE WE CHERISH MOST, KNOWING THAT THEY WILL NOT BE AROUND MUCH LONGER. CUT IN DIAMONDS AND INTERSPERSED WITH SECTIONS OF EGGPLANT, TOMATOES ARE USED HERE TO CREATE AN ARRESTING PLATE AND TABLE SETTING. SERVE THIS DISH COLD IN AUGUST WHEN THE TOMATOES ARE AT THEIR PEAK.

WILD MUSHROOM RAVIOLI WITH HERB SAUCE
RAVIOLIS D'AUTOMNE A L'HERBE SAUVAGE

PASTA

2	CUPS ALL-PURPOSE FLOUR
1	TEASPOON SALT
4	EGG YOLKS
1	TABLESPOON OLIVE OIL

FILLING

4	TABLESPOONS UNSALTED BUTTER
1	POUND FRESH WILD MUSHROOMS (CHANTERELLES, GIROLLES, PLEUROTTES, OYSTER), WASHED, DRAINED, AND CHOPPED
1	SHALLOT, MINCED
	SALT AND FRESHLY GROUND PEPPER

SAUCE

	SALT
1	SMALL BUNCH OF CHERVIL (ABOUT ½ CUP, LOOSELY PACKED)
1	BUNCH OF PARSLEY (ABOUT 2 CUPS, LOOSELY PACKED)
1	BUNCH OF FLAT-LEAF (ITALIAN) PARSLEY (ABOUT 2 CUPS, LOOSELY PACKED)
4	TABLESPOONS CHILLED UNSALTED BUTTER, CUT INTO SMALL PIECES
2	TABLESPOONS RED WINE VINEGAR
	FRESHLY GROUND BLACK PEPPER

PREPARE THE PASTA: Place flour, salt, egg yolks, oil, and 3 tablespoons water in a food processor and process until dough is smooth and forms a ball. Add a little more water if mixture is too dry. Wrap dough in plastic and refrigerate for 1 hour. Alternatively, place flour in a medium bowl. Make a well in center and mix together salt, egg yolks, olive oil, and water. Slowly incorporate flour into liquids until dough coheres. Remove to a floured work surface and knead until smooth and elastic, about 3 minutes. Cover and refrigerate for 1 hour.

PREPARE THE FILLING: Melt 2 tablespoons butter in a medium sauté pan. Add mushrooms and cook over medium high heat until they begin to give off liquid, about 3 minutes. Pour into a sieve and drain.

Melt remaining 2 tablespoons butter in a medium sauté pan; add shallot. Cook slowly over low heat, stirring often, until almost soft, about 5 minutes. Add drained mushrooms and heat through. Season with salt and pepper. Set aside.

PREPARE THE RAVIOLI: Cut pasta dough into 2 equal pieces. Using a pasta machine, roll out 1 piece as thin as possible. Place ½-teaspoon mounds of filling mixture 1 inch apart along rolled-out pasta.

Moisten exposed spaces around mushroom mounds with a pastry brush dipped in water. Roll out second piece of dough to same shape and thickness. Gently place on top. With flat side of your thumb, press sheets of dough together, working around mounds. Cut out ravioli with a 2-inch cookie cutter or a sharp knife. Place on a kitchen towel and cover with another towel.

PREPARE THE SAUCE: Fill a medium saucepan three-fourths full with water and bring to a boil. Add a pinch of salt. Meanwhile, wash herbs in cold water and plunge into boiling water. Cook for 5 minutes, remove from heat and let cool in the liquid for 15 minutes.

Using a slotted spoon, transfer cooked herbs to a food processor. Add 1½ tablespoons cooking liquid and process until sauce is smooth, about 1 minute. Remove to a small saucepan.

Bring sauce to a boil. Slowly add chilled butter, a piece at a time, whisking constantly. Add vinegar and season with salt and pepper to taste.

TO SERVE: Bring salted water to a boil in a large pot. Cook ravioli for 3 minutes. Remove with a slotted spoon and drain on paper towels.

Pour a small amount of sauce on each of 4 individual serving plates and carefully place cooked ravioli in a star pattern on top. Serve at once. *Makes 4 servings.*

IF CLIMATIC CONDITIONS HAVE BEEN FAVORABLE, AUTUMN IS THE TIME FOR A PLENTIFUL HARVEST OF WILD MUSHROOMS. IN FRANCE, THE FORESTS HIDE OVER 400 TO 500 SPECIES OF MUSHROOMS. SEVERAL DOZEN VARIETIES ARE EDIBLE, ALTHOUGH WE ARE PERHAPS MOST FAMILIAR WITH THE *CHANTERELLE* (OR *GIROLE*), EASILY IDENTIFIABLE BY ITS FUNNEL-SHAPED CAP. DICED, PEELED TOMATOES, FRESH CHERVIL, OR EVEN TRUFFLE JULIENNE COULD BE USED TO GARNISH THIS DISH OF WILD MUSHROOM RAVIOLI.

CANNELLONI WITH SWISS CHARD AND WALNUTS
CANNELLONI DE FEUILLES DE BLETTES AUX NOIX

THE UNJUSTLY NEGLECTED CHARD IS RELATED TO THE BEET, ALTHOUGH CERTAIN PEOPLE SAY THAT ITS TASTE IS SIMILAR TO THAT OF SPINACH. THERE ARE NUMEROUS VARIETIES OF THIS LEAFY GREEN VEGETABLE. FOR THIS DISH, FLAT NOODLES FOR CANNELLONI OR THE PREFORMED CYLINDERS AVAILABLE IN COMMERCIAL FOOD STORES COULD BE SUBSTITUTED FOR THE OMELETS. COOK IN

SALTED WATER WITH A SPOONFUL OF OLIVE OIL. THE FINISHED DISH COULD ALSO BE SERVED WITH A LIGHT TOMATO AND TARRAGON SAUCE INSTEAD OF THE WHITE SAUCE SUGGESTED HERE.

FILLING
2 POUNDS YOUNG SWISS CHARD, WASHED AND TOUGH OUTER STEMS REMOVED
8 TABLESPOONS UNSALTED BUTTER
3 SHALLOTS, MINCED
¼ CUP COGNAC
2 TABLESPOONS HEAVY CREAM
¾ CUP COARSELY CHOPPED WALNUTS
1 TABLESPOON GRATED SWISS CHEESE
1 WHOLE EGG, BEATEN WELL
SALT AND FRESHLY GROUND PEPPER
FRESHLY GRATED NUTMEG
CANNELLONI
3 WHOLE EGGS
SALT AND FRESHLY GROUND PEPPER
2 TABLESPOONS MINCED PARSLEY
2 TABLESPOONS UNSALTED BUTTER
SAUCE
1 CUP MILK
1½ TABLESPOONS UNSALTED BUTTER
1½ TABLESPOONS ALL-PURPOSE FLOUR
1 EGG YOLK
SALT AND FRESHLY GROUND PEPPER
FRESHLY GRATED NUTMEG
ASSEMBLY
½ CUP GRATED SWISS CHEESE
2 TABLESPOONS BUTTER, MELTED

PREPARE THE FILLING: Bring salted water to a boil in a large saucepan. Plunge chard into boiling water, bring back to a boil, and cook over high heat for 1 minute. Drain very well and coarsely chop.

Melt 4 tablespoons butter in a large skillet over medium heat. Add shallots and cook slowly until soft, about 5 minutes. Add Cognac, ignite, and stir until flames subside. Add cream and stir well. Add chopped chard and cook, tossing, over medium heat for 5 minutes.

Meanwhile, melt remaining 4 tablespoons butter in a large sauté pan over medium high heat. Allow butter to brown, without burning. Stir in walnuts, and then chard. Remove from heat. Mix grated cheese with beaten egg; add to chard mixture. Season with salt, pepper, and nutmeg to taste. The filling should hold together.

PREPARE THE CANNELLONI: Beat eggs well and strain. Season with salt and pepper; add parsley.

In a 5- or 6-inch crêpe pan, melt ½ tablespoon butter over medium high heat. When very hot, add 2 tablespoons egg mixture. Quickly rotate the pan to coat bottom evenly with egg mixture as for making crêpes. Cook until set, about 30 seconds. Carefully flip "cannelloni" over using a small spatula. Cook for 15 seconds. Turn out onto a plate. Repeat the procedure with the remaining butter and egg mixture. You should end up with 4 to 6 thin "cannelloni."

PREPARE THE SAUCE: In a small saucepan, scald milk; set aside. In a medium saucepan, melt butter over medium heat. Add flour and cook, whisking constantly, for 2 minutes. Add the milk all at once and bring to a boil, whisking constantly. Reduce heat to low and cook for 5 minutes, stirring often. Off heat, whisk in egg yolk. Season with salt, pepper, and nutmeg to taste.

ASSEMBLE THE DISH: Preheat oven to 450 degrees. Butter an 8-inch baking dish. Cut off sides of cannelloni omelets to make neat squares. Place a large spoonful of filling in the bottom third of each square and roll up into large cylinders. Place neatly, side by side, in prepared baking dish. Coat with sauce. Sprinkle on grated cheese and melted butter. Bake until browned on top, 5 to 10 minutes. *Makes 4 servings.*

CELERY AND RED BELL PEPPER REMOULADE
REMOULADE DE CELERI ET POIVRONS ROUGES
AUX COPEAUX D'AVOCAT

1 MEDIUM CELERY ROOT (CELERIAC, ABOUT 1 POUND), PEELED AND SHREDDED

1 MEDIUM RED BELL PEPPER, CORED, SEEDED, AND CUT INTO FINE JULIENNE

¾ TO 1 CUP WELL-SEASONED THICK HOMEMADE MAYONNAISE

1 AVOCADO

1 TABLESPOON OLIVE OIL
JUICE OF ½ LEMON
SALT AND FRESHLY GROUND PEPPER

THIS CLASSIC YET ORIGINAL DISH IS AN EASY ONE TO PREPARE, BUT IT IS IMPORTANT THAT THE MAYONNAISE BE THICK ENOUGH TO BIND THE CELERY ROOT AND RED PEPPERS. TOO THIN A MAYONNAISE COULD RUIN THE PREPARATION.

In a small bowl, combine celery root, pepper, and mayonnaise. Divide among four ½-cup ramekins and refrigerate for at least 2 hours.

Choose an avocado that is not too ripe. Peel avocado. Using a swivel vegetable peeler, remove strips of avocado as you would if peeling an apple. Place strips in a small bowl and sprinkle with olive oil and lemon juice. Season with salt and pepper.

Place a salad plate over each ramekin and invert to unmold. Garnish with avocado strips.

CREAM OF PUMPKIN SOUP WITH HERBS

SOUPE DE COURGE A LA CREME AUX HERBES

THE PUMPKIN IS ONE OF THE FAMILY OF SQUASHES THAT ARE HARVESTED IN LATE FALL. THIS BIG, RIBBED ORANGE VEGETABLE CAN BE PREPARED IN A VARIETY OF WAYS. IN NORTHERN FRANCE, IT APPEARS IN A TART WITH ONIONS; HERE IT IS USED IN A SOUP. A VEGETABLE STOCK MADE WITH THE GREEN PART OF LEEKS CAN REPLACE SOME OF THE CREAM IN THIS RECIPE. IT IS PREFERABLE TO DRAIN THE COOKED PUMPKIN WELL IN ADVANCE TO ELIMINATE AS MUCH WATER AS POSSIBLE. AN EXCELLENT GRATIN OF PUMPKIN CAN BE MADE BY COOKING THE VEGETABLES FOR A SLIGHTLY SHORTER AMOUNT OF TIME, DRAINING THEM CAREFULLY, AND CRUSHING THE PULP WITH A FORK IN A GRATIN DISH RUBBED WITH GARLIC. SEASON WELL AND COVER WITH HEAVY CREAM BEFORE PLACING IN A HOT OVEN FOR A FEW MINUTES TO OBTAIN A NICE GLAZE.

1　SMALL PUMPKIN (ABOUT 2½ POUNDS), PEELED, SEEDED, AND CUT INTO LARGE PIECES
4　CUPS HEAVY CREAM
1　TEASPOON SUGAR
　　SALT AND FRESHLY GROUND BLACK PEPPER
　　FRESHLY GRATED NUTMEG
2　TABLESPOONS UNSALTED BUTTER
2　TABLESPOONS VEGETABLE OIL
4　THIN SLICES OF WHITE BREAD, CUT INTO ½-INCH CUBES
½　CUP CHOPPED FRESH HERBS (PARSLEY, CHIVES, CHERVIL, OR TARRAGON)
½　CUP GRATED SWISS CHEESE

Cook pumpkin in boiling salted water until soft, about 20 minutes. Drain on paper towels for at least 1 hour. Press through a fine-mesh sieve or food mill. Place puree in a medium saucepan and add cream. Season with sugar, salt, pepper, and nutmeg. Cook over low heat for 10 to 15 minutes.

Meanwhile, melt butter with oil in a large skillet over medium high heat. Add bread and sauté until browned, about 1 minute on each side. Drain on paper towels.

Pour hot soup into 4 warmed rimmed soup plates. Sprinkle with chopped herbs. Float croutons on top, covered with a large pinch of the grated cheese. *Makes 4 servings.*

COMPOTE OF *SWEET* PEPPERS WITH RAW MUSHROOMS
COMPOTE DE PIMENTS DOUX ET D'AROMATES AUX CHAMPIGNONS CRUS

1	LARGE RED BELL PEPPER	¾	CUP DRY WHITE WINE
1	LARGE GREEN BELL PEPPER		SALT AND FRESHLY GROUND PEPPER
3	TABLESPOONS OLIVE OIL	½	POUND MUSHROOMS, WASHED AND
3	SHALLOTS, MINCED		WIPED DRY
10	SMALL CLOVES GARLIC, MINCED		JUICE OF ½ LEMON

Halve the red and green peppers lengthwise; remove core, ribs, and seeds. Rinse under running cold water. Cut lengthwise into very fine strips, then into ⅛-inch dice (called a *brunoise* in French).

In a small saucepan, heat the olive oil over medium heat. Add shallots and garlic and sauté for 3 minutes. Add peppers and cook, stirring, for 5 minutes. Pour in wine and bring to a boil. Season with salt and pepper to taste. Pour mixture into a bowl and let cool completely.

Just before serving, thinly slice mushrooms. Place in a bowl and sprinkle with lemon juice. Season with salt and pepper.

Spread the bottom of 4 individual plates with cooled pepper compote. Decoratively arrange mushroom slices on top. *Makes 4 servings.*

HERE, A WINEMAKER IN THE MACON REGION STANDS AMID HIS BARRELS. DON'T LEAVE OUT THE WHITE WINE IN THIS RECIPE FOR IT IS ESSENTIAL TO COMPLETE THE TASTE. TWO TEASPOONS OF A WELL-REDUCED TOMATO CONCASSEE MAY ALSO BE STIRRED INTO THE GREEN AND RED PEPPER COMPOTE IF DESIRED.

BALLOTTINE OF CABBAGE WITH CHESTNUTS
BALLOTTINE DE CHOU FARCI AUX MARRONS

1	POUND CHESTNUTS, BLANCHED AND PEELED	3	TABLESPOONS UNSALTED BUTTER
	SALT AND FRESHLY GROUND PEPPER	1	MEDIUM ONION, QUARTERED
	SMALL PINCH OF SUGAR	1	CLOVE GARLIC, MINCED
½	RIB CELERY	2	TABLESPOONS HEAVY CREAM
½	CELERY ROOT (CELERIAC), PEELED AND CUT INTO ¼-INCH DICE, OR 2 RIBS CELERY, PEELED, BLANCHED, AND CUT INTO ¼-INCH SLICES		FRESHLY GRATED NUTMEG
		2	CARROTS, PEELED AND CUT INTO 1-INCH ROUNDS
			SEVERAL BRANCHES OF FRESH THYME
		1	BAY LEAF
1	MEDIUM CABBAGE (ABOUT 2 POUNDS), CORED	1	CUP DRY WHITE WINE

Preheat oven to 350 degrees. Place peeled chestnuts in a small buttered baking dish and season with salt and pepper. Add sugar, celery rib, and enough water to barely cover. Butter a piece of parchment paper and place loosely on top. Braise in oven until tender, about 25 minutes. Set aside.

Place celery root in a buttered baking dish. Season with salt and pepper; cover with buttered paper. Braise in oven until soft and lightly colored, about 25 minutes. Set aside.

Bring salted water to a boil in a large saucepan. Plunge cabbage into boiling water and cook over high heat for 4 minutes. Drain well. Separate leaves without tearing them.

Overlapping edges, spread out cooked cabbage leaves on a clean tea towel or linen cloth to form a rectangle in the center about ¾ inch thick. Place another tea towel on top and press down to absorb moisture. Remove second towel and season cabbage leaves with salt and pepper.

Reserve half of the cooked chestnuts and half of the cooked celery root. Melt 1 tablespoon butter in a medium saucepan over medium heat. Thinly slice 1 onion quarter. Add sliced onion, garlic, remaining celery root, and chestnuts to saucepan. Cook until onions are almost translucent, about 5 minutes. Scrape mixture into a food processor and puree until somewhat smooth, about 30 seconds. With processor running, slowly add cream and puree until smooth. Season with salt, pepper, and a pinch of nutmeg.

Spread puree over cabbage leaves. Arrange reserved chestnut and celery root on top and press down gently. Starting with a long side of the rectangle in front of you, roll up, jelly-roll fashion, lifting up borders of tea towel. Enclose cabbage roll completely in towel and tie ends securely with kitchen string. The *ballottine* should form a tight, neat bundle.

Melt remaining 2 tablespoons butter in a large ovenproof casserole. Add carrots, remaining onion quarters, thyme, and bay leaf. Pour in wine and cook over high heat until reduced by one-fourth, about 10 minutes. Place *ballottine* on top of vegetables and add enough water to barely cover. Simmer over medium low heat for 25 to 30 minutes, turning *ballottine* frequently to prevent drying out.

Remove *ballottine* to a cutting board; gently remove tea towel. Cut into slices and serve warm. *Makes 4 servings.*

CABBAGE SEASON BEGINS IN JUNE BUT CONTINUES ALMOST THROUGHOUT THE YEAR. CABBAGES SHOULD BE VERY HEAVY AND WHEN THE LEAVES ARE STROKED THEY SHOULD GIVE OFF A LIGHT SQUEAK. BESIDES THE CLASSIC PREPARATION (BRAISED, STUFFED, OR IN *POTEE*), CABBAGE IS A PERFECT ACCOMPANIMENT TO PHEASANT, GUINEA FOWL, SAUSAGE, AND EVEN *CONFIT*. THIS BALLOTINE CAN BE ACCOMPANIED BY COOKED, SLICED MUSHROOMS. SERVE WITH A LEMON SAUCE.

POTATOES FILLED WITH CREAMED SALSIFY
PALETS GOURMANDS

4   LARGE BAKING POTATOES, WASHED AND
       DRIED
    ROCK SALT OR COARSE (KOSHER) SALT
1   TABLESPOON UNSALTED BUTTER
1   TABLESPOON SHAVED TRUFFLES,
       CHOPPED
1   TABLESPOON PORT WINE
1   TABLESPOON ALL-PURPOSE FLOUR
    JUICE OF ½ LEMON
4   SALSIFY, PEELED AND PLACED IN
       ACIDULATED WATER

SAUCE
4   TABLESPOONS UNSALTED BUTTER
3   TABLESPOONS ALL-PURPOSE FLOUR
1½ CUPS MILK
½   CUP HEAVY CREAM
    SALT AND FRESHLY GROUND PEPPER
    PINCH OF FRESHLY GRATED NUTMEG
ASSEMBLY
7   TABLESPOONS UNSALTED BUTTER
¾   CUP HEAVY CREAM
    SALT AND FRESHLY GROUND PEPPER
    PARSLEY SPRIGS

SALSIFY IS A ROOT GROWN IN THE HARSH EARTH OF THE NORD PAS-DE-CALAIS AND PICARDY. TO CLEAN SALSIFY, IT IS BEST TO WEAR GLOVES FOR IT GIVES OFF A STICKY LATEX WHICH STAINS THE HANDS. AFTER THE SALSIFY HAVE BEEN PEELED, THE ROOTS MUST BE DROPPED IN ACIDULATED WATER TO PREVENT OXIDATION. THIS LABOR ACCOMPLISHED, SALSIFY CAN BE PREPARED IN MANY WAYS TO ACCOMPANY WHITE MEAT OR POULTRY. HERE, IN THE CONSERVATORY, IS THE CHATEAU GARDENER AND A SIMPLE MEAL.

Preheat oven to 425 degrees. Push a 2-inch round or oval cookie cutter three-quarters of the way through the center of each potato. Pull out cutter but leave potato intact. Spread bottom of a large jelly-roll pan with a 1-inch-deep layer of rock salt. Place potatoes on top, pushing down slightly into salt. Bake for 45 to 60 minutes, or until done. Cooking time will depend on size of potatoes.

Melt 1 tablespoon butter in a small saucepan. Add truffles and cook over medium heat for 3 minutes. Add port and reduce over medium heat until syrupy, about 3 minutes. Set aside to cool.

Mix together flour, lemon juice, and 2 cups salted water in a medium saucepan. Bring to a boil and add salsify. Cook over medium high heat until tender, about 20 minutes. Drain and cut into small dice; set aside.

PREPARE THE SAUCE: Melt butter in a small saucepan over medium heat. Stir in flour. When foaming stops, add milk little by little, whisking constantly. Add cream, salt, pepper, and nutmeg. Remove from heat and set aside.

ASSEMBLY: Lift off cutout "plugs" from cooked potatoes and reserve. Carefully remove potato pulp, keeping potato shells intact. Place in a baking dish.

In a bowl, mash potato pulp with butter and beat vigorously with a wooden spoon. Add ½ cup cream and season with salt and pepper.

Add truffles and salsify to reserved sauce. Reheat over low heat and divide evenly among potato shells. Divide potato puree among shells. Smooth and decorate top with a knife. Add 1 tablespoon of heavy cream to each potato and place in the still hot oven. Bake until lightly browned on top, about 10 minutes. Place the reserved cutout "plugs" on top just before serving. Garnish with fresh parsley sprigs. *Makes 4 servings.*

HERB-FILLED CABBAGE "BEGGAR'S PURSES"
BOULANGERE AUX AUMONIERES FARCIES D'HERBES

WITH THIS MODERN RENDITION OF A CLASSIC RUSTIC DISH CALLED "POMMES BOULANGERES" THE CABBAGE SHOWS AGAIN HOW VERSATILE IT CAN BE. THESE UNUSUAL CABBAGE "PURSES" (PICTURED ON PAGES 218–219) ARE FURTHER ENHANCED BY THE DRAMATIC PRESENTATION OF THIS DISH. THE TRUFFLE BUTTER CAN BE RE-PLACED BY A BUTTER MIXED WITH A JUICE OF

FRESH HERBS. USE IT TO COLOR THE ROUNDS OF POTATOES.

"PURSES"

1	MEDIUM CABBAGE (ABOUT 1½ POUNDS), CORED
1	CUP DRY FRESH BREAD CRUMBS
1	CUP MILK
1	MEDIUM ONION, FINELY CHOPPED
1	CUP CHOPPED FRESH HERBS (PARSLEY, CHIVES, CHERVIL, OR TARRAGON)
	SALT AND FRESHLY GROUND PEPPER
	FRESHLY GRATED NUTMEG
1	BUNCH CHIVES
3	TABLESPOONS UNSALTED BUTTER

POTATOES

10	MEDIUM FIRM-FLESHED POTATOES (ABOUT 2½ POUNDS)
	SALT AND FRESHLY GROUND PEPPER
2	TABLESPOONS UNSALTED BUTTER
1	TABLESPOON VEGETABLE OIL
	VEGETABLE STOCK OR WATER

ONIONS AND TRUFFLES

6	TABLESPOONS UNSALTED BUTTER, SOFTENED
2	WHITE ONIONS, THINLY SLICED
2	TEASPOONS SUGAR
	SALT AND FRESHLY GROUND PEPPER
½	CUP TRUFFLE SHAVINGS, CHOPPED

PREPARE THE "PURSES": Place cabbage in a large saucepan and add salted water to cover by 2 inches. Cover and bring to a rapid boil. Spear cabbage through cored end with a large fork. As cabbage cooks, peel off outer leaves, keeping them intact. Cook leaves until soft, about 10 minutes. Remove and rinse under cold running water. Drain well on wire racks.

Meanwhile, soak bread crumbs in milk for 10 minutes. Drain well in a fine-mesh sieve. Combine bread crumbs, onion, and herbs in a food processor and add salt, pepper, and nutmeg to taste. Process until well blended, about 1 minute.

Shave stems of cabbage leaves so that they are as thin as the leaf. Place a spoonful of bread crumb filling in the center of each leaf. Fold up the sides and roll to form a bundle. Tie each bundle, using a chive as string.

Melt butter in a large skillet. Add bundles and gently braise, covered, over medium low heat until heated through, about 10 minutes.

PREPARE THE POTATOES: Preheat oven to 425 degrees. Peel and wash potatoes. Form into uniform shapes, each about the size of a large egg. Wipe dry. Season with salt and pepper. Melt butter with oil in a large ovenproof casserole with a cover. Brown potatoes, turning often over medium high heat, until uniformly colored, about 10 minutes. Add enough vegetable stock to reach about halfway up sides of potatoes. Cover and bake until tender, about 25 minutes.

PREPARE THE ONIONS: Melt 2 tablespoons butter in a large skillet. Add onions, sugar, salt, and pepper. Cook, stirring constantly, over medium high heat, until soft and caramelized, about 7 minutes.

TO SERVE: Cut potatoes crosswise into ¼-inch slices. Divide rounds decoratively among 4 dinner plates. Place some of caramelized onions in the center and 1 "beggar's purse" on top of each.

Mix together truffles and remaining 4 tablespoons butter. Season with salt and pepper. Top each bundle with a walnut-size piece of truffle butter to enrich this rustic preparation.

MUSHROOM TERRINE
WITH EGGPLANT AND *SWEET RED BELL PEPPERS*
TERRINE DE CEPES AUX AUBERGINES ET PIMENTS DOUX

OLIVE OIL

3   SMALL EGGPLANTS, EACH CUT
      LENGTHWISE INTO 8 PIECES
    SALT AND FRESHLY GROUND PEPPER

3   RED BELL PEPPERS, ROASTED AND
      PEELED

1   LARGE ONION, THINLY SLICED

2   TOMATOES, PEELED, SEEDED, AND
      COARSELY CHOPPED

1   SHALLOT, THINLY SLICED

½   POUND LARGE WHITE MUSHROOMS,
      CLEANED AND TRIMMED

2   EGGS

½   CUP HEAVY CREAM

Heat ¼ cup olive oil in a medium saucepan. Add eggplant pieces, season with salt and pepper, and cook, turning often, until soft, about 7 minutes. Drain on paper towels.

Cut roasted peppers into large pieces. Add ¼ cup olive oil to sauté pan and cook peppers over low heat until soft, about 10 minutes. Drain and reserve.

Heat ¼ cup olive oil in sauté pan and cook the sliced onion over low heat until soft, about 15 minutes. Reserve.

Heat 2 tablespoons olive oil in sauté pan and cook tomatoes over medium high heat until all water evaporates and mixture is thick and pulpy, about 10 minutes. Season with salt and pepper.

In same sauté pan, cook shallot in 1 tablespoon olive oil until soft, about 2 minutes. Finely chop mushrooms and add to shallot. Stir constantly over high heat until mushrooms give off all of their liquid and mixture thickens, about 10 minutes. Scrape mushroom filling into a fine-mesh sieve and drain to eliminate as much water as possible.

Place peppers, tomatoes, and onions in a food processor and process until smooth and creamy, about 1 minute. In a bowl, beat eggs with cream. With motor running, add to processor and mix well. Season with salt and pepper; set pepper filling aside.

Line an 8-inch loaf pan or terrine with parchment paper. Lightly oil paper.

Preheat oven to 350 degrees. Arrange eggplant tightly over bottom of terrine. Top with a layer of pepper filling. Carefully add a layer of mushroom filling. Repeat layering, using eggplant, pepper filling, and mushroom filling.

Place terrine in a baking dish. Add hot water to reach two-thirds up sides of terrine. Bake until set, about 45 minutes.

Remove terrine from oven and let rest for at least 1 hour. Serve at room temperature with butter sauce, or cold with a tomato-herb vinaigrette. *Makes 4 servings.*

NOTE: The original recipe offered by the chef calls for fresh *cèpes*. The recipe has been adapted to be made with a more accessible variety. If you can find fresh *cèpes*, cut into ¼-inch slices and sauté quickly in olive oil over high heat for 3 to 5 minutes. Drain on paper towels. They should replace the layer of cooked white mushrooms called for above.

THIS HEARTY VEGETABLE TERRINE IS FULL OF CHARACTER, COMBINING EGGPLANTS, RED PEPPERS, TOMATOES, AND MUSHROOMS. SINCE ANTIQUITY, MUSHROOMS HAVE HAD AN IMPORTANT PLACE IN COOKING. THE ROMANS HELD THEM TO BE A FOOD OF THE GODS, AND APICIUS, AUTHOR OF THE FIRST BOOK OF RECIPES SOME 2,000

YEARS AGO, DESCRIBED SEVERAL WAYS OF PREPARING MUSHROOMS.

CABBAGE *STUFFED WITH* SALMON
CHOU VERT FARCI AU *SAUMON*

COURT BOUILLON
1 BOTTLE (25.4 OUNCES) DRY WHITE WINE
 JUICE OF 1 LEMON
1 CARROT, CUT INTO 1½ INCH PIECES
1 ONION, QUARTERED
1 CLOVE GARLIC, MASHED
1 SPRIG OF FRESH THYME
1 BAY LEAF
¼ TEASPOON FRESHLY GROUND BLACK PEPPER
¼ CUP COARSE (KOSHER) SALT

CABBAGE
1 GREEN CABBAGE (ABOUT 2½ POUNDS)
¾ POUND FRESH SALMON, CUT INTO ¼-INCH SLICES
 SALT AND FRESHLY GROUND PEPPER

BUTTER SAUCE
2 TABLESPOONS HEAVY CREAM
1 CUP UNSALTED BUTTER, CHILLED AND CUT INTO SMALL PIECES
 JUICE OF 1 LEMON
2 TABLESPOONS RED WINE VINEGAR
 SALT AND FRESHLY GROUND PEPPER

THERE ARE NUMEROUS MEMBERS OF THE CABBAGE FAMILY; GREEN CABBAGE, USED IN THIS RECIPE, DOES NOT HAVE A FIRM HEART BUT IS RESISTANT TO THE COLD. THIS STUFFED CABBAGE, SERVED ON AN EARTHENWARE PLATTER, SITS ATOP A BRESSANE CHEST OF DRAWERS. TO ENRICH THIS RECIPE, ADD A SPOONFUL OF CAVIAR TO THE SAUCE JUST BEFORE ASSEMBLING THE DISH.

PREPARE THE COURT BOUILLON: In a nonreactive pot or saucepan large enough to hold stuffed cabbage, combine wine, lemon juice, carrot, onion, garlic, thyme, bay leaf, pepper, salt, and 2 cups water. Bring to a boil, reduce heat, and simmer for 20 minutes.

PREPARE THE CABBAGE: Cut out core from cabbage and discard outer leaves. Separate leaves, taking care to keep them intact. Reserve small leaves at heart of cabbage.

Plunge large leaves and heart into a large quantity of boiling salted water. Boil over high heat for 3 minutes. Drain and refresh under cold running water. Spread leaves on paper towels to dry.

Cut the salmon lengthwise into ⅛-inch strips. Season with salt and pepper. Reserve on a large plate.

Place a 2-foot-square double layer of cheesecloth on a flat work surface. Wrap a strip of salmon around the smallest part of the cabbage to form a round bundle. Cover with larger leaves of cabbage and enclose again with strips of salmon. Following the order of the dimensions of the leaves, continue forming a round that resembles the shape of a cabbage. Pull up ends of the cheesecloth and secure tightly with kitchen string.

Bring the court bouillon to a simmer over medium heat. Add the cabbage and simmer for 15 minutes. Gently turn over to finish on the other side for 5 more minutes. Reserve in the cooking liquid to keep warm while preparing the sauce.

PREPARE THE BUTTER SAUCE: In a nonreactive saucepan, bring ¼ cup court bouillon to a boil over high heat. Add cream and continue boiling until slightly thickened, about 2 minutes. Working on and off heat as necessary to achieve a thick emulsion, add pieces of butter, 1 at a time, whisking constantly. Pour in lemon juice, vinegar, and salt and pepper to taste.

TO SERVE: Remove cabbage from cheesecloth. Cut into quarters or neat slices. Spoon a small amount of sauce onto 4 large serving plates. Place portions of cabbage on top. Serve warm. *Makes 4 servings.*

LANGOUSTINES WITH TOMATO AND EGGPLANT PUREE IN SEA URCHINS

PISTOU DE TOMATE ET D'AUBERGINE A L'OURSIN ET AUX BROCHETTES DE LANGOUSTINES

12 LARGE SEA URCHINS
3 TO 4 MEDIUM TOMATOES (ABOUT 1½ POUNDS)
1 CUP OLIVE OIL
3 CLOVES GARLIC, MINCED
1 TABLESPOON CHOPPED FRESH BASIL
SALT AND FRESHLY GROUND PEPPER

1 MEDIUM EGGPLANT (ABOUT 1¼ POUNDS)
1 TABLESPOON RED WINE VINEGAR
24 LARGE LANGOUSTINE TAILS, SHELLED AND CLEANED
SEVERAL SLICES OF TOASTED BREAD

THIS DISH COMBINES A HARVEST FROM THE SEA WITH A HARVEST FROM THE GARDEN IN AN ENGAGING PRESENTATION. LANGOUSTINES, A RELATIVE OF THE CRAYFISH, (OR LANGOUSTINOS, SINCE IN THE U.S. THEY ARE OFTEN IMPORTED FROM CHILE) CAN SOMETIMES BE DIFFICULT TO OBTAIN. LARGE SHRIMP OR SCAMPI WILL MAKE A FINE SUBSTITUTE.

Using a kitchen towel for protection, hold a sea urchin in one hand, concave side up, and cut out the center with the other hand. Remove the eye and make an incision in the top, about 2 inches in diameter. Invert and thoroughly drain off liquid; discard liquid. Carefully scoop out the yellow pulpy flesh with a small spoon and reserve. Rinse out the shell and drain on paper towels. Repeat, reserving all flesh and 8 shells.

Core each tomato and remove seeds. Cut pulp into small dice. In a large skillet, combine 1 tablespoon olive oil, tomatoes, garlic, and basil. Season with salt and pepper. Cook, stirring often, over medium high heat until water evaporates, about 15 minutes.

Rinse, dry, and trim eggplant. Cut flesh into small dice without peeling. Pour ¼ cup olive oil into a large sauté pan. Add eggplant and stir well. Cook, stirring often, over medium high heat until tender, about 8 minutes. Season with salt and pepper.

Scrape eggplant into a food processor and puree until smooth, about 30 seconds. Scrape down sides as necessary. Pass through a fine-mesh strainer into a bowl. Add cooked tomatoes to processor and puree until smooth. Strain and add to eggplant puree. Add reserved flesh of the sea urchins; mix well. Adjust seasonings. Add 1 tablespoon olive oil and vinegar. Fill 8 sea urchin shells with puree and place 2 on each of 4 large serving plates.

Divide langoustines among 4 wooden skewers. Season with salt and pepper. Pour remaining ½ cup plus 2 tablespoons olive oil into a large sauté pan. Cook langoustines quickly over high heat until pink and firm, 2 to 4 minutes depending on size. Drain on paper towels.

TO SERVE: Surround filled sea urchins with cooked langoustines and accompany with toasts. Use puree as a dipping sauce. *Makes 4 servings.*

TERRINE OF POTATOES
AND RED SNAPPER WITH ANISE
TERRINE DE POMMES DE TERRE AU ROUGET A L'ANIS

THE ANISE BUTTER, WHICH ACCOMPANIES THE RED SNAPPER, CAN BE SERVED HOT, TEPID, OR COLD. IF IT IS TO BE SERVED COLD, DO NOT REFRIGERATE BUT KEEP IN A COOL SPOT. ADD A SPOONFUL OF WATER TO BRING THE SAUCE BACK TO A HOMOGENEOUS STATE IF IT SOLIDIFIES.

1 POUND MEDIUM RED SKINNED POTATOES
2 POUNDS ROCK SALT (OPTIONAL)
2 EGG WHITES (OPTIONAL)
4 RED SNAPPER FILLETS WITH SKIN INTACT OR 2 POUNDS OTHER FILLETS WITH SKINS
2 TABLESPOONS UNSALTED BUTTER
½ CUP OLIVE OIL
2 TABLESPOONS MINCED SHALLOTS
2 TABLESPOONS MAYONNAISE

1 SMALL BUNCH CHIVES, SNIPPED PLUS ADDITIONAL CHIVES FOR GARNISH
   SALT AND FRESHLY GROUND PEPPER
   ANISE BUTTER
¾ CUP UNSALTED BUTTER, CHILLED AND CUT INTO SMALL PIECES
2 SHALLOTS, MINCED
½ CUP DRY WHITE WINE
2 TO 3 TABLESPOONS *PASTIS* (ANISEED APERITIF)
   PINCH OF THREAD SAFFRON
   SALT AND FRESHLY GROUND PEPPER

Scrub potatoes. Cook in a large amount of salted water until tender, about 20 minutes. (Alternatively, bake in rock salt to concentrate the flavor: Preheat oven to 450 degrees. Mix rock salt and egg whites in a large bowl. Pour half of mixture into an ovenproof casserole. Place potatoes on top and cover with remaining rock salt mixture. Bake for 20 minutes, or until soft. Remove hardened crust, keeping potato skin intact.) When potatoes are cool, cut lengthwise into ¼-inch slices.

Lay each red snapper fillet on a flat surface. Using a sharp knife, cut each fillet into 2 thin fillets, making one thin fillet with skin and another that is all flesh. Wrap and reserve flesh fillets in the refrigerator. Cut skin sides crosswise into 1½-inch strips.

In a medium skillet, melt butter with olive oil. Cook strips of snapper over medium heat until just done, about 1½ minutes on each side. Remove to drain on paper towels. Add shallots to skillet and cook over low heat until translucent, about 5 minutes. Add reserved flesh of the snapper and cook over medium heat until firm, about 3 minutes. Scrape contents of skillet into a food processor and process until smooth but not pureed, about 15 seconds. Scrape into a mixing bowl. Add mayonnaise and chives. Mix well and season filling with salt and pepper.

Brush a small, straight-sided 8-inch cake mold or terrine with olive oil. Line with strips of fillets, skin side facing outward. Spread a thin layer of filling over the bottom. Place sliced potatoes on top. Repeat layering procedure until mold is three-fourths full. Top with any remaining fillets, skin side up. Cover and refrigerate overnight.

PREPARE THE ANISE BUTTER: Melt 1 tablespoon butter in a nonreactive saucepan. Add shallots and cook over low heat until soft and translucent, about 5 minutes. Pour in white wine, increase heat to medium high, and reduce by one-fourth.

Whisk in remaining pieces of butter, a bit at a time, beating constantly and working on and off heat until all butter is incorporated. Season to taste with the *pastis*, saffron, salt, and pepper. Gently bring sauce to a simmer.

To serve: Run a sharp knife around the terrine and dip into hot water for 15 to 20 seconds to unmold. Turn out onto a large serving platter. Cut into neat slices and serve with anise butter. Garnish with fresh chives if desired. *Makes 4 to 6 servings.*

Note: The original recipe calls for a popular French fish called *rouget*. These are almost impossible to find in North America. Should you have access to this fish, proceed as above with 8 rouget weighing ¼ to ¾ of a pound apiece.

In addition to breeding poultry from Bresse, Monsieur Catherin is an accomplished fisherman. At this time of day he likes to cast his net in the Veyle river.

LIME RISOTTO WITH FROG LEGS
RISOTTO AU CITRON VERT ET AU FUMET DE GRENOUILLES

RISOTTO

1   TABLESPOON SEA SALT
½   CUP LONG-GRAIN WHITE RICE
    GRATED ZEST OF 4 LIMES
4   TABLESPOONS UNSALTED BUTTER
20 SMALL FROG LEGS (ABOUT 1 POUND)
    SALT AND FRESHLY GROUND PEPPER

LEMON SAUCE

1   CUP DRY WHITE WINE
1   TABLESPOON RED WINE VINEGAR
3   TABLESPOONS MINCED SHALLOTS
⅓   CUP HEAVY CREAM
½   CUP UNSALTED BUTTER, CHILLED AND
      CUT INTO SMALL PIECES
4   LEMONS
    SNIPPED CHIVES OR PEELED SECTIONS
    OF TOMATO FOR GARNISH

IN THE DOMBES REGION, LAND OF FROGS LEGS AND CARP, EARLY MORNING POND FISHING IS A MEMORABLE RITUAL. THIS RISOTTO WITH FROGS LEGS IS FLAVORED WITH LIME AND THEN SERVED WITH A CREAMY LEMON SAUCE. THE RESULT IS A LIGHT, UNUSUAL, AND REFRESHING DISH.

PREPARE THE RISOTTO: Fill a large saucepan with water. Add sea salt and bring to a boil. Add rice and lime zest. Bring to a boil, reduce heat to low, and simmer for 15 minutes.

Melt butter in a large skillet. Wash and drain frog legs. Add to butter and cook, covered, over medium heat for 5 minutes. Pour into a colander set inside a large bowl; reserve cooking liquid. Without shredding meat, remove flesh from frog legs; add meat to cooking liquid.

Drain cooked rice and quickly rinse under running cold water to stop the cooking. Drain well but do not completely cool. Add to bowl and stir to combine with meat and cooking liquid. Add salt and pepper to taste. Butter four ½-cup ramekins. Fill with rice mixture. Cover and refrigerate.

PREPARE THE LEMON SAUCE: Combine wine, vinegar, and shallots. In a small nonreactive saucepan, reduce over high heat until only 1 tablespoon liquid remains. Add cream and cook to reduce slightly. Whisk in butter, piece by piece. Remove from heat and pass through a fine-mesh strainer. Keep warm.

Remove zest from lemons in large pieces. Blanch in boiling water for 3 minutes. Drain and refresh under running cold water. Set aside. Squeeze lemons and strain juice to remove seeds; reserve.

ASSEMBLY: Preheat oven to 325 degrees. Place ramekins in a deep baking dish. Add boiling water to reach halfway up sides of ramekins. Cover ramekins lightly with pieces of buttered aluminum foil. Cook until heated through, about 15 minutes.

Add lemon zest to butter sauce. Pour in lemon juice to taste. Season and heat but do not boil.

Unmold risotto onto each of 4 large serving plates. Pour lemon sauce around base and garnish with chives or tomato. Reserved pieces of frog legs can be used to enhance the presentation if desired. *Makes 4 servings.*

Near Saint-Paul de Varax, Sunday morning, the pond is almost empty. The owner, his farmers, and helpful neighbors direct, with their nets, the fish in the direction of the "thou," the low part of the pond with the sluice gates. There the carp, pike, perch, and other white fish are picked up with landing nets and sorted. Their sale takes place on the spot, according to their weight on the traditional Roman scale.

SAUTÉED WILD MUSHROOMS WITH SEA SCALLOPS
SAUTÉ DE CÈPES ET GIROLLES EN COQUE DE SAINT-JACQUES

In France, the *cèpe* (or boletus mush-room) is the king of autumn mushrooms, and it comes in at least two dozen varieties. *Cèpes* are recognized by their swollen stems and by the "beard" which lines the interior of their caps. They are not peeled but are wiped with a damp cloth. Cooking usually takes place in two

¼	POUND SMALL FRESH *CÈPES* (BOLETUS), TRIMMED
¼	POUND SMALL FRESH *CHANTERELLES*, TRIMMED
2	SHALLOTS, MINCED
⅓	CUP DRY WHITE WINE
2	TEASPOONS WHITE WINE VINEGAR
10	TABLESPOONS UNSALTED BUTTER, SOFTENED SLIGHTLY

1½	TABLESPOONS LEMON JUICE
½	TEASPOON SOY SAUCE
	PINCH OF CURRY POWDER
	SALT AND FRESHLY GROUND PEPPER
8	LARGE SEA SCALLOPS
4	TABLESPOONS OLIVE OIL
	COARSE SEA SALT

Quickly rinse mushrooms under cold water, keeping varieties separate. Dry mushrooms well in a towel. Slice *cèpes*. Halve chanterelles if large.

Preheat oven to 475 degrees. In a small saucepan, combine shallots, wine, vinegar, and 1 tablespoon water. Bring to a boil over high heat and cook until almost all liquid has evaporated, about 2 minutes. Reduce heat to low and whisk in butter, 2 tablespoons at a time. Add lemon juice, soy sauce, and curry powder; season to taste with salt and pepper. Strain and keep sauce warm over hot water.

Place scallops on a lightly buttered baking sheet. Bake, without turning, just until scallops whiten and lose their opaque quality, 6 to 8 minutes.

Meanwhile, heat 2 tablespoons olive oil in each of 2 medium skillets. Add *cèpes* to one skillet, *chanterelles* to other skillet. Sauté over high heat, tossing frequently, until lightly browned, about 4 minutes. Drain mushrooms on paper towels.

TO SERVE: Spoon sauce onto 4 heated shallow dinner plates and place 2 scallops, browned-side up, on each one. Sprinkle scallops with coarse sea salt and a grind of fresh pepper; top with sautéed mushrooms. Serve immediately. *Makes 4 servings.*

STAGES: THE FIRST TO MAKE THEM "SWEAT," THAT IS, GIVE UP THE WATER THEY CONTAIN. THE STALKS ARE EDIBLE BUT ARE USUALLY PUT ASIDE TO MAKE A HASH WHICH ACCOMPANIES THE *CÈPE* IN MANY RECIPES.

FLAGEOLET BEANS IN LEMON BUTTER WITH TROUT MOUSSE AND CHIVES
FLAGEOLETS VERTS AU SOUFFLE DE TRUITE A LA CIBOULETTE

BEANS

5   OUNCES FRESH SHELLED FLAGEOLET
    BEANS OR ⅔ CUP DRIED
1   CARROT, PEELED
1   ONION, PEELED AND STUDDED WITH 1
    CLOVE
1   SMALL BOUQUET GARNI
½   POUND SKINLESS SALMON TROUT
    FILLETS, CUT INTO CHUNKS

2   EGG WHITES, WELL-CHILLED
    SALT AND FRESHLY GROUND WHITE
    PEPPER
    PINCH OF CAYENNE PEPPER
¾   CUP HEAVY CREAM, WELL-CHILLED
LEMON BUTTER
¼   CUP STRAINED LEMON JUICE
14 TABLESPOONS UNSALTED BUTTER
1   BUNCH CHIVES, FINELY CHOPPED

TROUT AND FLAGEOLET BEANS MAKE A FLA-VORFUL COMBINATION. FRESH HARICOT BEANS FOR SHELLING, INCLUDING GREEN FLAGEOLET BEANS, REIGN OVER THE MARKETS FROM JULY TO OCTOBER. IT IS SAID THAT THE FIRST BEANS CULTIVATED IN FRANCE WERE GIVEN BY POPE CLEMENT VII TO HIS NIECE CATHERINE DE

PREPARE THE BEANS: If using dried flageolet beans, soak overnight in a large bowl with water to cover by 3 inches. Drain and rinse beans.

Place fresh or soaked, dried beans in a large saucepan with water to cover. Add carrot, onion, and bouquet garni and cook over medium high heat until tender, about 40 minutes for fresh beans and 1 hour for dried. Remove and discard carrot, onion, and bouquet garni.

While beans cook, preheat oven to 300 degrees. Puree salmon trout in a food processor. Strain puree through a fine-mesh strainer into a bowl. Using a wooden spoon, beat in egg whites until thoroughly incorporated. Season with ½ teaspoon salt, ¼ teaspoon pepper, and cayenne. Gradually beat in cream in a thin stream until thoroughly incorporated. (If you prefer, mousse can be made in food processor.)

Butter four 1-cup ramekins or dariole molds and fill with the trout mixture. Place molds in a hot water bath and bake until a skewer inserted in the center comes out clean, about 15 minutes.

PREPARE THE LEMON BUTTER: Bring lemon juice to a boil in a small nonreactive saucepan. Reduce heat to medium and whisk in butter, 1 tablespoon at a time, until sauce is thick and creamy. Drain beans and add to sauce to reheat. Stir in three-fourths of the chives and season to taste with salt and pepper.

TO SERVE: Unmold trout mousses onto 4 heated serving plates. Spoon beans and butter sauce around mousses and garnish each serving with remaining chopped chives. *Makes 4 servings.*

MEDICIS AT THE TIME OF HER MARRIAGE TO HENRI II.

AUTUMN FRUITS

THE FOUR FRUITS WHICH HOLD THE PLACE OF HONOR IN THE AUTUMN FRUIT BASKET ARE SOME OF THE OLDEST IN THE WORLD, AND WERE ALREADY PART OF OUR ANCESTORS' DIET SEVERAL THOUSAND YEARS AGO. GRAPES, APPLES, WAL-NUTS, AND FIGS ARE ALL REFERRED TO IN THE BIBLE AND THROUGHOUT HISTORY, ALTHOUGH THE FRUITS OUR ANCESTORS CONSUMED WOULD HAVE BORNE LITTLE RESEMBLANCE TO THOSE WE EAT TODAY.

DOUBLE APPLES WITH LEMON AND CINNAMON
DOUBLE POMME AU CITRON ET A LA CANNELLE

4   MEDIUM GOLDEN DELICIOUS APPLES,
      RINSED AND HALVED CROSSWISE
½   CUP GRANULATED SUGAR
      GRATED ZEST OF 2 LEMONS, BLANCHED
2   MEDIUM GRANNY SMITH APPLES,
      PEELED, CORED, AND GRATED
3   TABLESPOONS HEAVY CREAM

2   EGG YOLKS
      PINCH OF SALT
      PINCH OF GROUND CINNAMON
2   TABLESPOONS UNSALTED BUTTER, CUT
      INTO BITS
      BROWN SUGAR (OPTIONAL)
      POWDERED SUGAR

Preheat oven to 400 degrees. Remove the core and seeds from halved apples, cutting a cavity large enough to hold filling. Place apples, cut side up, in a buttered baking dish. Sprinkle with 6 tablespoons granulated sugar. Pour ¼ cup water into bottom of dish. Bake for 10 minutes. Leave oven on.

Meanwhile, in a bowl, combine lemon zest, grated apples, remaining 2 tablespoons granulated sugar, cream, egg yolks, salt, and cinnamon.

Stuff apple cavities with mixture and dot with bits of butter. Sprinkle with brown sugar if desired. Bake until the tops are golden amber, 15 to 20 minutes. Sprinkle with powdered sugar. Serve hot or cold. *Makes 8 servings.*

APPLES, THE MOST PLANTED FRUIT IN THE WORLD, COME IN SEVERAL THOUSAND VARIETIES, WHICH ARE THE SUBJECT OF INSURMOUNTABLE DEBATES BETWEEN CONNOISSEURS FAVORING ANCIENT KINDS AND THOSE WHO PREFER MODERN APPLES. DELICATE IN ITS SIMPLICITY BUT ALLURINGLY RUSTIC, THIS DESSERT COMBINES GOLDEN DELICIOUS WITH GRANNY SMITH APPLES AND COULD BE SERVED WITH A VANILLA-SCENTED SAUCE. HERE THE COOKED APPLES SIT ON A MOUSTIER PLATE IN FRONT OF A TAPESTRY.

ROASTED PEARS WITH MERINGUES AND BLACKBERRY SAUCE

POIRE ROTIE AUX ILES FLOTTANTES ET AUX MURES

THESE ROASTED PEARS SERVED WITH AN ENTICING BLACKBERRY SAUCE OFFER A PLEASANT UNION OF FLAVORS AND TEXTURES. THE ROASTED PEARS COULD ALSO BE SERVED WITH PISTACHIO, CARAMEL, OR VANILLA ICE CREAM. THE EXPRESSION *ENTRE LA POIRE ET LA FROMAGE* (BETWEEN THE PEAR AND THE CHEESE, OR BEFORE DESSERT) COMES FROM THE TIME WHEN A SWEET DESSERT

WAS SERVED BEFORE PASSING THE CHEESE PLATE, AS IS STILL DONE IN ENGLAND.

PEARS
3   TABLESPOONS UNSALTED BUTTER
4   MEDIUM PEARS, PEELED, CORED, AND QUARTERED LENGTHWISE

MERINGUES
4   EGG WHITES, AT ROOM TEMPERATURE
½   CUP GRANULATED SUGAR
½   CUP POWDERED SUGAR
   ALL-PURPOSE FLOUR AND SOFTENED BUTTER FOR BAKING SHEET

BLACKBERRY SAUCE
3   CUPS BLACKBERRIES, WASHED AND DRAINED
1   TABLESPOON POWDERED SUGAR
   JUICE OF ½ LEMON
   WHOLE BLACKBERRIES FOR GARNISH (OPTIONAL)

PREPARE THE PEARS: Preheat oven to 450 degrees. Melt butter in an ovenproof casserole or baking dish large enough to hold pears. Add pears and brown over medium heat, turning often to color evenly, about 10 minutes. Transfer to oven and cook until tender, about 7 minutes.

PREPARE THE MERINGUES: Preheat oven to 200 degrees. In a large bowl (preferably copper), combine egg whites with a small pinch of granulated sugar. Beat with a wire whisk until soft peaks form, about 5 minutes. Gradually add remaining granulated and powdered sugars and beat until stiff.

Butter and flour a large baking sheet. Fit a pastry bag with a ¼-inch round tip and fill with meringue. Pipe out small mounds about the size of a quarter. Bake until lightly browned and dry, about 45 minutes.

PREPARE THE BLACKBERRY SAUCE: Combine blackberries, powdered sugar, and lemon juice in a food processor and puree until liquid, about 30 seconds. Strain into a bowl through a fine-mesh sieve and reserve. (The recipe can be prepared ahead to this point.)

TO SERVE: Spread a small amount of sauce over each of 4 individual serving plates. Alternate pears with small meringues. Decorate with fresh blackberries if desired. *Makes 4 servings.*

FIG SOUP WITH CITRUS JUICE AND MINT

SOUPE DE FIGUES VIOLETTES AU SUC D'AGRUMES ET A LA MENTHE

1½ POUNDS FRESH FIGS (12 TO 24, DEPENDING ON SIZE)
1   CUP FRESHLY SQUEEZED ORANGE JUICE
1   CUP FRESHLY SQUEEZED GRAPEFRUIT JUICE
1   CUP LEMON JUICE
1½ CUPS SUGAR
1   SMALL BUNCH MINT

Peel figs being careful to retain their shape.

Combine citrus juices and sugar in a medium nonreactive saucepan. Bring to a boil over medium high heat, stirring to dissolve sugar.

Plunge peeled figs into boiling liquid and immediately remove from heat. Let cool completely. Refrigerate for at least 2 hours.

Serve in glass compote dishes, sprinkled with several mint leaves.
Makes 4 servings.

THE PORCH ENTRANCE OF THE SMALL MEDIEVAL CITY OF PEROUGES IN THE DOMBES REGION FRAMES THE STREET BEYOND. THE FRESH FIG IS FOUND IN MARKETS FROM JULY UNTIL THE END OF OCTOBER, BUT HAS A BRIEF LIFE OF ONLY 24 HOURS. VERY RICH IN SUGARS, THE FIG WAS FOR A LONG TIME USED TO SWEETEN FOOD; IT ALSO CONTAINS VITAMINS AND MINERAL SALTS, WHICH MADE IT THE FAVORITE FOOD OF ANCIENT GREEK ATHLETES. IT IS ALSO SAID THAT THE FIG AIDS DIGESTION, WHICH EXPLAINS THE CUSTOM OF EATING FIGS AT THE BEGINNING OF A MEAL, SOMETIMES WITH THIN SLICES OF BAYONNE OR PARMA HAM.

COOKIES WITH FRESH FIGS AND QUINCE
FEUILLANTINE DE FIGUES FRAICHES AU COING

FRESH FIGS ARE COMBINED WITH A QUINCE SAUCE IN THIS APPEALING DESSERT. THE QUINCE ONCE PLAYED THE ROLE OF "WELCOMING FRUIT," FOR IN THE MIDDLE AGES IT WAS OFFERED TO KINGS AND QUEENS WHEN THEY VISITED THE CITIES OF THEIR KINGDOM. THIS PEAR-SHAPED FRUIT WITH A HARD, TART FLESH IS NEVER EATEN RAW, AND IS MOST OFTEN MADE INTO COMPOTES,

JELLIES, OR PRESERVES. IT CAN ALSO BE USED IN ICE CREAM OR SHERBET. THE QUINCE IS NOT PEELED; BEFORE COOKING ONE NEED ONLY TO RUB IT TO REMOVE THE COTTONY DOWN THAT COVERS IT.

COOKIE LEAVES
- ⅔ CUP GRANULATED SUGAR
- ¾ ALL-PURPOSE FLOUR
- ½ CUP UNSALTED BUTTER, MELTED
- 4 EGG WHITES

FIGS AND QUINCE
- 1 POUND FIGS (12 TO 24, DEPENDING ON SIZE)
- 4 TABLESPOONS UNSALTED BUTTER, CUT INTO BITS
- ¾ CUP HEAVY CREAM
- 1 TABLESPOON POWDERED SUGAR, PLUS ADDITIONAL FOR DECORATION
- JUICE OF 1 ORANGE
- 2 CUPS GRANULATED SUGAR
- 1 VANILLA BEAN
- 4 TO 6 MEDIUM QUINCES, PEELED, SEEDED, AND QUARTERED

PREPARE THE COOKIE LEAVES: In a large bowl, combine sugar and flour. Add melted butter and stir well with a wooden spoon. Slowly incorporate the egg whites until a smooth batter is formed. Let mixture chill in refrigerator for at least 2 hours.

Preheat oven to 400 degrees. Lightly butter a large cookie sheet. Spread batter into thin 3- to 4-inch rounds with the back of a spoon, using ½ teaspoon batter for cookie. (The rounds should be almost transparent when spread out on the sheet.) Bake until golden brown, 3 to 5 minutes. Watch carefully as these cookies burn easily. Immediately remove to cool on wire racks. *Makes about 48.*

PREPARE THE FIGS AND QUINCE: Preheat oven to 450 degrees. Cut an X on the top of each fig. Place in a buttered baking dish and dot with pieces of butter. Bake for 5 minutes. Remove and drain on paper towels.

In a large bowl, lightly whip cream. Add powdered sugar and beat until soft peaks form. Add orange juice and beat just until mixed. Refrigerate until ready to assemble dish.

In a large saucepan, bring sugar and 4 cups water to a boil over medium high heat. Add vanilla bean. Stir just to dissolve sugar. Reduce heat and add quinces. Poach until tender, 30 to 45 minutes. Remove from heat and allow fruit to cool in liquid, at least 1 hour. Remove vanilla bean. Pour fruit and liquid into a food processor and puree until smooth, about 1 minute. Scrape into a bowl and reserve in a cool spot until ready to assemble dish. (The recipe can be prepared ahead to this point.)

ASSEMBLE THE DISH: Open cooked figs and carefully dig out pulp with a small spoon. On 4 individual serving plates, place a small amount of orange-flavored whipped cream. Add a spoonful of the fig pulp and cover with a thin cookie leaf. Top with a dollop of whipped cream, then another spoonful of fig, and another cookie. Continue this procedure until the plate is attractively layered with stacked cookies and cream, using 4 cookies for each serving. Dust with powdered sugar. Surround the bottom of the serving plate with the quince sauce. Serve immediately. *Makes 4 servings.*

PEAR CHARLOTTE WITH FRESH FIGS
CHARLOTTE A LA POIRE ET AUX FIGUES FRAICHES

PEAR CHARLOTTE
2 MEDIUM PEARS, PEELED, CORED, AND QUARTERED
⅔ CUP SUGAR
1 TABLESPOON LEMON JUICE
1 ENVELOPE UNFLAVORED GELATIN
⅔ CUP HEAVY CREAM, SLIGHTLY WHIPPED
FIG SAUCE
½ POUND FRESH FIGS (4 TO 8, DEPENDING ON SIZE)
JUICE OF ½ LEMON
JUICE OF 1 ORANGE
1 TABLESPOON GRENADINE
1 TABLESPOON SUGAR
ASSEMBLY
2 TABLESPOONS UNSALTED BUTTER
8 TO 12 FRESH FIGS, CUT INTO THIN SLICES

PREPARE THE PEAR CHARLOTTE: Place quartered pears in a medium saucepan and add water to cover. Simmer over medium heat until tender, about 15 minutes. Drain well. Place pears in a food processor and puree about 30 seconds. You will have about ¾ cup.

In a medium saucepan, mix pear puree with sugar. Bring to a boil over medium high heat. Stir in lemon juice. Set aside to cool for 10 minutes.

Sprinkle gelatin over puree and let dissolve for 5 minutes. Stir well. Set aside to cool completely.

Fold in lightly whipped cream. Cover and refrigerate until ready to assemble dish.

PREPARE THE FIG SAUCE: Carefully peel figs. Combine figs, lemon and orange juices, grenadine, and sugar in a food processor and puree until liquid and smooth, about 30 seconds.

ASSEMBLY: Lightly butter four 6-ounce ramekins. Melt butter in a small skillet over medium high heat. Working in batches if necessary, quickly cook fig slices for about 30 seconds on each side. Drain and cool on paper towels. Line molds with fig slices.

Divide charlotte mixture among molds. Chill overnight in the refrigerator.

TO SERVE: Unmold charlottes onto 4 individual serving plates. Surround with fig sauce. Decorate with additional slices of fresh fig if desired. *Makes 4 servings.*

PEARS AND FIGS PROVIDE A GOOD SEASONAL MARRIAGE OF TASTES. WHILE PEARS BEGIN TO APPEAR DURING THE SUMMER, THEY ARE A QUINTESSENTIAL AUTUMN FRUIT. PEAR CHARLOTTE, ALONG WITH PEARS BELLE-HELENE, PEARS IN WINE, AND PEAR GRANITE, IS ONE OF THE CLASSIC PREPARATIONS OF THIS FRUIT. STORED IN A DARK BUT WELL-AERATED CELLAR, PEARS CAN KEEP FOR SEVERAL MONTHS.

NOUGAT WITH ALMONDS, HAZELNUTS, AND GREEN PISTACHIOS
NOUGAT AUX AMANDES, AUX NOISETTES, ET AUX PISTACHES VERTES

WHILE HAZELNUTS AND ALMONDS MAY BOTH BE EATEN FRESH WHEN THEY RIPEN DURING THE SUMMER, THEY ARE OFTEN USED DRIED IN BOTH DESSERTS AND SAVORY DISHES. THE CUT SQUARES OF THIS NOUGAT CAN BE DIPPED IN MELTED CHOCOLATE. CHOPPED CANDIED FRUIT CAN BE SUBSTITUTED FOR THE HAZELNUTS IF DESIRED.

3	EGG WHITES	2½ CUPS ROASTED SLICED ALMONDS
2	CUPS POWDERED SUGAR	2½ CUPS HAZELNUTS, SKINS REMOVED AND
1	VANILLA BEAN, SPLIT LENGTHWISE	COARSELY CHOPPED
2	CUPS HONEY	
1½	CUPS UNSALTED GREEN PISTACHIOS,	
	SHELLED AND SKINNED	

In a large nonreactive bowl, mix together egg whites, sugar, vanilla bean, and honey. Place over a saucepan of simmering water and whisk vigorously for 30 to 45 minutes, or until the mass turns white, becomes thick, and takes on body. Use a wooden spoon if it becomes too difficult to work.

Stir in nuts. Turn nougat out onto a buttered work surface, preferably marble. Use 4 wooden rulers to make square borders and to prevent the nougat from spreading thin at edges. Alternatively, turn nougat out into a small buttered jelly-roll pan. Spread top of nougat smooth with a rolling pin. Let cool for 1 hour.

Cut into perfect squares with a ruler and sharp paring knife.

THIS SPLENDID GRANITE IS A FITTING HOMAGE TO THE GRAPE, THE FRUIT WHOSE FLAVOR, FRAGRANCE, AND COLOR IS AN EMBODIMENT OF THE SEASON. PERSONALLY, I SUGGEST INCORPORATING THE ICE INTO A COMPOSITION OF SEVERAL DESSERTS THAT CAN HARMONIOUSLY COMPLETE A MEAL.

GRAPE AND RED WINE ICE
GRANITE DE MUSCAT AU PINOT ROUGE

½	BOTTLE STRONG RED WINE (PREFERABLY BURGUNDY)	1 TABLESPOON CREME DE CASSIS (OPTIONAL)
1½	CUPS SUGAR	1 SMALL BUNCH GRAPES, HALVED AND
	ZEST OF 3 ORANGES	SEEDED FOR DECORATION
2	CUPS WHITE OR RED GRAPE JUICE	
	JUICE OF 1 LEMON	

Combine wine, sugar, and orange zest in a medium, nonreactive saucepan. Bring to a boil over medium high heat. Remove and let cool. Place grape juice in a large bowl. Pour wine mixture through a fine-mesh strainer into bowl. Add the lemon juice and crème de cassis and mix well. Chill several hours. Pour into an ice cream maker and freeze according to manufacturer's directions.

Serve in chilled tulip-shaped glasses. Garnish with grape halves. *Makes 8 servings.*

MELI-MELO WITH PRUNE SAUCE AND BASIL ICE CREAM

MELI-MELO DE FRUITS D'AUTOMNE AU COULIS DE PRUNEAUX ET A LA GLACE BASILIC

BASIL ICE CREAM
2 CUPS MILK
½ VANILLA BEAN
1 BUNCH BASIL, WASHED, DRIED, AND
  COARSELY CHOPPED
4 EGG YOLKS
1 CUP SUGAR
PRUNE SAUCE
12 PITTED PRUNES, SOAKED IN WATER FOR
  24 HOURS
½ CUP SUGAR
1 CUP STRONG RED WINE
1 CINNAMON STICK
  ZEST OF 4 ORANGES
  ZEST OF 4 LEMONS

1 TEA BAG
  JUICE OF 1 LEMON
MELI-MELO
1 PINEAPPLE
2 BANANAS
8 TO 12 FRESH FIGS
4 WALNUTS
4 SMALL PEACHES
2 MEDIUM PEARS
1 BUNCH GREEN OR PURPLE GRAPES
  CANDIED ORANGE PEEL (OPTIONAL)
  OTHER FRUITS, ACCORDING TO
   AVAILABILITY
  SPRIGS OF BASIL

A MELI-MELO, OR MIXTURE, OF SEASONAL FRUIT SITS BY THE WATERFALL THAT ESCAPES THROUGH THE SLUICES OF THE MILL CONVERT. WHILE PINEAPPLES AND BANANAS ARE BOTH IMPORTED FRUITS, THEY OCCUPY AN IMPORTANT PLACE IN FRENCH CUISINE. LOUIS XV, THE FIRST PERSON TO EAT A PINEAPPLE IN FRANCE AFTER IT WAS BROUGHT BACK FROM BRAZIL BY A FRENCHMAN, RESTRICTED ITS CONSUMPTION TO THE ROYAL TABLE FOR A LONG TIME.

PREPARE THE BASIL ICE CREAM: Bring milk, vanilla bean, and basil to a boil in a medium saucepan. Remove from heat, cover, and let infuse for 10 to 15 minutes.

Meanwhile, in a large heatproof bowl, whisk egg yolks and sugar until thick and creamy; the mixture should form a ribbon when whisk is lifted.

Pour infused milk into egg mixture and mix well. Pour back into saucepan and cook over low heat, stirring constantly with a wooden spoon, until a finger drawn across the back of the spoon leaves a trace, 5 to 7 minutes. Strain and set aside to cool completely.

Place ice cream custard in an ice cream maker and freeze according to manufacturer's directions. Scrape into a container and freeze until ready to assemble the dessert.

PREPARE THE PRUNE SAUCE: Drain prunes. In a medium saucepan, combine sugar, wine, cinnamon stick, and orange and lemon zests. Bring to a boil over medium high heat. Add prunes and cook for 5 minutes. Add tea bag, remove from heat, and let infuse for 5 minutes.

With a slotted spoon, transfer prunes to a food processor; reserve cooking liquid. Puree prunes until smooth, about 1 minute. Add small amounts of cooking liquid and continue processing to make a thin, pourable sauce. Add lemon juice to taste. Refrigerate sauce until ready to use.

ASSEMBLE THE MELI-MELO: Peel and cut seasonal fruits into bite-size pieces. Decoratively arrange fruit on 8 large plates. Place a large scoop of basil ice cream in the center of each plate. Pour the prune sauce between the fruits. Sprinkle with candied orange peel, if desired, and garnish the ice cream with sprigs of basil. Serve immediately. *Makes 8 servings.*

POACHED PEARS FILLED WITH CHOCOLATE
POIRE WILLIAM FARCIE AU CHOCOLAT AMER

A PEAR FILLED WITH BITTER CHOCOLATE SITS IN THIS FALL GARDEN AT EUGENIE-LES-BAINS IN THE REGION CALLED "LES LANDES." THE PEAR HAS VARIOUS HEALTH-INDUCING PROPERTIES. SUFFERERS OF HYPERTENSION HAVE EVEN BEEN KNOWN TO TAKE A "PEAR CURE" OF UP TO THREE POUNDS PER DAY TO REDUCE ARTERIAL TENSION.

1½ CUPS SUGAR
   JUICE OF 1 LEMON
4 MEDIUM PEARS, PEELED WITH THE
   STEM INTACT
¾ CUP HEAVY CREAM

8 OUNCES SEMISWEET CHOCOLATE,
   GRATED
1 CUP CREME ANGLAISE (SEE APPENDIX)
1 CUP GREEN PISTACHIOS, SHELLED,
   SKINNED, AND CHOPPED

In a deep nonreactive saucepan, bring sugar and 4 cups water to a boil. Add lemon juice and pears, reduce heat and poach pears until soft but not mushy, about 30 minutes. Remove from heat and allow pears to cool in syrup. Cover and chill overnight.

In a heavy nonreactive saucepan, bring cream to a boil. Remove from heat and stir in chocolate until melted completely, about 5 minutes. Set ganache aside in a cool place until ready to use.

Drain pears well on paper towels. Carefully cut off the top part of each pear closest to stem (about one-fourth the height of pear) and reserve. With a small spoon or melon-ball cutter, make a large cavity in the bottom part of each pear.

Carefully warm chocolate ganache over barely simmering water, stirring until the consistency is soft and spreadable. Fit a pastry bag with a ¼-inch star tip and fill each pear with ganache. Allow chocolate to overflow slightly. Replace reserved top part of pear.

Pour a small amount of crème anglaise on the bottom of 4 individual shallow dessert bowls. Carefully place a filled pear in the center of each. Garnish with chopped pistachios. *Makes 4 servings.*

VANILLA CRISPS WITH APPLES AND CIDER
CROQUANT A LA VANILLE ET POMME AU CIDRE

GRANITE
⅓ CUP POWDERED SUGAR
1 CUP DRY APPLE CIDER

APPLE JUICE
1 MEDIUM GRANNY SMITH APPLE, PEELED AND CORED
1 TABLESPOON POWDERED SUGAR
JUICE OF 1 LEMON

COOKIES
⅔ CUP UNSALTED BUTTER, SOFTENED
1¼ CUPS POWDERED SUGAR

1½ CUPS ALL-PURPOSE FLOUR
4 EGG WHITES

VANILLA PASTRY CREAM
1 CUP MILK
1 VANILLA BEAN, HALVED LENGTHWISE
3 EGG YOLKS
¼ CUP GRANULATED SUGAR
2 TABLESPOONS ALL-PURPOSE FLOUR
PINCH OF SALT
½ CUP HEAVY CREAM, WHIPPED

PREPARE THE GRANITE: Dissolve sugar in cider. Add ½ cup water and pour into an ice cream maker. Freeze according to manufacturer's directions. Alternatively, pour into an ice tray and place in freezer. Stir every hour or so until consistency is slushy but firm, 8 to 10 hours. Keep frozen until ready to use.

PREPARE THE JUICE: Cut apples into large pieces. Place in a juice extractor that works by centrifugal process. Extract as much juice as possible. Add sugar and lemon juice. Cover and chill in the refrigerator.

PREPARE THE COOKIES: In a large bowl, blend softened butter with powdered sugar. Slowly incorporate flour. Add egg whites, little by little, until a smooth batter is formed. Whisk well. Cover and chill in the refrigerator overnight.

Preheat oven to 350 degrees. Butter a large baking sheet. Spread out batter into thin 4-inch rounds, using about ½ teaspoon of batter per cookie. (The rounds should be almost transparent when spread on the sheet.) Bake for 3 to 5 minutes, watching carefully to avoid burning, until golden brown. Remove from baking sheet and form into cylinders by wrapping still warm cookies around a dowel, broomstick handle, or cannoli mold. Work quickly, as the cookies become brittle in a matter of seconds. Return cookies to oven for a few seconds if they become too brittle. Store cookies in an airtight container until ready to fill.

PREPARE THE VANILLA PASTRY CREAM: In a medium saucepan, scald milk with vanilla bean. In a heatproof bowl, combine egg yolks, granulated sugar, flour, and salt. Stir until smooth. Slowly add hot milk. Return to saucepan and bring to a boil over medium high heat, stirring constantly with a wooden spoon. Boil for 1 minute. Remove vanilla bean. Pour cream into a buttered baking dish and set aside to cool completely.

When completely cool, fold in whipped cream. Refrigerate until ready to use.

ASSEMBLY: Pipe or spoon cold vanilla cream into cookies. Place a spoonful of granité in the middle of 4 individual serving plates. Attractively arrange filled cookies around each mound. Use apple juice to fill in spaces between the filled cookies. *Makes 4 servings.*

IN LATIN *POMUM* MEANS FRUIT; THE FACT THAT IN FRENCH *POMME* BECAME THE WORD FOR APPLE SHOWS JUST HOW CENTRAL THIS FRUIT IS TO FRENCH CUISINE. THE ANCIENT GAULS MADE CIDER FROM IT, A PRACTICE THAT HAS BEEN PERPETUATED IN NORMANDY THROUGH TO THE PRESENT. THE GRANNY SMITH APPLE, USED TO MAKE THE APPLE JUICE IN THIS RECIPE, IS CRISPER AND MORE ACIDULATED THAN OTHER VARIETIES AND IS OFTEN USED IN FRUIT SALADS. THE RANGE OF POSSIBLE DESSERTS MADE WITH APPLES IS ENORMOUS—FROM *TARTE AUX POMMES* TO *POMMES SOUFFLES*.

PAPILLOTE OF BANANAS
AND GREEN FIGS WITH RUM

PAPILLOTE ALEXANDRE A LA BANANE ET AUX FIGUES VERTES

4	SMALL BANANAS	2	TABLESPOONS UNSALTED BUTTER
8	RIPE GREEN FIGS	2	TABLESPOONS UNSALTED BUTTER,
¼	CUP SUGAR		MELTED
¼	CUP RUM OR OTHER SPIRIT		

Preheat oven to 450 degrees. Peel bananas and cut into diagonal slices. Cut out 4 large heart shapes of parchment paper that measure 15 inches at widest part. Fold hearts in half to make a crease down the center. Fan out banana slices on one side of parchment near the crease.

Peel figs. Make a ½-inch-deep X in top of each one. Place 2 figs on each parchment heart, next to bananas. Sprinkle fruits with sugar and drizzle with rum. Place ½ tablespoon of butter on each portion.

Brush the free side of each heart lightly with water. Brush rims of hearts with melted butter. To close papillotes, fold loose side of heart over fruit and fold the border onto itself 3 times. Fold over in tiny pleats to seal.

Place papillotes on a baking sheet and bake until puffed and lightly browned, about 6 minutes. Place a papillote on each of 4 serving plates. Cut a small X in top of each one to facilitate opening. Let guests open their own. *Makes 4 servings.*

THE GERANIUMS ARE ALREADY SHELTERED FOR THE WINTER WHILE A PARCHMENT PAPILLOTE LIES AMIDST THE VIRGINIA CREEPER ON A BRIDGE OVER THE VEYLE RIVER. ONCE THESE PAPILLOTES ARE CUT OPEN, STRAINED FRESH RASPBERRY PUREE CAN BE POURED INSIDE TO COMPLEMENT THE FLAVOR OF THE COOKED FRUITS. THE FRUIT OF THE BANANA TREE, WHICH AN OLD LEGEND FROM SRI LANKA ASSERTS IS THE TRUE FORBIDDEN FRUIT, HAS BEEN KNOWN TO THE FRENCH SINCE THE RENAISSANCE.

W   I   N

T E R

WINTER VEGETABLES

THE GREAT FROZEN AND DESERTED PARK OF
WINTER IS ALSO THE GARDENER'S SEASON OF
ENJOYMENT RATHER THAN LABOR. BUT NEITHER
THE KITCHEN GARDEN NOR THE ORCHARD IS
COMPLETELY ASLEEP DURING THESE LONG, DARK
MONTHS. CERTAIN HARDY VEGETABLES RESIST THE
SEASON'S RIGORS WHILE OTHERS ADAPT TO THE
COLD EARTH. THE HARVEST OF NATURE'S PRO-
DUCE AND THE POSSIBILITIES FOR A NATURAL
CUISINE CONTINUE.

BRANDADE OF CELERY AND FENNEL
BRANDADE AU CELERI ET AU FENOUIL

1 MEDIUM CELERY ROOT (CELERIAC, ABOUT 1½ POUNDS), PEELED AND CUT INTO QUARTERS
2 FENNEL BULBS (ABOUT 1½ POUNDS), TRIMMED AND QUARTERED
2 LARGE WHITE-FLESHED POTATOES (1 POUND), PEELED AND QUARTERED
JUICE OF 1 LEMON

4 CLOVES GARLIC, MINCED
⅓ CUP OLIVE OIL
⅔ CUP HEAVY CREAM
1 STAR ANISE
SALT AND FRESHLY GROUND PEPPER
2 TABLESPOONS MINCED PARSLEY
2 SLICES FINE-TEXTURED WHITE BREAD, HALVED DIAGONALLY

Place celery root, fennel, and potatoes in a steamer. Sprinkle with half the lemon juice. Steam over boiling water until tender, about 20 minutes. Drain well.

Meanwhile, in a small skillet, sauté garlic in the olive oil over low heat for about 3 minutes; do not allow to brown. Heat cream in a small saucepan over low heat for 3 to 5 minutes.

Place the star anise in a spice grinder or coffee grinder and reduce to a fine powder.

Place steamed vegetables in a food processor. Set aside 1 tablespoon of oil used for garlic. Turn on processor and slowly add hot olive oil and garlic, processing until smooth and creamy, about 1 minute.

Pour puree into a large mixing bowl. Add hot cream and blend well. Season with powdered star anise, salt, pepper, and remaining lemon juice.

Heat reserved 1 tablespoon oil in a small skillet. When oil is very hot, add bread and brown quickly on both sides; drain croutons on paper towels.

Stir parsley into vegetable puree. Pour into a heatproof serving dish and smooth top. Place croutons on top. Serve hot. *Makes 4 servings.*

THE RENEWED INTEREST IN A NATURAL CUISINE, WHICH IS BOTH INNOVATIVE AND LOOKS WITH A NEW EYE AT TRADITIONAL FOODS, HAS SEEN TO THE REDISCOVERY OF FENNEL. THIS VEGETABLE BULB, WITH A SWEET, ANISELIKE TASTE, WAS BECOMING QUITE RARE UNTIL SEVERAL YEARS AGO. A TRADITIONAL FRENCH BRANDADE CONSISTS OF SOAKED, COOKED SALT COD

POUNDED WITH OLIVE OIL, POTATOES, AND GARLIC. THIS RECIPE EVOKES A SIMILAR TASTE AND TEXTURE YET USES ONLY VEGETABLES.

POTATO FRITTERS WITH TRUFFLES
BEIGNET DE POMME DE TERRE A LA TRUFFE

BUTTER SAUCE

1   CUP DRY WHITE WINE
2   MEDIUM SHALLOTS, MINCED
6   TABLESPOONS UNSALTED BUTTER, CUT INTO SMALL PIECES
⅛   TEASPOON CURRY POWDER
   JUICE OF ½ LEMON
   SALT AND FRESHLY GROUND PEPPER
   TRUFFLE JUICE (OPTIONAL)

FRITTERS

3   MEDIUM BOILING POTATOES (ABOUT 1 POUND), PEELED AND QUARTERED

¼   CUP MILK
3   TABLESPOONS POTATO STARCH
3   WHOLE EGGS
3   EGG WHITES
1   TO 3 TABLESPOONS HEAVY CREAM
   SALT AND FRESHLY GROUND PEPPER
1   CUP CLARIFIED BUTTER
   WHOLE FRESH TRUFFLES (ABOUT ⅓ OUNCE PER PERSON), CUT INTO THIN SLICES; RESERVE A FEW AND CUT INTO JULIENNE

PREPARE THE BUTTER SAUCE: In a nonreactive small saucepan, combine wine and shallots. Cook over medium high heat until less than 1 tablespoon liquid remains. Whisk in pieces of butter, little by little, working on and off heat as necessary, until butter is incorporated and emulsified. Add curry, lemon juice, and salt and pepper to taste. Season with a small amount of truffle juice, if desired. Set aside and keep warm.

PREPARE THE FRITTERS: Place potatoes in a large saucepan with salted water to cover. Cook until tender, about 20 minutes. Drain well and return potatoes to pan. Add milk and mash potatoes well. Pass puree through a fine-mesh sieve or work through a food mill to remove lumps. Stir in potato starch with a wooden spoon. One at a time, add whole eggs; add egg whites. Beat in enough cream, 1 tablespoon at a time, until batter is consistency of thick pastry cream. (Do not add the 3 tablespoons of cream all at once. Make a test by cooking a small amount of batter and eventually adding more cream, if necessary, to thin it.) Season batter with salt and pepper.

Heat a small amount of clarified butter until very hot in a large cast-iron skillet over medium heat. Pour in 1 tablespoon batter. Immediately place 1 truffle slice in the center of each round. As soon as truffle slice has penetrated into batter, turn over to cook on other side. (The fritters cook quickly; be careful not to let them dry out.) Drain slightly on paper towels before placing on individual serving plates. Continue making fritters, 6 or 7 at a time, until all of batter is used.

Place 2 or 3 fritters on each plate. Decorate with truffle julienne. Surround with a small amount of warm butter sauce. Serve warm. *Makes 10 servings.*

A WINTER GARDEN IN THE REGION OF PONT D'AIN LIES IN THE SHADOW OF THE FIRST FOOTHILLS OF THE BUGEY REGION. TRUFFLES AND POTATOES MAKE AN EXCELLENT COMBINATION OF TASTES AND FLAVORS, FITTING TO THIS SEASON, SINCE TRUFFLES ARE AT THEIR PEAK DURING THE WINTER. SUBSTITUTE THIN SLICES OF FRESH SALMON IF PREPARING THIS RECIPE DURING A SEASON WHEN FRESH TRUFFLES ARE DIFFICULT TO FIND. PLACE TWO PAPER THIN SALMON SLICES ON EACH FRITTER AFTER IT HAS BEEN TURNED OVER. THE FISH WILL COOK IN THE REMAINING MINUTE OR SO IT TAKES FOR THE FRITTER TO CONTINUE BROWNING ON THE SECOND SIDE. INTERSPERSE ROWS OF CAVIAR BETWEEN THE SLICES TO GARNISH IF DESIRED. THE FRITTERS CAN BE USED FOR DESSERT AS WELL IF SPRINKLED WITH A SMALL AMOUNT OF POWDERED SUGAR.

CORN FRITTERS
CREPE DE MAIS

CORN FRITTERS (PICTURED ON PAGE 266) SIZZLE IN THEIR FRYING PAN WHILE CLARIFIED BUTTER, USED IN THIS RECIPE AS WELL AS IN MANY OTHER DISHES, FILLS A BIG EARTHENWARE POT (PAGE 267). THE FRENCH HAVE ONLY RECENTLY BEGUN TO EAT FRESH SWEET CORN WITH ITS LIGHT, TENDER KERNELS; FRESH CORN MUST BE EATEN VERY QUICKLY AFTER IT HAS BEEN

BOUGHT—OTHERWISE THE SUGARS THAT SWEETEN THE CORN BEGIN TO TURN TO STARCH. THIS GARDEN HOUSE IS AT VAREY IN THE BUGEY REGION.

1½ CUPS FRESH CORN KERNELS		2	WHOLE EGGS
2	CUPS MILK	1	EGG WHITE
2	MEDIUM POTATOES, PEELED AND QUARTERED	1	TABLESPOON HEAVY CREAM
		1	CUP CLARIFIED BUTTER
3	TABLESPOONS ALL-PURPOSE FLOUR	1	CUP *BEURRE BATTU* (SEE APPENDIX)
	SALT		CHOPPED FRESH HERBS FOR GARNISH

Place corn in a medium saucepan and pour in 1 cup milk. Cook over medium heat until done, about 10 minutes. Drain well.

Meanwhile, cook potatoes in salted boiling water until soft, about 20 minutes. Drain and mash with the back of a large spoon. Add remaining 1 cup milk. Let mixture cool.

Strain potatoes and milk through a fine-mesh sieve into a large mixing bowl, working the pulp through to make a puree. Place flour in a small sieve and sprinkle over puree. Add salt and stir. One at a time, whisk in whole eggs. Add egg whites and cream. The batter should be the consistency of thick custard sauce. Sprinkle on an additional 1 to 2 tablespoons flour to thicken if needed.

Just before serving, heat 4 to 5 tablespoons clarified butter in a large cast-iron skillet over moderately high heat. When very hot, pour in ¼- to ⅓-cup batter to form 4-inch crêpes. Immediately sprinkle on a large pinch of corn. Turn at once with a spatula, taking care as crêpes are very delicate. The crêpes cook almost instantly. Add more clarified butter as needed and repeat crêpe-making process. Drain on paper towels; keep warm.

Serve 2 crêpes per person on warmed serving plates. Surround with a ribbon of *beurre battu*. Garnish with chopped fresh herbs. *Makes 4 servings.*

THE CHEF'S OWN POTATO PUREE
MA PUREE MOUSSELINE

4 TO 6 MEDIUM WHITE-FLESHED
  POTATOES, PEELED AND RINSED
¾ CUP UNSALTED BUTTER, CUT INTO
  SMALL PIECES

SALT
FRESHLY GRATED NUTMEG
½ TO ¾ CUP HEAVY CREAM

Cut potatoes into ¼-inch slices. Cook in salted simmering water until done, about 20 minutes. Press gently with fingers to test for doneness. The potatoes are perfectly cooked when they give slightly under pressure. Drain and let the water evaporate, not more than 2 minutes.

Immediately work through a food mill, a few slices at a time. Mix in butter, bit by bit, with a wooden spoon. Season with salt and nutmeg. Keep warm.

Heat cream. Slowly pour into potatoes, beating with a wire whisk. Add as much cream as is necessary to form a smooth, homogeneous consistency. The puree should be white. Adjust seasonings and serve immediately. *Makes 4 servings.*

NOTE: Steaming would be an ideal way to cook the potatoes.

Baked potatoes could be used as well. Remove the pulp from the skin and incorporate the butter and seasoning. Omit the cream and double the amount of butter.

General rules of thumb are: do not overcook the potatoes, and incorporate the butter right away to make the mixture smooth. Milk can be used to replace all or part of the cream.

Many varieties of purees can be made using this base: a puree of potatoes and green beans or a puree of potatoes with fennel, for example. Olive oil can be used to replace all or part of the amount of butter. Chopped chervil or parsley can be used to garnish.

Only one thing is essential: serve the finished puree as soon as possible.

WHEREAS THERE WERE ONLY 13 VARIETIES OF POTATO IN 1789, THERE WERE MORE THAN TWO HUNDRED BY THE END OF THE LAST CENTURY, ONLY ABOUT ONE HUNDRED OF WHICH REMAIN TODAY. IT IS ALSO IMPOSSIBLE TO MAKE AN EXHAUSTIVE LIST OF ALL THE USES OF THE POTATO; OVER A DOZEN WAYS OF CUTTING FRENCH FRIES ALONE HAVE BEEN COUNTED. AS

FOR THE REPUTATION THAT POTATOES MAKE ONE FAT, IT IS UNDESERVED—AND ORIGINATES LARGELY FROM THE WAY THEY ARE COOKED, OFTEN BY FRYING.

LIGHT CREAM OF GREEN LENTIL SOUP WITH CELERY

CREME LEGERE DE LENTILLES VERTES AU CELERI

1½ CUPS GREEN LENTILS, WASHED AND
    SOAKED OVERNIGHT IN A LARGE
    QUANTITY OF COLD WATER
3   TABLESPOONS UNSALTED BUTTER
1   MEDIUM CELERY ROOT (CELERIAC),
    PEELED AND CUT INTO 1-INCH
    JULIENNE; TRIMMINGS RESERVED
1   WHITE ONION, SLICED
1   MEDIUM LEEK, WHITE PART ONLY,
    CLEANED AND CUT INTO ⅛ INCH
    SLICES
2   SHALLOTS, COARSELY CHOPPED

1   CLOVE GARLIC, MASHED
    SALT AND FRESHLY GROUND PEPPER
½ SMALL BUNCH WATERCRESS, STEMS
    REMOVED
    JUICE OF 1 LEMON
2   TO 3 TABLESPOONS OLIVE OIL
2   SLICES FIRM-TEXTURED WHITE
    SANDWICH BREAD, CUT INTO
    ¼-INCH CUBES
1   TO 2 TEASPOONS DIJON MUSTARD
1   TABLESPOON RED WINE VINEGAR
½ CUP HEAVY CREAM

Drain lentils; set aside. Melt butter in a large saucepan and add celery root trimmings, onion, leek, shallots, and garlic. Cook over medium high heat until just wilted, about 5 minutes.

Add lentils to cooked vegetables and mix well. Pour in 1½ quarts water, season with salt and pepper, and bring to a boil. Reduce heat to low, and simmer for 1 hour. Add watercress leaves to soup during the last 5 minutes of cooking.

In the meantime, place celery root julienne in a medium nonreactive saucepan filled with cold water. Add lemon juice and bring to a boil. Cook until tender, about 10 minutes. Drain in a nonreactive sieve or colander and set aside.

In a medium skillet, heat olive oil until hot. Add bread cubes and fry over high heat until uniformly brown, about 2 minutes. Drain on paper towels.

Working in batches if necessary, pour soup into a food processor and puree until creamy, about 1 minute. Pass through a fine-mesh sieve into a medium saucepan and bring to a simmer over low heat. Add mustard and vinegar. Pour in cream and season with salt and pepper to taste. Serve croutons and additional cream, if desired, separately. *Makes 8 servings.*

ANDRE AND JANINE GUILLARD ARE THE GARDENERS AT THE CHATEAU OF PONT DE VEYLE. THEY GROW MARVELOUS VEGETABLES THAT "CONNOISSEURS" OF THE REGION APPRECIATE AND COME TO BUY DIRECTLY. OF ALL LEGUMES, THE LENTIL HAS THE MOST FLATTERING REPUTATION AND WHAT BETTER TIME TO EAT LENTILS THAN WHEN THE GARDEN IS BARE. WHILE THIS SOUP IS PREFERABLY SERVED HOT IN WINTER, IT CAN BE SERVED COLD IN THE SUMMER. SIMPLY REPLACE THE DICES OF FRIED BREAD WITH DICES OF TOMATO AND THE CELERY ROOT WITH CELERY BRANCHES.

FENNEL GRATIN
GRATIN DE FENOUIL

FENNEL

6 FENNEL BULBS
3 TABLESPOONS UNSALTED BUTTER
1 MEDIUM CARROT, THINLY SLICED
2 MEDIUM ONIONS, THINLY SLICED
1 BAY LEAF
2 SPRIGS OF THYME OR ½ TEASPOON
    DRIED
  SALT AND FRESHLY GROUND PEPPER
2 CUPS VEGETABLE STOCK OR WATER

CREAM SAUCE

3 TABLESPOONS UNSALTED BUTTER
3 TABLESPOONS ALL-PURPOSE FLOUR
2 CUPS MILK

1 SMALL ONION, FINELY CHOPPED AND
    COOKED SLOWLY IN 1 TABLESPOON
    BUTTER FOR 15 TO 20 MINUTES
  SALT AND FRESHLY GROUND PEPPER
  FRESHLY GRATED NUTMEG
2 TABLESPOONS HEAVY CREAM
1 EGG YOLK

SERVING SAUCE

½ CUP HEAVY CREAM
8 TABLESPOONS UNSALTED BUTTER, CUT
    INTO ¼-INCH CUBES AND CHILLED
  SALT AND FRESHLY GROUND PEPPER
1 TABLESPOON RED WINE VINEGAR

PREPARE THE FENNEL: Preheat oven to 400 degrees. Trim fennel bulbs, leaving about 1-inch branches on bulb. Wash and lightly peel, reserving all trimmings.

Melt 2 tablespoons butter in a large ovenproof casserole. Add carrot, onions, bay leaf, and thyme. Stir well and cook over medium heat for 1 to 2 minutes. Arrange fennel bulbs on top. Season with salt and pepper. Pour in vegetable stock and add more liquid, if necessary, to partially submerge fennel. Bring to a simmer over high heat. Cover with a buttered piece of parchment paper or aluminum foil. Place a heatproof plate on top to submerge vegetables. Place in oven and cook for 30 to 45 minutes, until fennel is barely cooked, not mushy or soft.

Remove fennel and reserve cooking liquid. Cut off inch-long branch stems; set aside. Cut bulbs lengthwise into ¼-inch slices.

Melt remaining 1 tablespoon butter in a large skillet. Add sliced fennel and cook over medium high heat until lightly colored and all of the water has evaporated, about 10 minutes. Set aside to cool slightly.

PREPARE THE CREAM SAUCE: Melt butter in a heavy saucepan over medium heat. Add flour and cook, stirring, for 1 to 2 minutes. Pour in milk, beating constantly with a wire whisk. Bring to a simmer. Add cooked onion; season with salt, pepper, and a pinch of nutmeg. Stir in cream. Pour half of the sauce into a small bowl. When slightly cooled, mix in egg yolk. Reserve remaining sauce. (The dish can be prepared to this point in advance.)

ASSEMBLE THE GRATIN: Preheat oven to 400 degrees. Spread a layer of fennel slices in the bottom of a buttered 8-inch gratin dish. Cover with the cream sauce made without egg yolk. Spread another layer of fennel on top. Top with egg-yolk enriched cream sauce.

PREPARE THE SERVING SAUCE: Just before serving gratin, combine ½ to 1 cup reserved fennel trimmings with cream in a small saucepan over medium high heat. Cook until liquid is reduced by half, about 5 minutes. Add ½ cup reserved fennel cooking liquid and cook until reduced by half again. One by one, whisk in pieces of butter, beating constantly until sauce is smooth and emulsified. Season with salt, pepper, and vinegar. Strain through a fine-mesh sieve and keep warm.

TO SERVE: Preheat broiler. Brown gratin under broiler for 1 to 2 minutes. Serve hot with serving sauce. *Makes 4 servings.*

NOTE: If desired, sprinkle gratin with 1 tablespoon Swiss cheese before browning.

HERE IS ANOTHER GRATIN FOR THOSE WHO ARE FOND OF THEM, USING THE UNUSUAL AND AROMATIC FENNEL BULB. FORMERLY CALLED *QUEUE DE POURCEAU* (PIG'S TAIL), ITS HEAD IS FORMED BY THE SWELLINGS OF ITS OVERLAPPING RIBS. FENNEL IS AVAILABLE IN MARKETS FROM OCTOBER UNTIL JANUARY OR FEBRUARY AND WHEN BOUGHT MUST BE QUITE WHITE, FIRM, AND WITHOUT BLEMISHES.

CLUSTER OF MACHE WITH TRUFFLES "EN SURPRISE"
BOUQUET DE MACHE A LA TRUFFE EN SURPRISE

Mache (lamb's lettuce or corn salad) is another salad green that grows either wild or in a garden, where it can survive the rigors of winter. Once picked, however, it becomes extremely fragile, and one must take great care when cleaning it. It is also better to season the leaves first with oil, salt, and pepper; add the vinegar at the last moment. Mache goes well with beets, or anchovies and hardboiled eggs, and is used in certain poultry stuffings.

¾ POUND *MACHE* (LAMB'S TONGUE LETTUCE, LAMB'S QUARTERS, CORN SALAD, ETC.)
8 MEDIUM ARTICHOKES
3 TABLESPOONS UNSALTED BUTTER
SALT AND FRESHLY GROUND PEPPER
¼ CUP HEAVY CREAM
3 MEDIUM TOMATOES, PEELED, SEEDED, AND CHOPPED

⅓ POUND TRUFFLES, FINELY CHOPPED
½ CUP VINAIGRETTE
2 TABLESPOONS WALNUT OIL
SEVERAL THIN SLICES OF FRESH TRUFFLE FOR GARNISH
COARSE SALT
8 CROUTONS (SEE RECIPE BELOW)

Wash and dry *mâche*. Wrap in a linen tea towel and set aside.

Cook artichokes in a large quantity of salted boiling water until tender, about 25 minutes. Remove and drain. Pluck off leaves and cut out fibrous chokes. Trim bottoms and cut into small cubes; pass through a fine-mesh strainer. Melt butter in a small saucepan over medium high heat. Add puree and cook, stirring constantly, until water evaporates, about 5 minutes. Season with salt and pepper; stir in cream and mix well. Pour puree into a bowl to cool; refrigerate.

In a small nonreactive saucepan, cook tomatoes, stirring often, over low heat until all water evaporates, about 15 minutes. Season with salt and pepper. Pass through a fine-mesh strainer and set aside.

In another bowl, mix together one-third of the tomato puree with two-thirds of the artichoke puree. Adjust seasonings and refrigerate for 20 minutes. (Reserve remaining purees for another use.)

Make walnut-size balls of chilled vegetable puree. Roll in chopped truffles until completely covered. Refrigerate until ready to serve.

Dress *mâche* with vinaigrette sauce and walnut oil. Arrange on 4 individual salad plates. Accompany with truffles *en surprise*. Garnish lettuce with thin slices of truffle that have been lightly oiled and seasoned with a pinch of coarse salt. Add 2 croutons and serve immediately. *Makes 4 servings.*

To make croutons: Cut day-old French bread into ¼-inch slices. Melt 2 tablespoons unsalted butter with 1 tablespoon vegetable oil in a medium sauté pan. Cook bread over medium high heat until golden brown, about 30 seconds on each side. Drain on paper towels.

CAULIFLOWER, CABBAGE, AND BROCCOLI MOLD
CHARTREUSE AUX TROIS CHOUX

Broccoli, with its long stalks and bluish-green flowers, was brought from Italy by Catherine de Medicis and is a kin of the winter cauliflower, whose stalk may reach five to six inches in length. The green cabbage, which is resistant to the cold, is another hardy winter vegetable. The three vegetables are here pureed and

layered in a chartreuse. Serve as a side dish or as a course in itself.

1	LARGE CAULIFLOWER	6	EGGS
	SALT	¾	CUP HEAVY CREAM
1	GREEN CABBAGE		FRESHLY GROUND PEPPER
4	TO 5 BUNCHES BROCCOLI (ABOUT 4 POUNDS)		CAYENNE PEPPER
2	TABLESPOONS UNSALTED BUTTER, SOFTENED		

Plunge whole cauliflower into boiling salted water. Return to a boil and cook for 1 to 2 minutes. Drain and refresh under cold water. Remove core; cut into florets. Fill a large saucepan with water, add salt, and bring to a boil. Cook cauliflower florets over high heat until tender, about 15 minutes. Drain and set aside.

Remove core from cabbage. Cut around core to release leaves; separate leaves, keeping them intact. Cook in a large pot of boiling salted water until soft but not mushy. Drain and reserve most attractive leaves. Shave down large veins so each leaf is uniformly thick. Dry reserved leaves in paper towels; reserve remaining cabbage.

Cut broccoli into florets. Blanch in a large pot of boiling salted water until tender, about 10 minutes. Refresh under cold water and drain.

Choose a stainless-steel or heatproof glass mixing bowl slightly larger than the head of cauliflower. Brush well with softened butter. Line bottom with several cauliflower florets, flowers facing outward. Make another ring of cauliflower florets, facing outward. Use broccoli florets to make another row, facing outward. Refrigerate.

Puree remaining cauliflower and broccoli separately in a food processor. Puree remaining cabbage. Pass each puree separately through a fine-mesh sieve into separate medium saucepans. Constantly stir each puree over medium high heat until all moisture has evaporated. The purees must be very stiff.

When very dry, add 2 eggs to each puree. Stir until well blended. Add enough cream to bind, about ¼ cup for each. Season with salt, pepper, and cayenne.

Preheat oven to 300 degrees. Remove bowl from refrigerator. Fill bottom with cabbage puree using the back of a spoon to press down into bowl. Cover surface with reserved cabbage leaves, allowing ends to overhang rim of bowl. Top with broccoli puree.

Fill a baking pan half full with boiling water. Placed filled bowl in baking pan. Bake for 20 minutes. Pour on cauliflower puree. Fold up overhanging cabbage leaves to completely cover top. Cover with a buttered piece of aluminum foil. Bake for 30 minutes. Test for doneness by piercing with a skewer or long, thin-bladed knife.

Let mold rest for 10 minutes. Unmold onto a large plate. Hold bowl gently and pour off any excess cooking liquid. Remove the bowl and serve as is, or with a lemon butter sauce with herbs. *Makes 8 to 10 servings.*

STUFFED ENDIVES
ENDIVES FARCIS

ENDIVES

8   BELGIAN ENDIVES, WASHED AND DRIED
PINCH OF SALT
PINCH OF SUGAR
2   TABLESPOONS UNSALTED BUTTER, CUT
INTO BITS

FILLING

¼   POUND MUSHROOMS, RINSED AND
WIPED DRY
JUICE OF 1 LEMON
2   TABLESPOONS UNSALTED BUTTER
2   TABLESPOONS HEAVY CREAM

½   CUP THICK WHITE SAUCE
1   EGG YOLK
1   CUP GRATED SWISS CHEESE
2   TABLESPOONS PARMESAN CHEESE
SALT AND FRESHLY GROUND PEPPER
FRESHLY GRATED NUTMEG

SERVING SAUCE

¼   CUP HEAVY CREAM
8   TABLESPOONS UNSALTED BUTTER, CUT
INTO BITS
SALT AND FRESHLY GROUND PEPPER

PREPARE THE ENDIVES: Preheat oven to 375 degrees. Butter a shallow baking dish that will snugly hold endives side by side. Place endives in dish and pour in boiling water to cover by half. Dot with butter and add salt and sugar. Cover with a piece of buttered parchment paper and place a heatproof plate on top. Cover and cook in oven until endive is tender, about 20 minutes. Remove endives and drain on wire rack. Reserve cooking liquid.

PREPARE THE FILLING: Finely chop mushrooms. Sprinkle with lemon juice to prevent discoloring. Place chopped mushrooms on a double layer of cheesecloth. Fold over and gently squeeze to wring out as much water as possible.

Melt butter in a medium saucepan. Add mushrooms and cook over high heat until all liquid evaporates, about 1 minute. Add cream and white sauce. Remove from heat and stir in egg yolk, ½ cup Swiss cheese, and Parmesan. Season with salt, pepper, and nutmeg.

ASSEMBLE THE DISH: Preheat oven to 350 degrees. Gently press cooked endives without crushing to extract as much water as possible. Melt 1 tablespoon butter in a medium skillet. Cook endives for 1 to 2 minutes to dry out well.

Cut each endive along one long side. Remove several leaves from center to make a cavity for the filling. Reserve leaves. Stuff endives with mushroom filling and gently reshape. Replace in buttered baking dish and sprinkle with remaining Swiss cheese. Dot with butter. Bake until lightly browned, about 10 minutes. Do not dry out by overcooking.

PREPARE THE SERVING SAUCE: In a medium saucepan, boil reserved endive cooking liquid with reserved endive leaves over high heat until reduced to 1 tablespoon. Add cream and boil until reduced to 1 or 2 tablespoons. One by one, whisk in pieces of butter, working on and off the heat, until sauce is thick and emulsified. Season with salt and pepper. Pass through a fine-mesh strainer.

TO SERVE: Place 2 stuffed endives on each of 4 individual serving plates. Cover with serving sauce. *Makes 4 servings.*

ENDIVES GROW IN A GREENHOUSE WHILE OUTSIDE WINTERY WEATHER CLOAKS THE WOODS OF BEOST IN VONNAS. THE HALF-DOZEN MEMBERS OF THE CHICORY TRIBE, COUSINS OF THE THISTLE, ARE ALL AVAILABLE IN WINTER FOR LOVERS OF LATE GREENS. ENDIVE, THE YOUNGEST MEMBER OF THE CLAN, WAS BORN TOTALLY BY ACCIDENT 150 YEARS AGO WHEN A GARDENER IN BRUSSELS FORGOT THE ROOTS OF WILD CHICORY IN A DARK BUT WARM CORNER OF HIS GARDEN. THE MAN SAW THAT HIS ABANDONED ROOTS HAD GIVEN BIRTH TO A NEW SALAD GREEN WITH

WHITE, CLOSELY PACKED, CRISPY LEAVES. THUS ENDIVE WAS "INVENTED."

BROCCOLI ASPIC WITH TRUFFLED VINAIGRETTE
ASPIC DE BROCOLIS A LA VINAIGRETTE DE TRUFFE

THIS ASPIC, USING BOTH THE STALK AND FLOWERS, IS A DRAMATIC WAY TO SERVE BROCCOLI. THE STALKS OF BROCCOLI MAY OTHERWISE BE EATEN LIKE ASPARAGUS WHILE THE TIPS, COOKED VERY RAPIDLY TO PRESERVE THEIR DELICATE HAZELNUT FLAVOR, COULD BE PREPARED LIKE CAULIFLOWER AND SERVED AS A GARNISH FOR ALL MEATS AND FISH. BROCCOLI IS ALSO

DELICIOUS COOKED WITH CREAM OR WITH BACON AND POTATOES. IN FRANCE, THE FIRST BROCCOLI APPEARS IN SEPTEMBER AND MUST BE HARVESTED WITH VERY COMPACT FLOWERS.

4   TO 5 SMALL BUNCHES BROCCOLI
    (ABOUT 5 POUNDS)
¼   CUP HEAVY CREAM
    SALT AND FRESHLY GROUND BLACK
    PEPPER
2   MEDIUM LEEKS
1   TABLESPOON UNSALTED BUTTER

1   ENVELOPE (1 TABLESPOON)
    UNFLAVORED GELATIN
2   TABLESPOONS OLIVE OIL
1   TABLESPOON FINELY CHOPPED TRUFFLES
1   CUP VINAIGRETTE
    SEVERAL LEAVES OF WATERCRESS
    (OPTIONAL)

Cut florets from broccoli stalks. Cook in a large amount of salted boiling water for 5 minutes. Remove 2 or 3 large florets after 5 minutes. Refresh under cold water and drain well. Reserve for interior of aspic molds. Continue cooking remaining broccoli until soft, about 5 minutes more. Drain well. Pass through a food mill and add cream. Season with salt and pepper; cover and refrigerate.

Cut green parts from leeks; reserve white stalks. Cut greens into ¼-inch pieces. Melt butter in a medium saucepan. Add leek greens and cook over low heat, stirring often, for 5 minutes. Pour in 1½ cups water and simmer for 15 minutes.

Meanwhile, place ½ cup water in a large mixing bowl. Sprinkle gelatin over and set aside to dissolve, about 5 minutes. Pour in leek greens and cooking liquid and stir well. Pass through a fine-mesh sieve into a bowl; cool. Refrigerate until aspic is almost set.

Cut whites of leeks into ¼-inch-long rounds. Carefully add to boiling water; immediately reduce heat to simmer, and cook until soft, about 3 minutes. Remove carefully with a slotted spoon and drain on paper towels.

Pour a small amount of aspic into four ½-cup ramekins. Tilt molds to coat sides. Refrigerate for 2 or 3 minutes to set.

Carefully place the white leek slices around the sides of the ramekin molds. Trim reserved large broccoli florets into small flowers. Use to line the bottom of molds, flowers facing downward. Add a spoonful of aspic and refrigerate until set, about 3 minutes.

Fill molds with broccoli puree. Gently tap to settle puree; refrigerate for at least 2 hours.

Stir olive oil and truffles into vinaigrette sauce.

TO SERVE: Dip bottom of molds into a bowl of hot water. Turn them out into the center of 4 individual serving plates. Surround with a ribbon of vinaigrette sauce and garnish with watercress or other greens. *Makes 4 servings.*

PASTORAL SALAD OF MUSHROOMS AND SAFFRON
SALADE PASTORALE AUX CHAMPIGNONS SAFRANES

	A MIXTURE OF SALAD GREENS (BOSTON, ESCAROLE, ROMAINE, RED LEAF, ENDIVE—CHOOSE ACCORDING TO MARKET AVAILABILITY AND SEASONAL FRESHNESS)	1	TABLESPOON OLIVE OIL SALT
¼	POUND WILD MUSHROOMS (ACCORDING TO AVAILABILITY), WASHED, DRIED, AND TRIMMED	2	TABLESPOONS DRY WHITE WINE PINCH OF THREAD SAFFRON
3	TABLESPOONS UNSALTED BUTTER	1	CUP CLASSIC VINAIGRETTE SNIPPED CHIVES, QUARTERS OF PEELED AND SEEDED TOMATOES, OR POACHED EGGS FOR GARNISH FRESHLY GROUND PEPPER

Wash and dry salad greens. Wrap in paper towels to remove as much moisture as possible.

Cut mushrooms into thin slices. Melt butter in a medium skillet over medium high heat. Add the olive oil. Add mushrooms and cook until soft and just beginning to release moisture, about 5 minutes. Season lightly with salt. Add wine and saffron; stir well.

Toss salad greens with vinaigrette sauce. Arrange a nice bouquet of salad on 4 individual serving plates. Remove cooked mushrooms with a slotted spoon and arrange attractively around greens. Coat with spoonfuls of cooking liquid. Garnish with the chives, tomato quarters, or eggs and add pepper to taste. *Makes 4 servings.*

ONION AND LEEK SOUP WITH JULIENNE OF TRUFFLE
SOUPE D'OIGNONS ET POIREAUX A LA JULIENNE DE CELERI ET DE TRUFFES

2	TABLESPOONS UNSALTED BUTTER	1	SMALL CELERY ROOT (CELERIAC, ABOUT ¾ POUND), PEELED AND CUT INTO THIN JULIENNE
4	TO 5 WHITE ONIONS (ABOUT 1 POUND), VERY THINLY SLICED		
2	MEDIUM LEEKS, WHITE PARTS ONLY, THINLY SLICED		SALT AND FRESHLY GROUND PEPPER
⅓	CUP TRUFFLE JUICE	1	OUNCE FRESH TRUFFLES, CUT INTO VERY FINE JULIENNE

Melt butter in a large saucepan. Add onions and leeks and cook over low heat, stirring often, until lightly colored, about 30 minutes.

Pour in truffle juice. Mix well and cook for 1 minute. Add 4 cups water and bring to a boil. Reduce heat and simmer for 15 minutes.

Add celery root and cook for 2 to 3 minutes; season with salt and pepper. Add truffles and pour into a large soup tureen or 4 individual wide-rimmed soup plates. *Makes 4 servings.*

WINTER COMES TO THE VEYLE RIVER. EVEN THOUGH IT IS THE SEASON OF COLD AND SNOW, WINTER CAN STILL BE THE TIME TO ENJOY A SALAD OF LEAFY GREENS AND WILD MUSHROOMS. ENDIVE, CHICORY, AND ESCAROLE ARE SOME OF OUR FINE WINTER GREENS. WINTER ESCAROLE IS THE GREEN WHICH KEEPS THE BEST IF ONE IS CAREFUL TO STORE IT COLD AND IN DARKNESS.

THIS SEASONAL ONION SOUP, PLACED IN A SETTING OF FROSTY LEEKS, FEATURES FRESH TRUFFLES, ONE OF WINTER'S TRUE DELIGHTS. TRUFFLES MAY BE EATEN RAW OR COOKED, IN SHAVINGS, SLICES, OR DICES. PURISTS SAY THAT THE TRUFFLE IS BEST WHEN EATEN WHOLE, AS IN THE DISTANT PAST WHEN THE EGYPTIANS ATE THEM COVERED IN GOOSE FAT. TODAY TRUFFLE CONNOISSEURS EAT THEM RAW WITH SALT AND BUTTER OR IN CHAMPAGNE (THEY COOK IN ABOUT TEN MINUTES IN A REDUCTION OF VERY RICH TRUFFLE JUICE, CHAMPAGNE, COGNAC, AND PEPPERCORNS). CROUTONS FRIED IN BUTTER CAN ALSO BE USED TO GARNISH THIS SOUP.

Iɴ ᴇᴀʀʟʏ Fᴇʙʀᴜᴀʀʏ ᴛʜᴇ ᴛʀᴜғғʟᴇ ᴍᴀʀᴋᴇᴛ ᴀᴛ Cᴀʀᴘᴇɴᴛᴀs ɪs ᴀᴛ ɪᴛs ʜᴇɪɢʜᴛ. Uɴғᴏʀᴛᴜɴᴀᴛᴇʟʏ, ᴛʜɪs sᴜʙᴛᴇʀʀᴀɴᴇᴀɴ ғᴜɴɢᴜs ғᴏᴜɴᴅ 10 ᴛᴏ 15 ɪɴᴄʜᴇs ᴜɴᴅᴇʀɢʀᴏᴜɴᴅ ɪɴ ᴛʜᴇ sʜᴀᴅᴇ ᴏғ ᴏᴀᴋs, ʜᴀᴢᴇʟɴᴜᴛ ᴛʀᴇᴇs, ʟɪɴᴅᴇɴs, ᴄʜᴇsᴛɴᴜᴛs, ᴀɴᴅ sᴏᴍᴇᴛɪᴍᴇs ʙᴇᴇᴄʜ ᴛʀᴇᴇs ɪs ʙᴇᴄᴏᴍɪɴɢ ɪɴ- ᴄʀᴇᴀsɪɴɢʟʏ ʀᴀʀᴇ. Nᴏ ʟᴏɴɢᴇʀ ᴀʀᴇ ᴡᴇ ɪɴ ᴛʜᴇ ᴅᴀʏs ᴏғ Lᴏᴜɪs XIV, ᴡʜᴇɴ ᴄᴏᴏᴋs ᴘᴜᴛ ᴛʀᴜғ- ғʟᴇs—"ᴛʜᴇ ʙʟᴀᴄᴋ ᴅɪᴀᴍᴏɴᴅ ᴏғ ᴛʜᴇ ᴋɪᴛᴄʜᴇɴ"—ɪɴ ᴀʟᴍᴏsᴛ ᴀʟʟ ᴅɪsʜᴇs ᴡɪᴛʜᴏᴜᴛ ᴅɪsᴄʀɪᴍɪɴᴀᴛɪᴏɴ. Sᴛɪʟʟ, ᴛʜᴇ sᴇᴀʀᴄʜ ғᴏʀ ᴛʀᴜғ- ғʟᴇs ʀᴇᴍᴀɪɴs ᴀ ʟᴏᴄᴀʟ ᴄʀᴀғᴛ ᴡʜɪᴄʜ ᴇᴍᴇʀɢᴇs ᴡɪᴛʜ ᴛʜᴇ ғɪʀsᴛ ғʀᴏsᴛ ɪɴ ᴛʜᴇ sᴏᴜᴛʜ ᴏғ Fʀᴀɴᴄᴇ ᴀɴᴅ ʜᴀs ʜᴀʀᴅʟʏ ᴄʜᴀɴɢᴇᴅ ɪɴ ᴄᴇɴᴛᴜʀɪᴇs. Tʜᴇ *ᴄᴀᴠᴇᴜʀ*, ᴛʜᴇ ᴍᴀɴ ᴏʀ ᴡᴏᴍᴀɴ ᴡʜᴏ ɢᴀᴛʜᴇʀs ᴛʀᴜғғʟᴇs, ɪs ᴀʟᴡᴀʏs ᴀᴄᴄᴏᴍᴘᴀɴɪᴇᴅ ʙʏ ᴀ ᴘɪɢ ᴏʀ ᴅᴏɢ ᴛᴏ sɴɪғғ ᴏᴜᴛ ᴛʜᴇ ᴛʀᴜғғʟᴇs. Hᴇʀᴇ, Mᴏɴsɪᴇᴜʀ Pᴇʙᴇʏʀᴇ, "ᴋɪɴɢ ᴏғ ᴛʀᴜғғʟᴇs," ʜᴜɴᴛs ғᴏʀ ᴛʜᴇ ғᴜɴɢᴜs ᴏɴ ᴛʜᴇ sʟᴏᴘᴇs ᴏғ Mᴏɴᴛ- Vᴇɴᴛᴏᴜx ᴡɪᴛʜ Bᴇᴅᴏɪɴ, ʜɪs ᴛʀᴜғғʟᴇ ᴅᴏɢ. Bᴇғᴏʀᴇ ᴛʜᴇ ʜᴜɴᴛ ᴏɴᴇ ᴍᴜsᴛ ʜᴀᴠᴇ ᴀ ʙɪᴛᴇ ᴛᴏ ᴇᴀᴛ, sᴏ ᴛʜᴇ ᴘᴀʀᴛʏ—ᴡʜɪᴄʜ ɪɴᴄʟᴜᴅᴇs Aʟᴀɪɴ Sᴇɴᴅᴇʀᴇɴs, Mᴀʀᴄ Mᴇɴᴇᴀᴜ, ᴀɴᴅ ᴍʏsᴇʟғ— sɴᴀᴄᴋs ᴏɴ ᴛʜʀᴜsʜ ᴘâᴛé, sᴀʟᴛᴇᴅ ᴛʀᴜғғʟᴇs, ᴛʀᴜғғʟᴇ ᴏᴍᴇʟᴇᴛ, ᴀɴᴅ ɢᴏᴀᴛ ᴄʜᴇᴇsᴇ ᴀᴛ Mɪᴄʜᴇʟ Bᴏsᴄ's ʙɪsᴛʀᴏ ɴᴇᴀʀ Gᴏʀᴅᴇs.

SLIVERED ENDIVES
WITH LEMON AND ROASTED SCALLOPS
EFFILOCHEE D'ENDIVES AU CITRON ET AUX SAINT-JACQUES ROTIES

ENDIVE AND SCALLOPS ARE A MARRIAGE OF TASTES SUITED TO THE SEASON. WHEN ENDIVE ARRIVES IN OUR MARKETS, IT MUST BE WHITE, FIRM, AND SWOLLEN. AT THE TIME OF PREPARATION, IT SHOULD BE PASSED UNDER WATER AND WIPED. ENDIVE MAY BE SERVED IN A SALAD WITH HARDBOILED EGGS, WALNUTS, BEETROOT, AND ROQUEFORT, SEASONED WITH A STRONG VIN-

AIGRETTE AND EMBELLISHED WITH APPLE QUARTERS OR ORANGE SECTIONS. STEWED AND DRAINED, IT CAN ALSO BE PREPARED WITH A BECHAMEL, IN MEAT GRAVY, OR EVEN MADE INTO FRITTERS.

6 LARGE ENDIVES, WELL-RINSED AND TRIMMED
8 TABLESPOONS UNSALTED BUTTER
3 TABLESPOONS LEMON JUICE
SALT

16 SEA SCALLOPS
FRESHLY GROUND PEPPER
COARSE SEA SALT

Preheat oven to 500 degrees. Halve endives lengthwise; cut out tough inner cores. Thinly slice lengthwise.

Melt 3 tablespoons butter in a large skillet. Add endives and cook over medium heat, tossing, until liquid evaporates and they are quite tender, about 8 minutes. Remove from heat; stir in 1½ tablespoons lemon juice and season with salt. Keep warm.

Place scallops an inch or so apart on a buttered baking sheet. Bake until they just begin to lose their opaque quality, about 6 minutes.

Meanwhile, in a small saucepan, combine remaining 1½ tablespoons lemon juice with 1 tablespoon of water. Bring to a boil. Reduce heat to low and whisk in the remaining 5 tablespoons butter, 1 tablespoon at a time. Remove from heat; season sauce with salt and pepper.

TO SERVE: Reheat endives, if necessary, and divide them among 4 serving plates. Place 4 scallops on each plate, browned-side up; sprinkle with pepper and a pinch of sea salt. Drizzle lemon butter over endives and scallops; serve immediately. *Makes 4 servings.*

BRUSSELS SPROUTS AND CROSNES SOUP WITH MUSSELS

SOUPE DE CHOUX DE BRUXELLES ET DE CROSNES AUX MOULES

2½ POUNDS BRUSSELS SPROUTS
    SALT
¼ POUND *CROSNES* (SEE CAPTION)
1 TEASPOON ALL-PURPOSE FLOUR
    JUICE OF ½ LEMON

2½ POUNDS MUSSELS, SCRUBBED CLEAN
2 CUPS HEAVY CREAM
4 TABLESPOONS UNSALTED BUTTER
    FRESHLY GROUND PEPPER

Trim Brussels sprouts, removing any torn or yellow outside leaves. Tear off 8 or 12 nice, very green leaves; plunge them into boiling salted water. Bring back to the boil and cook over high heat for 2 minutes. Drain and refresh leaves under cold water. Dry on paper towels; reserve for decoration.

Fill a large pot with water and add a pinch of salt. Bring to a boil and add Brussels sprouts. Bring back to a boil and blanch for 2 to 3 minutes. Refresh under cold water. (This operation reduces the acidity of the vegetable and makes it more digestible.) Return sprouts to pot and add 1 quart cold water or enough to cover. Add a pinch of salt and bring to a boil. Reduce heat and simmer until sprouts slightly crush when pressed between two fingers; drain well. Place in a food processor and puree, about 30 seconds. Pass through a fine-mesh strainer into a clean saucepan.

Clean *crosnes* by rubbing them with coarse salt or scrape with a sharp paring knife. Rinse well and place in a small saucepan. Cover with cold water. Add the flour, lemon juice, and a pinch of salt. Bring to a boil; cook until tender, about 15 minutes. Drain and add to Brussels sprout puree.

Place mussels in a large saucepan. Cover and cook over medium high heat until opened, about 5 minutes. Remove mussels from shells and combine with Brussels sprout puree and *crosnes*. Pour any liquor from mussels through a double thickness of dampened cheesecloth. Add to soup. Bring to a boil over medium high heat and cook for 1 minute.

Add cream and butter; stir gently. Season with salt and pepper. Serve in a soup tureen and garnish with the reserved sprout leaves. *Makes 4 servings.*

CROSNE IS A ROOT, ORIGINALLY FROM THE FAR EAST; ITS DELICATE, SLIGHTLY SWEET TASTE IS HALFWAY BETWEEN THAT OF SALSIFY AND THE ARTICHOKE, AND MADE IT A FAVORITE EXOTIC VEGETABLE IN NINETEENTH-CENTURY FRANCE. *CROSNES* ARE NOT AVAILABLE IN AMERICA, BUT JERUSALEM ARTICHOKES MAKE AN EXCELLENT SUBSTITUTE. PEEL AND TRIM 5 TO 6 CHOKES

(ABOUT ½ POUND). CUT IN ¼ INCH SLICES AND PROCEED AS FOR THE *CROSNES*. COOK FOR ONLY 10 MINUTES.

WINTER FRUITS

WHILE THE BRANCHES OF THE FRUIT TREES
BARE THEMSELVES TO FACE THE WINTER AND WAIT
FOR BETTER DAYS, FRUIT AND NUTS MAY STILL BE
HARVESTED AT WINTER'S ONSET AND STORED FOR
THE BLUSTERY MONTHS AHEAD. WHEN THE DAYS
GROW COLDER, WE CAN ALWAYS TURN TO THE
IMPORTED DELIGHTS OF EXOTIC FRUITS TO PLEASE
OUR PALATES.

ORANGE LACE COOKIES
DENTELLE A L'ORANGE

1½ CUPS SUGAR
1   CUP CHOPPED ALMONDS
¾   CUP ALL-PURPOSE FLOUR
    JUICE OF 1 ORANGE

8   TABLESPOONS UNSALTED BUTTER,
    MELTED
2   TEASPOONS GRATED ORANGE ZEST

Preheat oven to 400 degrees. In a large mixing bowl, combine sugar, almonds, and flour. Pour orange juice and melted butter in the center. Add grated zest. Stir well with a wooden spoon.

Using a teaspoon, make uniform mounds at least 2 inches apart on a nonstick or buttered baking sheet. Even the tops with a fork dipped in cold water. Bake for 5 to 7 minutes, until lightly browned at edges. Watch carefully as these fragile cookies burn easily.

Remove from oven and let rest until slightly firm, about 1 minute. Working quickly before cookies become too brittle, use a metal spatula to transfer to a rolling pin. Gently shape to form a curved cookie called a *tuile* in French. Store in a cool, dry place. *Makes about 3 dozen.*

PINEAPPLE BANANA SORBET
FLEURS DES ILES SORBET

4   CUPS SUGAR
1   VANILLA BEAN, SPLIT LENGTHWISE
1   PINEAPPLE, PEELED, CORED, AND
    TRIMMED

2   RIPE BANANAS, PEELED
    JUICE OF 6 LEMONS
    JUICE OF 4 ORANGES
1   TABLESPOON GRENADINE SYRUP

In a nonreactive medium saucepan, dissolve sugar in 4 cups water over moderately high heat. Add vanilla bean, remove from heat, and let mixture infuse until cool. Pass through a fine-mesh strainer; discard solids.

Quarter pineapple; cut into chunks. Puree pineapple and bananas in a food processor. Add lemon and orange juices; process just until mixed. Stir in grenadine. Pour mixture into an ice cream maker and freeze according to manufacturer's directions until firm. *Makes 8 servings.*

NAVELS, THOMSONS, AND JAFFA BLONDS ARE AMONG THOSE ORANGES PREFERRED AS DESSERT FRUIT AND WITH THEM ONE CAN MAKE FRUIT SALADS, DESSERT CREAMS, OR SOUFFLES. THE FRUIT SHOULD BE SMOOTH BUT NOT TOO SHINY AT THE TIME OF PURCHASE. IF THE PEEL IS TO BE USED, ONE SHOULD BE SURE THE FRUIT HAS NOT BEEN TREATED.

THE ACIDIC CITRUS JUICES ARE BALANCED BY THE SWEETER FRUIT PULP IN THIS WINTER SORBET. LIKE THE ORANGE, THE LEMON WAS FIRST BROUGHT TO FRANCE BY THE CRUSADERS, ALTHOUGH IT ORIGINATED IN THE ANCIENT COUNTRY OF ASSYRIA, AT THE FEET OF THE HIMALAYAS. THE LEMON IS INCREASINGLY USED IN COOKING, PARTICULARLY THE JUICE, OBTAINED BY PRESSING FIRMLY AND TURNING A FORK IN THE PULP OF A LEMON HALF.

GRAPEFRUIT WITH ZESTS AND HONEY
SUC DE PAMPLEMOUSSE AUX ZESTES ET AU MIEL

THIS SIMPLE, FRESH, AND NATURAL PREPARA-TION CAN SERVE AS A HEALTHY FIRST COURSE TO BEGIN A SUBSTANTIAL MEAL. THE CITRUS JUICE IS SLOWLY ABSORBED AND CONSTITUTES AN IDEAL APERITIF TO CALM THE EXCITEMENT OF AN IMPATIENT STOMACH.

THIS CITRUS PLATE CELEBRATES THAT BEAU-TIFUL TRIAD OF WINTER FRUITS: ORANGES, LEMONS, AND GRAPEFRUIT.

4   GRAPEFRUIT
¼   CUP HONEY

Grate zests from 2 grapefruit. Place in a small nonreactive saucepan, add water to cover, and bring to a boil over medium high heat. Boil for 2 minutes. Drain zest in a fine-mesh strainer and refresh with cold water. Repeat blanching procedure 3 times, changing water each time.

Using a sharp knife with a supple blade, cut off top and bottom of each grapefruit. Cut off skin and white pith in a circular motion, moving from top to bottom. Cut out sections from between membranes and drain on paper towels. Place grapefruit membranes and skin in a strainer over a bowl and press down to extract juice. Discard pulp and skins. Whisk honey and zests into juice. Cover and refrigerate for at least 1 hour.

Arrange grapefruit sections in the form of a flower in individual dessert bowls or crystal glasses. Cover with the chilled juices and zest. Serve cold. *Makes 4 servings.*

WINTER CITRUS PLATE
ASSIETTE D'AGRUMES A L'AGRUME

4   PINK GRAPEFRUITS   LEMON JUICE AND ADDITIONAL SUGAR
4   ORANGES   FOR GARNISH
2   CUPS SUGAR

Choose ripe, juicy fruit. Cut off tops and bottoms of grapefruits and oranges. Using a sharp knife with a supple blade, cut around fruit in a circular motion to remove skin and pith. Working over a bowl to collect the juices, cut into sections by slicing between membranes. Refrigerate juice.

Cut grapefruit peels into uniform pieces 2½ inches long by ¼ inch wide. Place peels in a nonreactive medium saucepan. Add cold water to cover and bring to a boil over high heat. Boil for 1 minute. Drain and rinse under cold water. Repeat blanching procedure 2 more times, always starting with cold water.

In a medium saucepan, combine sugar and ¼ cup water. Heat slowly until sugar dissolves, about 2 minutes. Add grapefruit peels and cook over very low heat until translucent, about 30 minutes. Remove with a slotted spoon and drain on a rack.

Arrange grapefruit and orange sections on individual serving plates, alternating colors. Add a squeeze of lemon juice and sprinkle with sugar to taste. Pour over a small amount of reserved grapefruit and orange juices. Roll candied grapefruit zest in crystalized sugar and use to garnish citrus plates.

ORANGE AND GRAPEFRUIT ASPIC WITH CARAMEL APPLE SAUCE

ASPIC D'ORANGES ET PAMPLEMOUSSES SAUCE POMME AU CARAMEL

THE FRUITS OF THE CITRUS FAMILY—ORANGES, LEMONS, AND GRAPEFRUITS—BRING THE SUN TO OUR TABLES WHEN NATURE HAS DARKENED AND THE FIELDS ARE BARE. THE ORANGE IS THE OLDEST AND MOST PREFERRED OF THE THREE, AND AFTER THE APPLE IT IS THE FAVORITE FRUIT OF THE FRENCH. THIS SIMPLE AND ATTRACTIVE DESSERT COMBINES CITRUS FRUIT IN AN ASPIC WITH A SAUCE MADE OF APPLES. ONCE ORANGES WERE SUCH A LUXURY THAT ONE OR MORE OF THESE FRUITS IN A CHRISTMAS STOCKING WAS THE RAREST AND MOST PRECIOUS OF GIFTS. THE GOLDEN APPLES OF THE GARDEN OF THE HESPERIDES, FAMED IN GREEK MYTHOLOGY, WERE NO DOUBT PICKED FROM THE ORANGE TREE, WHICH PROBABLY ORIGINATED IN CHINA. NOW, THE ORANGE IS NO LESS TREASURED BUT LUCKILY MORE PLENTIFUL, EVEN IF WE DO NOT GO AS FAR AS ROBESPIERRE, WHO DEVOURED A "PYRAMID" OF ORANGES AT EACH MEAL.

ASPIC

2 PINK GRAPEFRUITS
4 ORANGES
1 ENVELOPE (1 TABLESPOON) UNFLAVORED GELATIN
1 CUP SAUTERNES OR OTHER SWEET WHITE WINE

CARAMEL APPLE SAUCE

½ CUP SUGAR
JUICE OF 2 GRANNY SMITH APPLES
JUICE OF 2 LEMONS
4 TABLESPOONS UNSALTED BUTTER

PREPARE THE ASPIC: Cut off tops and bottoms of grapefruits and oranges. Using a sharp knife with a supple blade, cut around fruits in a circular motion to remove peel and bitter white pith. Working over a bowl to collect juices, cut between membranes into sections. Measure juice and add additional orange or grapefruit juice to make ⅔ cup. Pour into a medium mixing bowl.

Sprinkle gelatin over fruit juices and let dissolve, undisturbed, for 10 minutes.

Meanwhile, place sectioned fruit on paper towels and let dry, uncovered, for at least 6 hours. Arrange attractively in the bottoms of four ½-cup ramekins.

In a nonreactive small saucepan, heat wine to almost simmering. Pour over dissolved gelatin and stir well. Set over a larger bowl of ice and water and stir until thick and syrupy. Pour into ramekins and refrigerate until set, at least 4 hours.

PREPARE THE SAUCE: In a heavy, medium saucepan, combine sugar and 2 tablespoons water. Bring to a boil over medium high heat and cook until lightly caramelized. As soon as the caramel is dark amber, add 2 tablespoons water and the apple juice. Stir in lemon juice and butter. Let cool but do not refrigerate.

Unmold the ramekins by dipping quickly in hot water and inverting onto 4 individual serving plates. Surround with sauce. *Makes 4 servings*.

NOTE: The chef's original recipe calls for blood oranges. The color will enhance the presentation. Proceed as for above, if available.

TULIPS OF FROZEN PRUNE MOUSSE
TULIPE DE MOUSSE GLACEE AUX PRUNEAUX

Here is a winter tulip for those who like prunes and want a change from the eternal compote. While prunes are appreciated for their digestive powers and laxative properties, they have a long history as a delicacy; as far back as the Middle Ages itinerant merchants sold them in the streets. Prunes should not be bought too

dry and before eating should be washed and left to soak overnight in a light tea. A variety of other frozen mousses using fresh fruits, red fruits, or exotic fruits could be substituted in this recipe. Adapt the sauce as necessary and be sure to verify the consistency. If the mousse is too liquid it can ruin the dessert.

MOUSSE AND PRUNE SAUCE
20 LARGE PRUNES, PITTED AND SOAKED IN COLD WATER OVERNIGHT
2 CUPS FULL-BODIED RED WINE
1 ENVELOPE (1 TABLESPOON) UNFLAVORED GELATIN
1½ CUPS HEAVY CREAM, WHIPPED WITH 2 TABLESPOONS SUGAR
⅓ CUP SUGAR
JUICE OF 1 LEMON

TULIPS
⅔ CUP SUGAR
¾ CUP ALL-PURPOSE FLOUR
½ CUP UNSALTED BUTTER, MELTED
4 EGG WHITES

PREPARE THE MOUSSE AND THE PRUNE SAUCE: Drain prunes. Place in a medium nonreactive saucepan and cover with wine. Bring to a boil and remove immediately from heat. Let prunes cool in liquid for 4 to 6 hours.

With a slotted spoon, remove 10 prunes and place in a food processor. Puree until smooth, about 1 minute. Pass through a fine-mesh strainer into a small saucepan.

Warm puree over low heat. Remove from heat when hot to the touch but not quite simmering. Sprinkle gelatin evenly over puree. Set aside to melt, about 10 minutes. Stir gently. Strain again.

Reserve a small amount of the whipped cream for decoration. Gently fold prune puree into remaining whipped cream. Spoon into 4 small dariole molds or ½-cup ramekins. Cover and freeze for at least 3 hours.

Place remaining 10 prunes in a food processor and puree until smooth, about 1 minute. Pass through a sieve into a bowl. Add sugar and lemon juice. Blend well. Refrigerate until ready to serve. Add water if necessary; sauce should be thin.

PREPARE THE TULIPS: Mix sugar and flour in a large bowl. Add melted butter and stir well with a wooden spoon. Slowly whisk in egg whites until a smooth batter forms. Cover and refrigerate for at least 2 hours. (The batter can be made in a food processor.)

Preheat oven to 400 degrees. Lightly butter a large cookie sheet. Spread out chilled batter into thin 4- to 5-inch rounds, using about ¾ teaspoon of batter per cookie. (The rounds should be almost transparent when spread out on the sheet.) Bake until golden brown, 3 to 5 minutes. Watch very carefully as these thin cookies burn easily.

Using a spatula, lift an edge of each cookie and transfer to an inverted small ramekin or the bottom of a narrow drinking glass. Form into tulip shapes by gently pressing the sides of cookie around mold. Work quickly before cookies cool and become brittle. Store in a cool, dry place. (The recipe can be prepared ahead to this point.)

ASSEMBLE THE DESSERT: Place 1 tulip in the center of 4 individual serving plates. Unmold frozen mousse and place in each tulip. Surround with a small amount of prune sauce. Garnish with reserved whipped cream. *Makes 4 servings.*

SABAYON OF CLEMENTINES WITH RUM
SABAYON DE BANANE ET CLEMENTINES AU RHUM

Tangerines are a small citrus fruit with a thin, orangey skin that is easily peeled. The tangerine also has seeds, unlike the clementine—a more recent creation, dating from the eighteenth century. Both have a sweet and fragrant flesh and are eaten above all for dessert: plain, iced, in a cake, or savored in this dramatic sabayon.

4	EGG YOLKS	4	CLEMENTINES
2	TABLESPOONS CLEMENTINE JUICE	1	BANANA
1	TABLESPOON RUM	1	TABLESPOON POWDERED SUGAR
1	TABLESPOON GRANULATED SUGAR		

PREPARE THE SABAYON: Place the egg yolks, clementine juice, rum, and granulated sugar in a medium, heavy nonreactive saucepan. Whisk vigorously over very low heat, making sure that the bottom of the pan is never too hot to the touch. Whisk constantly on and off the heat until sabayon emulsifies and becomes the consistency of a creamy mousse, about 8 minutes. Keep warm on a corner of the stove.

PREPARE THE FRUIT: Preheat oven to 500 degrees. Peel clementines. Cut away tough membrane that runs lengthwise along the straight end of each section. Carefully squeeze out any seeds. Remove as much of the white pith as possible. Arrange sections in a spiral on 4 warmed heatproof plates. Peel banana. Cut into ¼-inch rounds. Cut each round in half and arrange in the center of the clementine spiral.

Whisk the sabayon to revive the emulsion. Coat fruit with a small amount of the sabayon and sprinkle with powdered sugar.

Carefully place plates in hot oven for 2 to 3 minutes, rotating plates to brown evenly. Watch carefully and serve hot. *Makes 4 servings.*

PEAR TART WITH ALMOND CREAM
TARTE AUX POIRES A LA CREME D'AMANDES

THIS PEAR TART (PICTURED ON PAGES 302–303) MANAGES TO BE BOTH DRY AND MOIST AT THE SAME TIME, AND DELIGHTFULLY COMBINES THE SEASONAL FLAVORS OF PEARS AND ALMONDS. LIKE MANY OF OUR FRUITS, THE PEAR ORIGINALLY CAME FROM CHINA WHERE IT WAS GROWN 4,000 YEARS BEFORE OUR TIME. IN FRANCE, THE PEAR HAS CHANGED NAMES THROUGH THE CENTURIES. FOUR CENTURIES AGO, ONE SPOKE OF THE *PETITE MUSCADINE*, OR THE *DOREE* "SO CALLED FOR THE GOLD WITH WHICH SHE IS PAINTED ON THE SIDE FACING THE SUN," OF THE *BRUTE-BONNE*, THE *MUSCATELE*, AND THE *BERGAMOTE*.

PASTRY

2	CUPS ALL-PURPOSE FLOUR
1	CUP GRANULATED SUGAR
	PINCH OF SALT
⅔	CUP UNSALTED BUTTER, CUT INTO SMALL PIECES
1	EGG

ALMOND CREAM

¾	CUP UNSALTED BUTTER, SOFTENED
1½	CUPS POWDERED (PULVERIZED) ALMONDS
2	EGGS
1	TABLESPOON RUM

ASSEMBLY

4	PEARS (ABOUT 1½ POUNDS), COOKED IN SYRUP
	APRICOT JELLY (OPTIONAL)

PREPARE THE PASTRY: Place flour, sugar, and salt in a food processor. Add pieces of butter and process until blended, about 15 seconds. Add egg and process until pastry masses into a ball, about 30 seconds. Turn out onto a floured work surface and form into a neat round. Wrap in plastic and refrigerate at least 1 hour.

PREPARE THE ALMOND CREAM: Using an electric mixer, blend together softened butter and powdered almonds in a bowl. One at a time, add eggs; add rum. Mix well, cover, and refrigerate until ready to use.

ASSEMBLE THE TART: Preheat oven to 400 degrees. Roll out pastry and line a 11- to 12-inch removable-bottom tart pan. Chill for 30 minutes before filling.

Cut cooked pears lengthwise into quarters, removing cores and seeds.

Spoon almond cream over bottom of tart shell. Arrange quartered pears on top in a star pattern.

Bake for 30 minutes, watching carefully toward the end to prevent burning. Unmold the tart when cool.

Glaze the top with melted apricot jelly if desired. *Makes 6 servings.*

FROZEN NOUGAT
WITH CANDIED FRUITS AND NUTS
NOUGAT GLACE AUX NOIX ET AUX FRUITS CONFITS

NOUGAT

¾ CUP POWDERED SUGAR

2 CUPS HONEY

½ CUP LIGHT CORN SYRUP

8 EGG WHITES

1 QUART HEAVY CREAM

¾ CUP GOLDEN RAISINS

1 CUP CANDIED RED CHERRIES, COARSELY
   CHOPPED

½ CUP CANDIED ORANGE PEEL, CHOPPED
   INTO SMALL PIECES

¾ CUP ASSORTED CANDIED FRUIT,
   CHOPPED

1½ CUP WALNUT HALVES

1 CUP SLICED ALMONDS

KIWI SAUCE

4 KIWI FRUITS, PEELED

1 CUP GRANULATED SUGAR
   JUICE OF 1 LEMON

PREPARE THE NOUGAT: Mix together powdered sugar, honey, and corn syrup in a large nonreactive saucepan. Cook over medium high heat until mixture reaches 120 degrees (verify with a candy thermometer).

In a large bowl, beat egg whites with electric mixer until soft peaks form. Add hot liquid in a thin stream and continue beating until cooled. Slowly add cream and beat until well incorporated. Fold in the raisins, candied fruits, and nuts.

Pour nougat into two oiled 8-inch loaf pans. Cover and freeze overnight.

PREPARE THE KIWI SAUCE: Chop kiwi fruit. Place in a food processor and puree until almost smooth, about 10 seconds. Add granulated sugar and puree until smooth, about 20 seconds. Strain into a bowl through a fine-mesh sieve. Add lemon juice, cover, and refrigerate.

TO SERVE: Remove nougat from freezer; dip mold into a large bowl of warm water. Unmold onto a large cutting surface and, using a sharp thin-bladed knife dipped in hot water, cut into slices about 2 inches thick. Place a slice on each of 8 individual dessert plates, and surround with a small amount of the sauce. *Makes 8 servings.*

THIS DELICATE NOUGAT IS SERVED WITH A BRILLIANTLY GREEN KIWI SAUCE. THE KIWI, A NATIVE OF THE FAR EAST, HENCE ITS NICKNAME OF CHINESE GOOSEBERRY, IS A VERY RECENT INTRODUCTION TO OUR CUISINE. UNKNOWN TO US TWENTY YEARS AGO, IT HAS BEEN PERFECTLY ACCLIMATED IN FRANCE, ALTHOUGH ITS CULTURE HAS BEEN ESPECIALLY DEVELOPED IN NEW ZEA-

LAND. THE KIWI MUST BE BOUGHT RIPE, WHEN IT IS POSSIBLE TO PEEL IT LIKE A WELL-RIPENED PEACH; THEN IT MAY BE MIXED WITH CERTAIN MEATS AND FISH, MADE INTO A SAUCE, SERVED IN SEAFOOD SALADS AND AS A DESSERT.

APPLE BUTTERFLIES WITH CARAMEL
PAPILLON DE POMMES AU CARAMEL

ICY WINTER GRIPS THE VEYLE RIVER IN VONNAS, AND WHAT BETTER TIME TO DELIGHT IN THIS UNUSUAL BUTTERFLY WITH ITS WINGS OF APPLE SLICES AND BODY OF CARAMEL CUSTARD. STORED AWAY FROM HUMIDITY AND HEAT, APPLES MAY KEEP FOR A FEW MONTHS TO BE ENJOYED EVEN AFTER THE ORCHARDS ARE BARE AND THE

BUTTERFLIES THAT DART THROUGH SUMMER GARDENS ARE FAR AWAY.

VANILLA CUSTARD
½ CUP SUGAR
1 CUP MILK
½ VANILLA BEAN, SPLIT LENGTHWISE IN HALF
3 EGGS, BEATEN TOGETHER WITH ⅓ CUP ADDITIONAL SUGAR

SAUCE
½ CUP SUGAR
½ CUP APPLE JUICE

DECORATION
3 GRANNY SMITH APPLES, PEELED AND CORED
¼ CUP CLARIFIED BUTTER
ZEST OF 1 LEMON, CUT INTO THIN STRIPS
SLIVERED ALMONDS (OPTIONAL)

PREPARE THE VANILLA CUSTARD: Preheat oven to 325 degrees. Combine sugar and 2 tablespoons water in a small saucepan. Bring to a boil over medium high heat. Cook sugar until amber colored, about 5 minutes. Immediately pour a ⅛-inch-thick layer of caramel into four ¾ cup dariole molds or ramekins. Let cool completely.

In a small saucepan, over medium heat, bring milk and vanilla bean to a boil. Pour milk into beaten, sweetened eggs and mix well. Strain through a fine-mesh sieve into a bowl. Skim off froth. Fill caramelized molds with custard.

Choose a baking dish just large enough to hold the filled molds. Fit the bottom with a piece of parchment paper to prevent the molds from moving about. Place molds in dish and add boiling water to reach halfway up sides of molds. Bake until set, about 30 minutes. Let cool completely before unmolding.

PREPARE THE SAUCE: In a small saucepan, combine sugar and ¼ cup apple juice over medium heat. Cook until mixture becomes a lightly colored caramel, about 5 minutes. Remove from heat and stop cooking by pouring in remaining ¼ cup apple juice. Cover and refrigerate until ready to serve.

PREPARE THE DECORATION: Just before assembling the dessert, cut apples into quarters and then into ¼-inch-thick slices. Heat clarified butter in a small sauté pan over medium high heat. When very hot, add apple slices. Brown quickly, turning frequently to ensure uniform coloring and to prevent burning. Drain on paper towels.

TO SERVE: Unmold 1 caramel custard in the center of each of 4 individual serving plates. Pour a small amount of sauce over the caramel. Arrange apple slices along both sides of the caramel, to resemble butterfly wings. Use lemon zests to make antennas. Complete decoration by placing a sliver of almond on each of the apple slices. *Makes 4 servings*.

Traditionally in this region, at the beginning of the year, each village pays homage to its conscripts, those who have reached the age of twenty and are going off to carry out their obligatory military service. All those born in the same year gather together for high mass in the village church. Afterwards, there is a parade, then dancing in the streets with all sorts of municipal fanfare and a laying of a wreath at the local war memorial. Then there is the "grand banquet" that ends late and allows everybody to call up childhood memories. The "fete" continues the following morning with the day of the "matefaim." These rather thick crepes are prepared in the Festival Hall, where the entire village joins together in this celebration of friendship.

CONVERSION CHART

LIQUID MEASURES

FLUID OUNCES	U.S. MEASURES	IMPERIAL MEASURES	MILLILITERS	FLUID OUNCES	U.S. MEASURES	IMPERIAL MEASURES	MILLILITERS
	1 TSP	1 TSP	5	25		1¼ PINTS	700
¼	2 TSP	1 DESSERTSPOON	7	27	3½ CUPS		750
½	1 TBS	1 TBS	15	30	3¾ CUPS	1½ PINTS	840
1	2 TBS	2 TBS	28	32	4 CUPS OR 2 PINTS		900
2	¼ CUP	4 TBS	56		OR 1 QUART		
4	½ CUP		110	35		1¾ PINTS	980
	OR ¼ PINT			36	4½ CUPS		1000,
5		¼ PINT OR 1 GILL	140				1 LITER
6	¾ CUP		170	40	5 CUPS OR	2 PINTS OR 1 QUART	1120
8	1 CUP OR		225		2½ PINTS		
	½ PINT			48	6 CUPS OR 3 PINTS		1350
9			250,	50		2½ PINTS	1400
			¼ LITER	60	7½ CUPS	3 PINTS	1680
10	1¼ CUPS	½ PINT	280	64	8 CUPS OR 4 PINTS		1800
12	1½ CUPS OR ¾ PINT		240		OR 2 QUARTS		
15		¾ PINT	420	72	9 CUPS		2000,
16	2 CUPS OR 1 PINT		450				2 LITERS
18	2¼ CUPS		500,	80	10 CUPS OR	4 PINTS	2250
			½ LITER		5 PINTS		
20	2½ CUPS	1 PINT	560	96	12 CUPS OR 3 QUARTS		2700
24	3 CUPS OR 1½ PINTS		675	100		5 PINTS	2800

SOLID MEASURES

U.S. AND IMPERIAL MEASURES		METRIC MEASURES		U.S. AND IMPERIAL MEASURES		METRIC MEASURES	
OUNCES	POUNDS	GRAMS	KILOS	OUNCES	POUNDS	GRAMS	KILOS
1		28		27		750	¾
2		56		28	1¾	780	
3½		100		32	2	900	
4	¼	112		36	2¼	1000	1
5		140		40	2½	1100	
6		168		48	3	1350	
8	½	225		54		1500	1½
9		250	¼	64	4	1800	
12	¾	340		72	4½	2000	2
16	1	450		80	5	2250	2¼
18		500	½	90		2500	2½
20	1¼	560		100	6	2800	2¾
24	1½	675					

OVEN TEMPERATURE EQUIVALENTS

Fahrenheit	Gas Mark	Celsius	Heat of Oven	Fahrenheit	Gas Mark	Celsius	Heat of Oven
225	¼	107	VERY COOL	375	5	190	FAIRLY HOT
250	½	121	VERY COOL	400	6	204	FAIRLY HOT
275	1	135	COOL	425	7	218	HOT
300	2	148	COOL	450	8	232	VERY HOT
325	3	163	MODERATE	475	9	246	VERY HOT
350	4	177	MODERATE				

TERMINOLOGY EQUIVALENTS

U.S.	British	U.S.	British
DRY WHITE BEANS	HARICOT BEANS	CHEESECLOTH	MUSLIN
EGGPLANT	AUBERGINE	BROIL	GRILL
ZUCCHINI	COURGETTE	PIT	STONE
HEAVY CREAM	DOUBLE CREAM	SKILLET	FRYING PAN
SUGAR, GRANULATED SUGAR	CASTOR SUGAR	BROILER	GRILL
POWDERED SUGAR	ICING SUGAR		

APPENDIX

TOMATO CONCASSE

1 TABLESPOON UNSALTED BUTTER	2 CLOVES GARLIC, PEELED
¼ CUP OLIVE OIL	BOUQUET GARNI: 1 BAY LEAF,
2 LARGE SHALLOTS, FINELY CHOPPED	2 THYME SPRIGS, 2
1½ POUNDS RIPE TOMATOES, PEELED, SEEDED, AND FINELY DICED	PARSLEY SPRIGS, 1 CELERY RIB, AND GREEN LEEK TOPS TIED IN CHEESECLOTH
2 TEASPOONS TOMATO PASTE	COARSE SEA SALT
½ TEASPOON SUGAR	FRESHLY GROUND PEPPER

Heat butter with oil in a heavy medium saucepan. Add shallots and cook over medium heat until they just begin to color, about 4 minutes. Add tomatoes, tomato paste, sugar, garlic, bouquet garni, and a little salt and pepper; cook over low heat, stirring occasionally, for 20 minutes. Remove from heat and discard bouquet garni and garlic. Season with salt and pepper to taste. *Makes about 1¾ cups.*

NOTE: This chunky tomato sauce is used in the preparation and the garnishing of various dishes.

FRESH TOMATO COULIS

1 TABLESPOON UNSALTED BUTTER	2 CLOVES GARLIC, PEELED
¼ CUP OLIVE OIL	BOUQUET GARNI: 1 BAY LEAF,
2 LARGE SHALLOTS, FINELY CHOPPED	2 THYME SPRIGS, 2
2 TEASPOONS TOMATO PASTE	PARSLEY SPRIGS, 1 CELERY RIB, AND GREEN LEEK
1½ POUNDS RIPE TOMATOES, PEELED, SEEDED, AND COARSELY CHOPPED	TOPS TIED IN CHEESECLOTH COARSE SEA SALT
½ TEASPOON SUGAR	FRESHLY GROUND PEPPER

Heat butter with oil in a heavy medium saucepan. Add shallots and cook over medium heat until they just begin to color, about 4 minutes. Stir in tomato paste until blended, and then add tomatoes, sugar, garlic, bouquet garni, and a little salt and pepper. Bring to a boil, stirring frequently, over medium high heat. Reduce heat to medium, cover, and cook, stirring occasionally, for 30 minutes. Remove from heat.

Remove and discard bouquet garni and garlic. Transfer tomato mixture to a blender and puree until smooth. If the *coulis* seems too fluid, pour it into a small saucepan and reduce slightly over medium heat until the desired consistency is reached. Season with salt and pepper to taste. *Makes about 1¾ cups.*

NOTE: Tomato *coulis* can be used on its own as a sauce, or it can be embellished with fresh herbs, olive oil, crème fraîche, or a little beurre blanc.

BEURRE BLANC

¼ CUP DRY WHITE WINE	1 CUP COLD UNSALTED BUTTER, CUT INTO SMALL CHUNKS
2 TABLESPOONS WHITE WINE VINEGAR	
3 SHALLOTS, FINELY CHOPPED	SALT AND FRESHLY GROUND WHITE PEPPER

In a medium nonreactive saucepan, combine wine, vinegar, and shallots. Bring to a boil over medium high heat and cook until liquid reduces to 1½ tablespoons, about 3 minutes. Reduce heat to very low and whisk in butter, a few chunks at a time. As it melts, butter should become creamy, not oily. Remove from heat if butter seems to be melting too fast, and continue whisking until all of the butter has been incorporated. Season the sauce with salt and white pepper to taste and serve. (If necessary, this sauce can be held for a short period of time over very warm water.) *Makes 1 cup.*

BEURRE BATTU

½ CUP COLD UNSALTED BUTTER, CUT INTO SMALL PIECES	SALT FRESH LEMON JUICE

Place ½ cup water in a heavy nonreactive saucepan and bring to a boil over high heat. Reduce heat to medium; add butter, a few pieces at a time, and whisk vigorously until thoroughly incorporated. Remove sauce from heat and season to taste with salt and lemon juice. Keep the sauce warm in a water bath until ready to use. *Makes about 1 cup.*

CREME ANGLAISE

1 CUP MILK
⅓ VANILLA BEAN, SPLIT
LENGTHWISE

3 EGG YOLKS, AT ROOM
TEMPERATURE
3 TABLESPOONS SUGAR

Place milk and vanilla bean in a heavy medium saucepan and slowly bring to a simmer over medium low heat.

Meanwhile, combine egg yolks and sugar in a medium bowl and whisk until light and thick. Gradually whisk half of the hot milk into egg yolks until thoroughly blended. Return mixture to the saucepan and whisk well. Cook custard over medium heat, stirring constantly with a wooden spoon, until it thickens slightly; do not let it boil. The custard is done when it lightly coats the back of a spoon and a clear trail is left when a finger is drawn across, about 7 minutes.

Strain custard into a heatproof bowl. Scrape seeds from vanilla bean and stir them into the custard. Cover and refrigerate until ready to use. (The custard can be prepared up to 1 day ahead.) *Makes 1 cup.*

CREME PATISSIERE

1 CUP MILK
⅓ VANILLA BEAN, SPLIT
LENGTHWISE
3 EGG YOLKS, AT ROOM
TEMPERATURE

3 TABLESPOONS PLUS 1
TEASPOON SUGAR
2 TABLESPOONS ALL-PURPOSE
FLOUR

Set aside 2 tablespoons milk. Pour remaining milk into a small heavy saucepan; add vanilla bean and slowly bring to a simmer over medium low heat.

Meanwhile, place egg yolks and sugar in a bowl and whisk until thick and light. Whisk in flour until thoroughly blended, then stir in reserved 2 tablespoons cold milk. Gradually whisk in hot milk until smooth. Return mixture to saucepan and cook over medium high heat, whisking constantly, until thick and boiling. Whisk for 30 seconds longer, then remove from heat and transfer the pastry cream to a heatproof

bowl. Remove vanilla bean, scrape seeds into the cream and stir well to blend. Press a piece of plastic wrap directly on the surface of the cream and refrigerate until chilled. (The pastry cream can be made up to 2 days ahead.) *Makes 1 cup.*

CREME FRAICHE

1 CUP HEAVY CREAM, AT ROOM
TEMPERATURE
2 TABLESPOONS BUTTERMILK

Combine cream and buttermilk in a clean, warm glass jar. Cover securely and set the container in a warm place (about 75 degrees). Allow to thicken for 6 to 8 hours or more. Refrigerate and use as needed. This crème fraîche will keep for up to 10 days. *Makes about 1 cup.*

STRAWBERRY COULIS

½ POUND RIPE STRAWBERRIES,
RINSED AND HULLED
1 TO 1¼ CUPS POWDERED
SUGAR

LEMON JUICE
CLUB SODA OR SELTZER
(OPTIONAL)

Place strawberries and powdered sugar in a food processor and puree until smooth. Strain through a fine mesh strainer and stir in a little lemon juice to taste. If the *coulis* seems too thick, stir in a little club soda.

NOTE: This recipe also works with other red berries, such as raspberries.

INDEX

DESIGNED BY RITA MARSHALL

COMPOSED IN NICHOLAS COCHIN AND BERKELEY OLD STYLE
BY TRUFONT TYPOGRAPHERS, INC., HICKSVILLE, NEW YORK

JACKET TITLE COMPOSED IN NICHOLAS COCHIN
BY AFFOLTER & GSCHWEND AG., BASEL, SWITZERLAND

PRINTED AND BOUND BY DAI NIPPON PRINTING CO., LTD.,
TOKYO, JAPAN